The Politics of Conducting Research in Africa

Lyn Johnstone
Editor

The Politics of Conducting Research in Africa

Ethical and Emotional Challenges in the Field

Editor
Lyn Johnstone
Royal Holloway, University of London
Egham, UK

ISBN 978-3-319-95530-8   ISBN 978-3-319-95531-5   (eBook)
https://doi.org/10.1007/978-3-319-95531-5

Library of Congress Control Number: 2018948723

Cover image: © Westend61
Cover design: Tjaša Krivec

This Palgrave Macmillan imprint is published by the registered company Springer Nature Switzerland AG
The registered company address is: Gewerbestrasse 11, 6330 Cham, Switzerland

CONTENTS

1   Introduction: Conducting Fieldwork in Africa   1
Lyn Johnstone

2   'Good That You Are One of Us': Positionality and
Reciprocity in Conducting Fieldwork in Kenya's
Flower Industry   13
Nungari Mwangi

3   Being Familiar, and Yet Strange: Conducting Research
as a Hybrid Insider-Outsider in Uganda   35
Christine van Hooft

4   Multi-positionality and 'Inbetweenness': Reflections
on Ethnographic Fieldwork in Southern Eastern Malawi   53
Maddy Gupta-Wright

5   Landscapes of Desire: The Effect of Gender, Sexualized
Identity, and Flirting on Data Production in Rwanda
and Zimbabwe   75
Lyn Johnstone

6   Fieldwork and Emotions: Positionality, Method Choices,
    and a Radio Program in South Sudan   97
    Kerstin Tomiak

7   Researching Diaspora Citizenship: Reflections on
    Issues of Positionality and Access from a Zimbabwean
    Researching Zimbabweans in South Africa   115
    Langton Miriyoga

8   Gatekeeping Success in the Namibian CBNRM Program   133
    Carolin H. Stamm

9   Failed Fieldwork in Senegal: Give Up or Continue?   153
    Elizaveta Volkova

10 Negotiating Research Access: The Interplay Between
    Politics and Academia in Contemporary Zimbabwe   171
    Joshua Pritchard

Bibliography   191

Index   213

Notes on Contributors

Maddy Gupta-Wright is a Ph.D. student with the London School of Hygiene and Tropical Medicine, UK. She first trained as a medical doctor and specializes in public health in the UK. She has undertaken Masters level training in public health and medical anthropology and is a member of the UK Faculty of Public Health. She is keen to combine a career in public health and medical anthropology and is particularly interested in exploring health and disease as biosocial phenomena, critically analyzing approaches to infectious disease control, and the development of ecological public health methods to health inequalities. Her Ph.D. research in Malawi is intended to help shape local and national policy approaches to trachoma, as well as contribute to the anthropological literature on biosocial approaches to health and disease.

Lyn Johnstone completed her Ph.D. at Royal Holloway, University of London in 2016. Her research explored ideas of family, the Commonwealth, and Africa with specific focus on Rwanda and Zimbabwe. Since completing her Ph.D., Lyn has been teaching African Politics and International Relations Theory to undergraduate students in the Politics and International Relations Department at Royal Holloway.

Langton Miriyoga completed his Ph.D. at Royal Holloway, University of London in 2018. His thesis explored the changing conceptions and practices of citizenship in the context of transnational migration, with a specific focus on Zimbabweans living in South Africa and the UK. Since completing his Ph.D., Langton has been working, among other projects, with Global Witness—a London-based environmental and anti-corruption campaign organisation.

Nungari Mwangi is currently a Ph.D. candidate with the Center of Development Studies, at the University of Cambridge. Her research is on the political economy of the Kenyan cut flower industry and focuses on how small holders survive and thrive in an industry dominated by giants. In 2016, Nungari received the Andrew E. Rice award for a young professional in International Development awarded by the Society of International Development (SID) in Washington, DC for her commitment to in-the-field engagement in her work.

Joshua Pritchard is a Ph.D. Candidate with the Faculty of History, University of Cambridge. Joshua is a CHSS-funded doctoral candidate in the Faculty of History, University of Cambridge. His thesis explores the interactions between race and the nationalist movement in Zimbabwe during the early years of the liberation struggle, 1957–1967. He has a Masters in African History from SOAS, and a B.A. in Modern History from Aberystwyth University.

Carolin H. Stamm is a research associate at SRH University of Applied Sciences, Berlin, Germany. Carolin recently completed her Ph.D. at University of Lincoln, UK. Originally departing from the domain of tourism studies, Caro's overall research interest is centered on tourism as a catalyst for regional development and community empowerment in rural areas in southern Africa. For her Ph.D. thesis, she assessed joint-venture tourism partnerships between community-based organizations and private tourism operators in the Namibian community-based natural resource management program (CBNRM). Here, she focused on the extensive technical/financial assistance provided by a network of national and international non-governmental organizations (NGOs) and how this impacts on the long-term viability of community-based tourism ventures.

Kerstin Tomiak gained her Ph.D. in 2017 from Cardiff University, with a thesis on media development. She has been working as a media expert for nongovernmental and international organisations such as NATO in Afghanistan and South Sudan. She currently holds the GLOCAL-Davis postdoctoral fellowship for research related to Africa at the Hebrew University of Jerusalem.

Christine van Hooft is a development economist specialising in public financial management. She is currently completing a Ph.D. at the Center of Development Studies at the University of Cambridge. Christine has previously been engaged as an ODI Fellow at the Ministry of Finance in Kampala, Uganda; a development specialist and diplomat with the Australian Agency for International Development (AusAID) in Jakarta, Indonesia; and an economist at AusAID in Canberra, Australia. She holds a Bachelor of Economics (Monash), a Master of Public Policy (ANU) and an M.Phil. in Development Studies (Cambridge).

Elizaveta Volkova is a Ph.D. candidate at *Ecole Pratique des Hautes Etudes* and *Institut des mondes africains* in Paris. Elizaveta is originally from Russia. She is currently completing her Ph.D. thesis on 'joking relations' among the Joola and among the Mandinka in Casamace in Senegal.

CHAPTER 1

Introduction: Conducting Fieldwork in Africa

Lyn Johnstone

Much of the literature on conducting fieldwork is received by research students in a polished and often sanitized style in which the realities of fieldwork are tidied up and presented in 'persuasive chunks' passing through a filter from the field to the literature (Harrowell et al. 2018, p. 230). Surprisingly little of the mess or uncertainly that we encounter during our first few fieldwork experiences is reflected in the narratives researchers tell when returning from the field and writing up their findings. Many researchers tend to rationalize problems and bring to the fore achievements, leaving the messier and often embarrassing parts, or instances of failure, on the cutting room floor (Shore 2010; Jones and Evans 2011; Kay and Oldfield 2011). One reason for this might be that years of positivist-inspired thinking have ingrained themselves in social science research practice teaching researchers that impersonal, emotionless and neutral detachment underlies good research (England 1994).

The idea that researchers can detach themselves from their research and don an academic cloak of neutrality ignores the openness and culturally constructed nature of the social world which is, as England (1994, p. 81) points out, 'peppered with contradictions and complexities.' Many

L. Johnstone (✉)
Royal Holloway, University of London, Egham, UK

© The Author(s) 2019
L. Johnstone (ed.), *The Politics of Conducting Research in Africa*,
https://doi.org/10.1007/978-3-319-95531-5_1

1

of the complexities that England describes here revolve around questions of positionality, a concept concerning where one stands in relation to 'the other' and in regard to the politics of knowledge construction (England 1994; Rose 1997; Merriam et al. 2001). In recent years, positionality has begun to assume a central position in the discourse surrounding research and methodology and, as a result, the recognition of the need to situate knowledge has seen an influx of studies which are devoted to reflexivity exploring and analyzing how researchers might better understand how their identity and research relationships affect data production.

My purpose in producing this edited volume is to add to the existing literature on positionality. For those questioning the decision to focus on an area that has amassed rather a large literature since the constructivist turn loosened the grip of positivism on social science research, the answer is simple. Many of the contributors to this volume found themselves facing challenges during their first fieldwork experiences, for which they struggled to find advice in the existing literature. These challenges revolved around issues of positionality, as well as access, and raised questions around identity, race, and gender such as: how does one cope with the feeling of failure in the field? What is a researcher to do when their path to potential fieldwork is blocked by the government of the country to which they are seeking access? And, how might a researcher interpret the effect that flirtatious behavior between the research participant and the researcher has on the quantity and quality of data produced? These questions, along with other issues around positionality and access, are discussed in this volume, which uses the fieldwork experiences of the contributing authors to address gaps in the existing literature and take the discussion of positionality in new directions.

The book contains case studies from doctoral research in Malawi, South Sudan, Kenya, South Africa, Rwanda, Zimbabwe, Senegal, Namibia, and Uganda and represents the combined knowledge of nine researchers from the fields of anthropology, development, history, tourism and hospitality, and political science who all found themselves navigating around issues of positionality and access while conducting fieldwork in Africa. But, why focus only on Africa?

As more and more doctoral researchers, beyond the discipline of anthropology, choose to carry out fieldwork on the African continent, the rise in publications on the findings of such research has far surpassed the rather slender body of literature that focuses on the research process itself.

For researchers from any discipline or background, the culmination of methodological and ethical issues that researchers might find themselves facing when conducting fieldwork in Africa can present challenges for academics of any discipline, level of experience, or background. This observation is one of the reasons why the editors of *African Affairs*, the top-ranked journal in African studies, decided recently to devote space in the journal to research notes focusing on methodological and ethical issues arising from fieldwork in Africa. This edited volume is produced with similar intentions, with this in mind, however, the themes analyzed here are in no way unique to the African field-site. The positionality challenges of conducting research in one's home country, the ways in which emotions, gender, and gatekeepers might affect data production, and the challenges of failed fieldwork, are all applicable to fieldwork carried out in other geographical locations, whether Africa or elsewhere.

This volume is dedicated to the ethical and emotional challenges that accompany fieldwork. It demonstrates how who we are shapes what we research and the knowledge we produce. All of the chapters collected here analyze different aspects of positionality gleaned from first-hand experience of how our subjective positions affect every stage of the research processes, and focus on the following questions:

1. What effect do our identity, role, and position as a researcher have on the ways in which our research subjects perceive us and on the data we collect?
2. How does a researcher's position evolve over time and what effects might this have on our research projects?
3. How do the emotional reactions we have affect the ways in which we interpret the data that we collect?
4. What options are open to a researcher when access to data is denied?
5. How might we adapt our methodologies in order to be flexible to the challenges of conducting research in hostile environments and authoritarian regimes?

Overview of Chapters

As I noted above, the content of this edited volume is based on the positionality challenges and access frustrations that each contributor faced in some way while out in the field. One such frustration that has received only scant attention in the scholarly literature to date is the complex web of emotions and challenges facing researchers who return home to conduct research. In Chapter 2 of this volume, Nungari Mwangi illuminates some of these issues with an exploration of the positionality challenges that she faced when she returned to Kenya to carry out fieldwork for her doctoral research. While we might expect a researcher who returns home to conduct research to have an easier ride in terms of identity and access, Mwangi argues that positionality for African researchers reorienting themselves toward home means a deeper critical engagement with a variety of selves. For Mwangi, her identity as female, Kenyan, and a Cambridge University student all added layers of complexity to the way she positioned herself and the ways in which her research participants positioned her also. Bringing to life encounters which saw her at times emphasizing some aspects of her Kenyan identity while downplaying others, and at other times slipping in between identities, Mwangi disrupts well-worn dichotomies that position researchers as either inside or outside of the community being researched. In sharing her approach to questions about identity and reciprocity, she provides an avenue for researchers to consider the ways in which positionality differs for scholars researching back home while adding a female African voice to debates around ideas of strangeness and belonging.

Strangeness and belonging are well-known concepts for researchers heading to the field. Feelings of strangeness in particular often accompany the beginning stages of research which can destabilize the researcher (Agar 2006; Jackson 2010; Rancatore 2010). The author of Chapter 7 in this volume, Langton Miriyoga understands destabilization well. Like Mwangi, Miriyoga returned home to conduct research, but with one significant difference. Rather than returning to his native home of Zimbabwe, Miriyoga conducted research in his adopted home of South Africa. Adding further layers of complexity to the process of data collection and interpretation, Miriyoga's research focus was the plight of Zimbabwean migrants, like himself, living in the townships of Cape Town and Johannesburg. Far from the ease of access he anticipated in the planning stages of his research, Miriyoga describes how shared identity does not always open doors to people and knowledge when the target research population is vulnerable and rumors about spies from back home abound. In examining his strategies for gaining access to vulnerable migrants, Miriyoga conveys a valuable lesson to researchers returning home: no matter how hard we try it is difficult to close off our own bias and memories of places and people. The mere observation of this fact, however, does not prevent us from successfully conducting research back home; as both Miriyoga and Mwangi show in this volume, it simply means that we have to problematize the idea of home which, following Mandiyanke (2009), carries a lot more baggage when we return as researchers with intimate knowledge of the field-site and its people.

The chapters from Mwangi and Miriyoga detail specific strategies that researchers can employ to come to terms with the positionality challenges of conducting research 'back home.' Both chapters consider it critical that researchers think about how prior relationships, and the ways in which fellow country men and women perceive us, can affect both the ways in which we collect and interpret data. In Chapter 3 of this volume, Christine van Hooft discusses a similar issue in her exploration of the ways in which prior relationships with one's research subjects can both help and hinder data collection. Early research in sociology and anthropology posited the dichotomous doctrine of the insider and the outsider, with each position bringing both benefits as well as challenges (Pike 1967; Merton 1972). More recent research has looked beyond this dichotomization, recognizing that research relationships are much more multidimensional and specific to research projects with relationships mediating research positions of status or difference (Bourdieu 1977; Merriam et al. 2001; Serrant-Green 2002; Cargo and Mercer 2008; Dwyer and Buckle 2009). Banks (1998) points to the spaces in between creating a more complex range of positionalities that are based on differences in researcher socialization within specific ethnic, racial, and cultural communities. In Chapter 3, van Hooft explores these spaces in between with an analysis of the ways in which her previous role as a civil servant with the Ugandan Ministry of Finance, Planning and Economic Development added an extra layer of complexity to data production. Drawing on what she refers to as a third category of researcher—the hybrid insider–outsider who shares some characteristics of the studied group, but nonetheless is an outsider in regard to other important characteristics—van Hooft looks particularly at the unique challenges her hybrid insider–outsider status posed in terms of the care needed in collecting, interpreting, and presenting data. She joins Mwangi and Miriyoga in showing how having prior relationships or identification with research participants can both impede as well as facilitate data production.

Throughout the research process, our role, position, and identity change. Additionally, people's image of a researcher's identity and agenda may shift over time. Maddy Gupta-Wright's contribution in Chapter 4 is specifically dedicated to this theme. Like van Hooft's chapter on hybrid identity and positionality, Gupta-Wright's chapter in this volume is concerned with the multidimensional aspects of research relationships, but with an important distinction: Gupta-Wright is a former medical doctor by training, making her role, position, and identity as an anthropologist conducting research on disease particularly problematic at times. Reflecting on her experience conducting fieldwork in Malawi, Gupta-Wright discusses the ways in which she navigated ethical and moral quandaries that emerged as she attempted to leave her identity as a medical doctor behind. She discusses the ways in which she struggled with the different positions, that she both assumed and were thrust upon her, showing how *multi-positionalities* are constructed from assumptions and impressions, both of and by researchers and research participants, and how these slowly change over time.

Assumptions and impressions accompany all fieldwork encounters. When we enter the field, we enter as members of groups about which our research participants already have preconceived notions about who we are. Since the 1990s, feminists have positioned the analytical lens on gendered positionality and the effects that perceived gender roles, and the power relations that often accompany gender issues, have on all stages of the research process from the design of the research proposal to the collection and analysis of data (McDowell 1992; England 1994; Rose 1997). Feminist research has recognized that researchers and their research participants have a 'different and unequal relation to knowledge' (Glucksmann 1994, p. 150) and that within most research projects, 'the final shift of power between the researcher and the respondent is balanced in favor of the researcher' (Cotterill 1992, p. 604). Acknowledging that power relations are a given in research relationships, more recent feminist scholarship has now moved toward an analysis of *how*, rather than *whether*, gender and power influence knowledge production and construction processes. But when Lyn Johnstone, in Chapter 5 of this volume, searched the literature for examples of how to deal with an issue that problematized understandings of gender and power—that of flirtation directed by the research participant toward the researcher—she found very little acknowledgment of the existence of what she calls 'sexualized identity' in research, outside of accounts of sexual harassment in the field. Through a discussion of the ways in which she encountered and reciprocated flirtatious banter directed by male interviewees during fieldwork in Rwanda and Zimbabwe, Johnstone adds nuance to the discussion on gender and power relations exploring the role that agency, power, and performance play when flirtation enters a research encounter and addressing the effect that flirtatious banter has both on the production and interpretation of data. In particular, she discusses performance and the ways in which flirtation and the performance of perceived gender roles can both impede and facilitate data production.

Like Johnstone, Carolin Stamm's contribution in Chapter 8 also explores a specific way in which access to knowledge and data is negotiated as she uses her fieldwork with CBOs and NGOs in rural conservation projects in Namibia to reconceptualize gatekeeper-researcher relationships. Stamm argues that research that heavily relies on fieldwork is profoundly influenced by the opportunities and constraints encountered during data collection, which often lie in the hands of gatekeepers. Taking a different approach to the usual focus in the literature on the role of the gatekeeper as a static instrumental figure to navigate around, Stamm critically evaluates the role that gatekeepers play in the data collection process, analysis and formation of research findings. She finds that the manner in which access to knowledge is negotiated should not be divorced from the results generated.

In the sixth chapter of this volume, Kerstin Tomiak takes this important insight one step further with a focus on how our emotional responses affect the ways in which we interpret data. Tomiak opens up discussion of identity within the discourse around positionality and writes of the need to add a further category to the list of gender, ethnicity, race, class, culture and so on—that of emotions. Tomiak's suggestion connects to Madge's argument that many researchers writing on their experiences in the field have pointed out that it is crucial to consider 'the role of the (multiple) "self", showing how a researcher's positionality (in terms of race, nationality, age, gender, social and economic status, and sexuality) may influence the "data" collected and thus the information that becomes coded as "knowledge"' (Madge 1993, p. 296). Tomiak adds a layer of nuance to this discussion in examining the links between the personal emotions of researchers, which, as Meyer (2007) notes, often receive little attention in the set-up of a research project, and method choices going forward. Grappling with her reactions to the deeply emotional responses of South Sudanese refugees, Tomiak offers insight into the ways in which emotions affect our present and future positionalities during fieldwork. She concludes that the experiences made in the field, and the emotions that these experiences trigger, play an important and often overlooked part in a researcher's positionality and in turn are carried with us into the planning stages of future research projects. Tomiak's contribution provides an avenue for researchers to consider how or whether our emotional experiences on one project might come to affect our methodological choices at a later date.

The observation of the way in which emotional responses affect future method choices opens up the discussion to other factors which might influence or affect the collection of data. While all of the chapters in this volume reflect on the ways in which positionality affects the collection and production of data, two chapters stand out for their discussion of failure in this respect. Firstly, Elizaveta Volkova in Chapter 9 of this volume on coping with the possibility of failed fieldwork in Senegal reflects upon the issues that can accompany research which is heavily reliant on gatekeepers who act as the bridge between researcher and research participants. Taking a different view of gatekeepers to that taken by Stamm in Chapter 8, Volkova tells the story of the challenges she faced while attempting to access information about the joking relationships between members of the Joola community in Emanpore in the Casamance region of Senegal. Connecting both the access challenge and the positionality focus of the book, she discusses different attributes that might impact the researcher's ability to successfully collect data. In her case, a push by the tourist board in the Casamance region to boost the tourism-fueled economy led to gatekeeper distortion of the questions Volkova was attempting to ask and the answers she was seeking, which led her to believe that her research was failing. Volkova's experience connects to Nilan's (2002, p. 368) observation that 'the researcher as human subject is […] in flux, dealing with shifting realities and contradictions.' Her discussion provides an important lesson that managing our own fear of failure is a common feature of research. Volkova's chapter also alerts us to the fact that there is very little scholarly literature on the theme of failed research and what a researcher might do to overcome the emotional and practical challenges of the threat of failure. Observations such as Volkova's shine a light on the fact that the more challenging aspects of access are very rarely discussed and fly in the face of observations by some researchers that 'anyone can go to the field, observe, conduct interviews, and gather evidence' (Thomson et al. 2013, p. 6).

Josh Pritchard's chapter also speaks to the theme of failure and how access challenges and positionality often go hand in hand. Pritchard, in Chapter 10 of this volume, addresses the question of how we might adapt our methodologies in order to be flexible to the challenges of gaining access to data in authoritarian regimes. Pritchard writes on his lengthy negotiations with the Zimbabwean authorities to secure a research permit in order to conduct historical research in the National Archives of Zimbabwe. He offers essential advice in his chapter: applying for a research permit to conduct research can be a very lengthy process and we should be prepared with a contingency plan in case our application is unsuccessful. Despite lengthy negotiations and the assistance of Zimbabwean academics, Pritchard never was successful in gaining an official permit, ultimately because of the fact that he was from Britain—a country hostile to Zimbabwe. In this respect, Pritchard's discussion teaches an important lesson: positionality and access are two concepts that are entirely connected to one another whether we realize it or not.

Conclusion

I began this introduction with the observation that the messiness of conducting fieldwork is often concealed at the writing up and submission stage of a researcher's project. Increased attention to issues around positionality and the ways in which our identity affects every stage of the research process have seen a steady growth in publications that look behind the polished and sanitized research reports to tell the 'stories behind the findings' (Thomson et al. 2013). Fieldwork is not always easy and access to the field and research participants is rarely straightforward, but once in the field—if indeed we do successfully gain entry—we are forced to confront a multitude of ways in which our identities, roles, and positions affect our research relationships and knowledge production. Due to the diversity of field-sites as well as the diversity of research projects, and as the scholarly literature begins to offer less sanitized narratives of fieldwork endeavors, researchers faced with positionality and access challenges during fieldwork can often find examples in the literature of other researchers who have experienced issues along similar lines. For some of us, advice is found easily in the existing literature; for others, however, perhaps because of issues specific to the environment of the field-site where our research takes place, it is not always possible to find ready made solutions to the challenges we encounter. This was the case for some of the contributors to the following chapters in this volume. The discussion and analysis over the following pages take the existing literature on positionality and access in new directions with the aim of providing insight into ethical and emotional issues that the authors found challenging during their first forays into the field.

REFERENCES

Agar, M. (2006). An Ethnography by Any Other Name. *Forum: Qualitative Social Research Socialforschung, 7*(4). http://www.qualitative-research.net/index.php/fqs/article/view/177. Accessed December 15, 2017.

Banks, J. (1998). The Lives and Values of Researchers: Implications for Educating Citizens in a Multicultural Society. *Educational Researcher, 27*(7), 4–17.

Bourdieu, P. (1977). *Outline of a Theory of Practice.* Cambridge: Cambridge University Press.

Cargo, M., & Mercer, S. (2008). The Value and Challenges of Participatory Research: Strengthening Its Practice. *Annual Review of Public Health, 29,* 325–350.

Cotterill, P. (1992). Interviewing Women: Issues of Friendship, Vulnerability and Power. *Women's Studies International Forum, 15,* 593–606.

Dwyer, S., & Buckle, J. L. (2009). The Space Between: On Being an Insider-Outsider in Qualitative Research. *International Journal of Qualitative Methods, 8*(1), 54–63.

England, K. (1994). Getting Personal: Reflexivity, Positionality, and Feminist Research. *Professional Geographer, 46*(1), 80–89.

Glucksmann, M. (1994). The Work of Knowledge and the Knowledge of Women's Work. In M. Maynard & J. Purvis (Eds.), *Researching Women's Lives From a Feminist Perspective* (pp. 149–165). London: Taylor & Francis.

Harrowell, E., Davies, T., & Disney, T. (2018). Making Space for Failure in Geographic Research. *The Professional Geographer, 70*(2), 230–238.

Jackson, M. (2010). From Anxiety to Method in Anthropological Fieldwork: An Appraisal of George Devereux's Enduring Ideas. In J. Davies & D. Spencer (Eds.), *Emotions in the Field: The Psychology and Anthropology of Fieldwork Experience* (pp. 35–45). Redwood City, CA: Stanford University Press.

Jones, P. J., & Evans, J. (2011). Creativity and Project Management: A Comic. *ACME: An International E-Journal for Critical Geographies, 10*(3), 585–632.

Kay, R., & Oldfield, J. (2011). Emotional Engagements With the Field: A View from Area Studies. *Europe-Asia Studies, 63*(7), 1275–1293.

Madge, C. (1993). Boundary Disputes: Comments on Sidaway (1992). *Area, 25,* 294–299.

Mandiyanike, D. (2009). The Dilemma of Conducting Research Back in Your Own Country as a Returning Student: Reflections of Research Fieldwork in Zimbabwe. *Area, 41,* 64–71.

McDowell, L. (1992). Doing Gender: Feminism, Feminists and Research Methods in Human Geography. *Transactions, Institute of British Geographers, 17,* 399–416.

Merriam, S. B., Johnson-Bailey, J., Lee, M.-Y., Kee, Y., Ntseane, G., & Muhamad, M. (2001). Power and Positionality: Negotiating Insider/ Outsider Status Within and Across Cultures. *International Journal of Lifelong Education, 20*(5), 405–416.

Merton, R. (1972). Insiders and Outsiders: A Chapter in the Sociology of Knowledge. *American Journal of Sociology, 78*(1), 9–47.

Meyer, S. (2007). *From Horror Story to Manageable Risk: Formulating Safety Strategies for Peace Researchers.* Thesis for Master Degree Programme in Peace and Conflict Transformation, Centre for Peace Studies, Faculty of Social Science, University of Tromsø, Norway.

Nilan, P. (2002). 'Dangerous Fieldwork' Re-examined: The Question of Researcher Subject Position. *Qualitative Research, 2*(3), 363–386.

Pike, K. (1967). *Language in Relation to a Unified Theory of the Structures of Human Behavior* (2nd ed.). The Hague: Mouton.

Rancatore, J. (2010). It Is Strange. *Millennium: Journal of International Studies, 39*(1), 65–77.

Rose, G. (1997). Situating Knowledges: Positionality, Reflexivities and Other Tactics. *Progress in Human Geography, 21*(3), 305–320.

Serrant-Green, L. (2002). Black on Black: Methodological Issues for Black Researchers Working in Minority Ethnic Communities. *Nurse Researcher, 9*(4), 30–44.

Shore, C. (2010). Beyond the Multiversity: Neoliberalism and the Rise of the Schizophrenic University. *Social Anthropology, 18*(1), 15–29.

Thomson, S., Ansoms, A., & Murison, J. (2013). Introduction: Why Stories Behind the Findings? In S. Thomson, A. Ansoms, & J. Murison (Eds.), *Emotional and Ethical Challenges for Field Research in Africa: The Story Behind the Findings* (pp. 1–11). Basingstoke: Palgrave Macmillan.

CHAPTER 2

'Good That You Are One of Us': Positionality and Reciprocity in Conducting Fieldwork in Kenya's Flower Industry

Nungari Mwangi

African researchers conducting qualitative fieldwork 'back home' have been writing increasingly about navigating a maze of intersecting identities, positionalities and the reciprocity involved in knowledge exchange (See Mandiyanike 2009; Faria and Good 2012; Kiragu and Warrington 2013; Thomson et al. 2013; Geleta 2014; Siwale 2015). In this writing, they acknowledge the totality of the research experience, rather than only reporting on the results, and in a reflexive exercise place themselves at the centre of the analysis. As will be elaborated in the next section of this chapter, *positionality* for African researchers reorienting themselves towards home means a deeper critical engagement with 'the variety of selves' (Reinharz 1997) we bring to the field, the various ways in which we might be or not be considered 'one of them', and the implications for knowledge exchange. While acknowledging that the term 'African researcher' is in itself complex and layered, this paper takes it to mean rootedness in one or more African countries as home, which therefore shapes one's politics and perspectives.

N. Mwangi (✉)
Centre of Development Studies, University of Cambridge, Cambridge, UK

© The Author(s) 2019
L. Johnstone (ed.), *The Politics of Conducting Research in Africa*,
https://doi.org/10.1007/978-3-319-95531-5_2

13

The very notion of 'returning home' to do fieldwork also needs to be problematized as Sultana (2007) argues, because the field context can, and often does, differ from the familiar for African researchers. The experiences of African scholars based in the Western academy while conducting research in their home countries tend to be totalized, rather than problematized, in terms of the varying positionalities undertaken to negotiate knowledge exchange with research participants. Critical narratives of the complexities of African female researchers' fieldwork experiences are especially difficult to find. In my fieldwork in Kenya's flower industry, women comprised on average eighty percent of farm labour force, and were twenty-five percent of the total ninety interviews that I conducted along the value chain. Yet, the majority of the scholarship in this field is authored by European men. This reality reinforces the (re) creation of 'master narratives' in the post-colony that support the status quo or dominant group perspective on reality (McHugh in Leavy 2014, p. 151). It is with this context in mind that I argue it is important and urgent to give voice to the experiences of African women not only as research participants but also as lead researchers conducting fieldwork back home.

My fieldwork interactions in Kenya's flower industry brought out various gendered, intersecting and alienating positionalities. At the point of introduction and from my name, I was encountered as a young lady from Nairobi of Kikuyu origin and foreign-educated from my presentation. I was also seen as a doctoral researcher coming from an elite university, and secondarily a development professional from having previously worked in a development consulting firm in Nairobi. At the same time, the elderly smallholder flower farmers from Central Kenya, whom I interviewed, referred to me as *Mwari wa Nyumba* which translates as 'a daughter of the home'. After interacting with them in my mother tongue Kikuyu, they often exclaimed that it was 'good that I was one of them'. In Nairobi, I was seen to be a mentee by various older industry professionals, a potential advocate for salient industry issues, as well as a future ally by various industry stakeholders.

It is also important to understand the various forms of alienation African researchers experience when we go back home. In my case, being a Kenyan researcher in a field where scholarship is dominated by European researchers, an urbanite from Nairobi conducting research in rural areas, an outsider to the flower industry, and also an outsider to the local system of higher education, contributed significantly to the many ways in which I was a stranger at home. With this 'otherness' in mind, it is important to then consider how *reciprocity*, which is how we negotiate access to insider information and knowledge exchange, enables and enriches the fieldwork experience. Reciprocity deals with the ways in which we shift between the variety of selves in order to facilitate knowledge exchange on as equal terms as possible. This chapter will argue that there is, in fact, a performative element in that we can 'slip between', emphasize or downplay some identities, and 'play along' to create a rapport with fieldwork participants.

The purpose of this chapter is to add to the burgeoning methodological literature on experiences of African doctoral students conducting research 'back home'. It draws on and analyses my own fieldwork experiences in the Kenyan cut flower industry, often locally perceived as an obscure, elitist and foreign industry, to explore how positionality and reciprocity interact in seeking fieldwork access. In doing so, the chapter makes three main contributions to the literature. The first is to elucidate the identity-based challenges of 'going back' home as a researcher, seeking access to and conducting fieldwork on the Kenyan flower industry. The second contribution elaborates on shifts in a researcher's various positionalities—that is, how one moves through various identities in the field in order to gain access to research participants and exchange knowledge. I build on Reinharz's (1997) typology of the research self, the brought self and the situationally created self to argue that the performativity of these various selves in various field settings includes 'slipping between', emphasizing or downplaying some identities and 'playing along' or acquiescence as a means of negotiating access during fieldwork. The third and final contribution is to discuss reciprocity in fieldwork as a means of negotiating access highlighting knowledge exchange and material exchange as modes of reciprocity mitigating the power dynamics between researcher and research participants.

To make my case, I first discuss the literature on positionality, reflexivity and reciprocity with emphasis on scholars who have conducted qualitative fieldwork in Africa. I then discuss the peculiarities of the research context in the Kenyan cut flower sector highlighting its elite perception in Kenyan society, historicizing its relative aversion to researchers and the guarded silences within it. In order to foreground the challenges of access I faced while researching the industry, I explore ethnicity, gender, class privilege and the performance of shifting between various positionalities. I then discuss reciprocity of knowledge exchange negotiated with various institutional interlocutors and how this process was informed by the various positionalities highlighted above. Lastly, I outline the impact on my findings of having obtained access to interviewees primarily through the Kenya Flower Council (KFC), the industry representative body. I conclude by providing a summary of the main arguments in the chapter, underscoring the relationship between positionality and reciprocity for knowledge exchange and some lessons learnt for researchers working in similar or comparable contexts.

Positionality and the 'Variety of Selves' in Fieldwork

Questions of positionality and reflexivity as part of a researcher's identity politics have been widely explored in social science literature on fieldwork methodologies. Positionality can be understood as a coming to terms with the intersecting, changing aspects of our identities or the 'plurality of selves' that we bear as researchers simultaneously dislocated from the familiarity of home and the university and 'othered' in fieldwork sites (Mollinga 2008). We engage in debates on positionality in fieldwork because the researcher's position is situated within a social hierarchy in light of race, class, gender, and ethnicity, and this matters because it broadens our understanding of 'the other' and of local phenomena (Wolfe 1996).

Writing on positionality emerging from her own fieldwork experience, Reinharz (1997) observes that our identities are made up of a 'variety of selves'. She provides a useful typology from the analysis of her field work notes from a Kibbutz in which she identified twenty selves and categorized them into three types—*the research based self* (transient researcher, listener), the *brought self* (academic, Kenyan, Kikuyu, unmarried woman) and the *situationally created self* (friend, advocate, go-between) (Reinharz 1997, p. 5). Implicit within the notion of a variety of selves is the idea that a researcher shifts between these various positionalities and indeed that they change over the duration of research. Chereni (2000) discussing his fieldwork in South Africa raises the issue of the dynamic nature of positionality, that is, the manner in which a researcher's identity unfolds over the course of his fieldwork. In my fieldwork, I see this dynamism as part of the performative nature of fieldwork and I characterize the shifts between positionalities in three ways: 'slipping between', emphasizing or downplaying some positionalities, and 'playing along' or acquiescence. These shifts are part of the process of seeking access and building rapport and collaboration with participants.

Situating my own experiences in the field in the context of Reinharz's typology involved a critical awareness of the privileges and pitfalls of class, ethnicity, nationality, and of gender. In particular, it is important to highlight the gender-specific challenges faced by African women and written by female African researchers either working in their home countries or in different parts of Africa. This methodological literature is hard to come by and seems to be present mostly in public health (see for example Abrahams-Gessel et al. 2015), and peace and security research in Africa around gender-based violence (Jewkes et al. 2000). The voices of African women scholars studying themselves and their home environments and phenomena in the developing world must emerge in order to re-enter epistemologies around the authority of our perspectives, and to challenge the dominance and inaccuracies of the Western gaze even, and especially, when coming from an often-well-meaning liberal white feminist lens.

That said, there is an expansive and rich body of work linking positionality and gender more generally, spearheaded by feminist scholars across the social sciences working in developing countries particularly in Geography, Anthropology and Education. They discuss a myriad of themes such as being granted insider status due to an implicit bond among women speaking to women (Sultana 2007); danger and violence as gendered phenomena (McCorkel and Myers 2003, p. 209) and using women's personal narratives to challenge master narratives (Romero and Stewart 1999; Ali 2015). While acknowledging that there can be no one singular African female narrative of the researcher, we can build strive to solidarities across the diversity of our contributions. As an African woman conducting research at home, my gaze over local phenomena and experiences is *bifocal* in the sense that I am able to ground my fieldwork with an understanding of local norms and contested meanings, and also have the analytical distance that my foreign academic training offers me, the combination of which enriches the quality and diversity of narratives about the developing world.

Reflexivity is the process of making sense of the various selves that researchers embody while conducting fieldwork. England (1994, p. 82) describes reflexivity as 'self-critical sympathetic introspection' coupled with 'the self-conscious analytical scrutiny of the self as researcher'. Since the 1980s, debates on ethics in fieldwork particularly in anthropology, have linked the positionality of the researcher with reflexivity— what became known as the 'reflexive-turn' (Babcock 1980; Foley 2002; Herzfeld 2009; Taggart and Sandstrom 2011). This approach centres the researcher by acknowledging that the researcher is the key fieldwork tool (Reinharz 1997, p. 3) and the work is therefore a process of ongoing mutual shaping between researcher and research (Attia and Edge 2017). I take reflexivity both as a posture and as a mindful process of how a researcher may critically acknowledge the self in research and the subjectivities thereof. This process is particularly important for emerging African researchers researching and writing on subjects that have previously only been articulated in the academy through the Western gaze. After all, as Cousin (2010, p. 10) aptly put it, 'The self is not some kind of virus that contaminates the research'. As a process, it means problematizing the various lenses through which our fieldwork interactions are seen and introspecting with humility about our vulnerabilities, partnerships as well as our power over research participants and the fieldwork environment and vice versa.

Considerations of positionality and reflexivity have been criticized particularly by feminist scholars for being inward looking and self-indulgent (Kobayashi 2003, p. 348; Bondi 2009, p. 328). Cousin (in Savin-Baden and Howell Major 2010, p. 24) further warns that the reflexive turn can lead to *positional piety* 'in which either moral authority is claimed through an affinity with subjects (such as working-class woman) or through a confessional declaration of difference and relative privilege (such as white middle-class man)'. Indeed, an important question arises of whether researchers' increasing focus on their positionality actually helps to produce better research (Patai 1994, p. 69). Foley (2002), an ethnographer, responds by arguing that adopting a reflexive posture enables researchers to adopt a genuine, narrative style that helps them to communicate their work and struggles more clearly. The reflexive exercise is about communicating honestly and openly about the messy, uncertain process of gathering first-hand knowledge rather than curating polished outcomes. Ultimately, the researcher's positionality feeds into the partial nature of knowledge produced from fieldwork processes and experiences and is therefore an important epistemological consideration.

THE RESEARCH CONTEXT

My doctoral research developed out of an interest in the power structures that underlie agricultural development in Kenya. The flower industry emerged in particular as a point of interest because of its elite ownership structure which, as Mulangu's (2016) research shows, is made up largely of commercial farms owned by Kenyans of Indian or European descent, and by the Kenyan political elite.[1] The sector is also influential in Kenya's economic development as the second highest earner of foreign exchange in the Agriculture sector after tea,[2] employing approximately 100,000 people in basic wage labour jobs. However, its developmental contributions and practices have not been fully explored in the literature. For example, there is little discussion about the knowledge impact of the industry locally, and limited literature differentiating the specific market practices and value chain relationships of mid-scale and small-scale producers that ensure their survival in an industry dominated by giants. With this in mind, I set out to explore the various ways in which these Kenyan flower producers negotiate for greater bargaining power in light of formative shifts in end markets from the Dutch auction towards sales in 'direct markets' (supermarkets and large retailers).

Between January and September 2016, I conducted eighty-three in-depth semi-structured interviews with a range of actors along the value chain in Kenya. My research area included Nairobi, Naivasha and the Mount Kenya region where large-[3] and mid-scale commercial farms are found, and Central Kenya (Njabini, Thika, Murang'a and Nyeri) where smallholders grow cut flowers. I also carried out seven interviews in the Netherlands at the Aalsmeer and Naaldwijk flower auctions. To help gain access to these key research sites, I approached the KFC, a membership and lobbying association for growers and exporters of cut flowers, who agreed to help mediate with key actors on my behalf.

Having the KFC as mediator was crucial to my research because, over the past two decades, the industry has had a reputation for being averse to researchers since a series of scathing reports were published, by a number of international NGOs as well as the Kenyan Human Rights Commission, exposing the industry's reputation for labour rights violations, tax dodging and environmental pollution (Bolger 1997; Wolf 1997; Oxfam 2004; Opondo 2006; Christian Aid 2008; Kenya Human Rights Commission 2012). As the industry embraced reform thereafter, it also carefully managed its public image, and with that research access, that might shed light on other issues in the industry, was policed. Trust flows predominantly through informal, familial or kinship-based affiliations, which is compounded by the industry norm of not using contracts to secure deals. I noted that the introductions I received from gatekeepers and farm managers to their peers were references within their ethnic groups. Outside of these gendered, ethnicized insider groups, only a strong personal reference and introduction from a respected industry figure within the KFC could provide access.

Just as much of the industry's research and development is centred in Europe and done by Europeans, so is much of the scholarship. The academic literature on and around the political economy of the Kenyan flower industry has been dominated by Western researchers (see, for example, Hughes 2000; Jaffee 1992; Thoen et al. 2000; Dolan 2007; Riisgaard 2009, 2011; Buxton 2012; Buxton and Vorley 2012). With the exception of Magdalene Opondo (Dolan et al. 2004; Dolan and Opondo 2005; Hale and Opondo 2005; Opondo 2006; Barrientos et al. 2015) and Maurice Bolo (Bolo et al. 2006; Bolo 2010, 2012), there are very few Kenyan academics who write consistently on the political economy of the Kenyan cut flower industry. This could be in part because there is a greater research funding pool for scientific agricultural research pertaining to food security challenges and African researchers are more likely to respond to this rather than political economy analyses of non-food luxury export crops such as cut flowers. While it is relatively easy to find publications by Western-trained African social scientists, it is rare to find writing that gives texture to their fieldwork experiences. This rarity is what makes their articulation so urgent. I found that local research organizations that I interacted with were pleased with my coming home to conduct research and expressed confidence that the knowledge produced from my fieldwork stood a better chance of being institutionalized locally rather than exported abroad, as happened with many foreign researchers. This shifted ever so slightly southwards the arc of the geopolitics of knowledge production that leans ever towards the European academy.

'GOING HOME' AS A KENYAN RESEARCHER FROM THE UNIVERSITY OF CAMBRIDGE

Going home to Kenya as a researcher was an alienating experience for me as I had had no prior contact with the flower industry. I also found myself alienated from the system of higher learning because my higher education had all been conducted abroad. This meant that I had no pre-existing institutional relationships in the Kenyan academy, which made me unfamiliar and therefore less trustworthy. One thing that rather surprisingly worked in my favour and allowed me to mitigate my 'otherness' was the class privilege that accompanied my affiliation with the University of Cambridge.

In Kenya, Cambridge, perhaps more than other elite universities, elicits both a curious sense of awe and cautionary distance. This is perhaps because, historically the Cambridge School Certificate was the ultimate academic credential and was instrumental in creating and positioning Kenya's colonial and post-colonial ruling elite (Sandgren 2012).[4] The legacy of this access to power that the Cambridge name offered persists in the public imagination and this was repeatedly brought home to me during the introduction stage of many of my interviews. Upon introduction, the mention of my Cambridge affiliations tempered the relaxed attitude that many of the mostly male participants appeared to have adopted on first experiencing me as a young Kenyan female. What began as slightly dismissive, 'How can I help you young lady?', turned into a more open 'Oh, miss, you're so young. And you're doing a PhD at Cambridge?!'. As an outsider to the industry, the recognizability of Cambridge enabled me to get my foot in the door. And yet, while the Cambridge identity provided some privilege that was useful in negotiating access, it was not quite synonymous with fully open doors. This became apparent to me through the reservations of certain industry officials who believed that because any research coming out of Cambridge would be 'taken very seriously', they might potentially be the subject of an exposé. In this way, the power which I wielded as a researcher from Cambridge shaped the seriousness with which my fieldwork and its potential future outcome were received. The reception I received was also startlingly indicative of a neo-colonial deference accorded to knowledge on local phenomena produced in the Western academy.

A mitigating factor in levelling interactions with research participants beyond the class differences imbued by education and urban bias was the selective use of language. The power of ethnic affiliation and use of three different languages—Kiswahili, English and Kikuyu—enabled me to slip between various positionalities in different fieldwork contexts. The idea of 'slipping between' was first articulated by Rossman and Rallis (1998, p. 161) in reference to an interview setting in which an English-speaking researcher might conduct an interview in a language other than English, or if the researcher and participants are fully fluent and bilingual and they slip between two languages in the interview. Srivastava (2006) who conducted comparative education research in India in Hindi and English, discusses the notion of mediating a researcher's multiple positionalities with fieldwork participants through the selective use of language as currency. The idea of currency, as she uses it, is powerful in unpacking the mechanisms of reciprocity in field work because it implies 'a medium of exchange to achieve temporary shared positionalities between researcher and participant to mediate relations of power and, ultimately, ease the exchange' (Srivastava 2006, p. 211).

Being able to slip between Kikuyu, Kiswahili and English for me was very useful in terms of building rapport with a wide variety of research participants. For example, while conducting interviews with smallholder flower farmers in rural central Kenya, which is predominantly inhabited by the Gikuyu, I communicated in my mother tongue, Kikuyu. My use of Kikuyu broke down urban bias and any class barriers that might have been metaphorically erected during my introduction of myself as a researcher from Cambridge. It led the farmers to regard me as *mwari wa nyumba* (a daughter of the home), who was respectful enough to address them in the language in which they were most comfortable. The use of Kikuyu language helped to transform the knowledge exchange relationship from being perceived as extractive to being relational.

While conducting fieldwork at the Nairobi flower market among traders and smallholder farmers, the language of research encounter shifted to Kiswahili. Using Kiswahili in the city is common since, as the national language, it has historically been the language of trade and commerce. It also allows those conversing to circumnavigate biases that might arise around ethnic cleavages. The language of choice for *Wananchi* (citizens), Kiswahili levels differences in class and education at the point of interaction. Conversing with research participants in Kiswahili enabled me to create a camaraderie with the traders and smallholder farmers. This was not the case with managers in the commercial flower farms around the Lake Naivasha and Mount Kenya regions. Here, I conducted interviews in English. English is the official language of Kenya and its use indicates a professional distance between those conversing. As the medium of instruction in schools, and in many ways the language of data, English demarcated the fieldwork interview as an academic space. Using it therefore effectively positioned me as a student and researcher.

Harking back to Reinharz's (1997) typology, the choice of language use enabled me to slip between positionalities: my research self in English, my brought self as a Kikuyu speaker, kinswoman and daughter, and my situational self-speaking Kiswahili as a potential advocate or client in the market place. This slipping between positionalities—the daughter, the ally, and the professional—through the selective use of language facilitated the search for common ground in meaning between my research participants and me.

In addition to language, my ethnicity played a role in seeking access to smallholder farmers in rural Kenya and insider groups, particularly farm managers. Language and ethnicity are inextricably intertwined in the Kenyan context, and further ethnic awareness tends to be more pronounced in rural areas where ethnic communities exist in enclaves. Productive conversations with smallholder farmers depended on building rapport which depended on how naturally they were able to relate to me. The sample of smallholders I interviewed were all from Central Kenya and were all Agikuyu, as am I. Upon saying my name ('Mwangi' is a common Kikuyu surname) and explaining my work in Kikuyu, I often received welcoming comments such as, 'Oh, it is good that you are *mwari wa nyumba*', referring to membership of the Agikuyu community. I am not entirely sure the reception would have been as warm were I unable to converse in the language. While ethnic kinship extended me a warm reception, it was encouraging to see that I was not barred from accessing information from farmers from other communities. A gatekeeper from the Luo community, which has been historically politically construed as rival to the Kikuyu, confessed that he initially struggled to find a reason to assist me, as he put it, 'Why should I help a privileged Kikuyu lady?' Nevertheless, he confessed that he felt compelled to assist me since he was impressed by my academic effort. I noted that thereafter all the farm manager networks he proceeded to introduce me to were also all his Luo kinsmen. African researchers returning home to conduct fieldwork would do well to be aware of possible ethno-centric dimensions influencing access and reception of the researcher and prepare to navigate them through the selective use of language, gatekeepers or translators.

Access in my research encounters was also shaped by gendered (mis)perceptions in the overwhelmingly male-dominated research participants. These views played out in fieldwork interactions along three main considerations—ambition and intelligence, societal status and gendered roles. Being in a highly competitive industry, a number of informants made remarks to the effect that, as a young woman I 'simply didn't look threatening', meaning that I did not seem capable of using the information shared to compete with or undermine them. Male research participants appeared to relax in my presence making them often more willing to speak at length. When I learned about the communicative power of being deemed non-threatening, I played along with it in order to obtain more information. Research participants' reactions sometimes stiffened, however, when they learned that I was a Cambridge doctoral student, and therefore 'very serious and sharp'. At this point, some refused for the interview to be recorded and became more guarded in the conversation.

My societal status as an unmarried woman and research student also granted varying degrees of access. When I interviewed women in senior positions, they often remarked that they were encouraged to find a young woman researching the industry and were therefore forthcoming and generous with their information. There was generally an empathetic mirroring where they saw me as a younger version of themselves. Many men interviewed in senior positions made what appeared to be patronizing references to my unmarried status and took on the role of benevolent benefactors who 'indulged' me with their time and information. Acquiescing to this power relational stance in the interviews actually worked in my favour as the participants offered data, information and access to their networks. Counter-intuitively, in this patriarchal environment and male-dominated industry, stereotypes of women as vulnerable and non-threatening worked to increase and enhance my access.

Also surprising was the notion that, as a Kenyan woman, I had internalized and could understand the male farm managers' patriarchal use of gender stereotypes. In explaining why ninety percent of his greenhouse workers were women, a flower farm manager elaborated on his preference of female employees because of their docility, risk-aversion, dutifulness, attention to detail, delicacy and superior ability to work on monotonous tasks. While describing this preference, the farm manager asked me, 'In the family who takes care of things at home?', to which I responded, 'Traditionally, it's the woman'. He then proceeded to ask who was more responsible in the home. When I responded that both the men and women were responsible in the home, the farm manager corrected me explaining that it was precisely women's responsibilities in the home, as well as their long suffering, risk-averse, non-confrontational demeanour, that made them great flower farm plantation employees.

My gut reaction was to speak out against these sexist views. However, I realized that in this scenario, the flower farm manager provided more information in reaction to acquiescence rather than a challenge to his deeply stereotyped views on women's roles. Getting the most out of this situation meant dialling back my moral outrage at the situation and balancing my roles as a researcher with my role as a Kenyan woman familiar with the farm manager's patriarchal views. This interaction was performative, in that I had to give answers that played along with the farm managers' expectations of my understanding of Kenyan society in order to keep the conversation going. In these examples, in the interests of easing access, positionality is experienced as playing along with, rather than resisting, otherwise disagreeable gendered assumptions. To ease knowledge exchange, where power dynamics are deeply gendered and unequal something has to give, and in this gendered scenario it was my freedom to critique the perspectives with which I disagreed.

RECIPROCITY: INSTITUTIONALIZING KNOWLEDGE IN LOCAL INSTITUTIONS

While much of this chapter has been concerned with positionality and how the different aspects of my identity and position have influenced access to research informants and data, here in this final section, I want briefly to discuss reciprocity and what this means for African researchers conducting research back home. The concepts of positionality and reflexivity are self-critical, inward-looking and centred on unpacking the specificities of being a researcher in the field; however, reciprocity acknowledges the inherently relational nature of field work. Just as researchers have expectations about the data and information they hope to gain and the relationships they have to build to do so, research participants also cultivate spaces of intention in the encounter which researchers inhabit. Discussing reciprocity allows us to develop an awareness of ways in which this encounter can be positively balanced to steer it away from extraction and towards partnership.

Reciprocity as a practice of mutual exchange in fieldwork matters because it mitigates imbalances of power, enabling us to conduct research 'with' rather than 'on' (Pillow 2003). As part of this practice, negotiating institutional permissions was important for my research for ethical and relational reasons. Sultana (2007, p. 375) explains that, 'ethical research is produced through *negotiated spaces* and practices of reflexivity that are critical about issues of positionality and power relations at multiple scales'. From a critical historical perspective, the acquisition of knowledge from developing countries by Western researchers[5] has been by and large, extractive and exploitative (Lewis 1973, p. 582). By wielding class and educational privileges over research participants, researchers today can also become agents of domination and control. Institutional permissions exist to place checks on those relationships and institutionalize knowledge generated locally. The time-consuming, repetitive process of seeking institutional permissions illustrates the profoundly relational nature of fieldwork. It goes to show that access is not a one-off event but a series of interactions and relationship building. Writing on the complexities of conducting fieldwork in primary schools in Kenya and the importance of systematic building of relationships in the process of fieldwork, Kiragu and Warrington (2013) advise foreign researchers seeking to conduct fieldwork in the global South to mitigate power dynamics and build relationships by partnering with local researchers.

The government of Kenya requires academic researchers conducting fieldwork locally to apply for permits from the National Commission for Science, Technology and Innovation (NACOSTI). Having had difficulties submitting my application online, I visited the administrator on several occasions, and my proposal was processed. This process speaks to the importance of building rapport and inter-personal relationships, especially when considered an outsider. One of the conditions of obtaining this permit was that the researcher be locally affiliated with an institution in Kenya and commit to sharing their work with NACOSTI. This requirement is an attempt to build up and locally house the body of knowledge produced within Kenya with Kenyan research bodies. Seeking out local institutional backing is also a way for the researcher to respect the role of the research bureaucracy in localizing and making public knowledge produced through field work. The process creates a shared sense of public responsibility in the researcher as co-creator of knowledge with and through the society from which it finds its meaning.

To meet the stipulations of the research permit, I decided to apply for affiliation as a research associate with the Institute of Development Studies (IDS) at the University of Nairobi. This was a less than straightforward process and my application suffered through four months of bureaucratic delays.[6] This was in part because I began the application while away. However, as soon as I followed through in person, the process accelerated. Throughout this process, I felt the need to emphasize certain positionalities and downplay others. For example, I did not speak much about my overall higher education abroad in order not to seem as foreign and elite as I appeared on paper. There have been reports of foreign-educated students having a difficult time gaining acceptance within local institutions partly because they are perceived as competitors, and because their foreign education can be resentfully perceived as a rejection of the local system of higher education. The fact that I could slip between and accentuate various positionalities (that is being Kenyan and an insider while being foreign as a Cambridge student) in order to build rapport as required, manifests the privileges of class access. I was granted the research associate position on the condition that I would share with IDS knowledge gained in the process of my research.

Many researchers will attest to the critical role of gatekeepers in setting the tone of relationships with research participants and negotiating access to data during fieldwork. The most important gatekeeper in terms of providing direct access to a wide range of flower industry officials was the KFC. The KFC has about 180 flower farms as members and is responsible for issuing internationally benchmarked certification after rigorous audits, which ensure the quality and reliability of the flower production process. I found the Council to be very welcoming to researchers. In an introductory meeting with the CEO, Jane Ngige, she asked whether I would be 'coming back' after my doctoral studies had finished to 'make use of the knowledge gained in Kenya'. In this case, the concern was not so much for the institutionalization of knowledge but rather the localization and utility of my findings for the local context. This matters because as Zakri (2006) notes, gaps persist in the relevance of scholarship from many African universities to the national agenda and developmental priorities. To gain access in this setting, I therefore had to emphasize the *situationally created self* of possible future advocate for the industry. The encounter with the CEO of the KFC sheds light on the dynamism of positionalities and indeed how the performance of 'shape-shifting' to emphasize some and downplay others is beneficial for negotiating access and building rapport with research participants.

REFLECTIONS AND CONCLUSION

The impetus behind writing this chapter was to add my voice to the body politic of African researchers writing about various fieldwork experiences that render complex the notion of home as the familiar. As I have elaborated over these pages, my experience of conducting fieldwork in the flower industry in Kenya as a young female Kenyan made me engage various positionalities which lie at the intersection of gender, ethnicity, class privilege and as a Kenyan researcher in a field researched mostly by foreigners. Many of these challenges manifest in the struggle for access to research participants in an industry known for its reticence. Coming to terms with various positionalities meant seeking out institutional mediators to negotiate access. In so doing, I learned more about the nature and dynamics of reciprocity in knowledge exchange. This reflexive exercise enables me to retrospectively see how I negotiated access by shifting between various positionalities. I show that I arrived at these positionalities in different ways—'slipping between', emphasizing or downplaying some identities and 'playing along' where they enabled access. The dynamism of this process of shifting positionalities depicts fieldwork as performance on the part of the researcher.

The second lesson learnt was that knowledge exchange rested on a mutual understanding of reciprocity with the research participant. On the part of the institutional gatekeepers, reciprocity was premised on the desire to locally institutionalize the knowledge, or to establish the local utility of the knowledge generated from fieldwork, which is a matter of particular importance for developing countries which have long been sites of knowledge capture and extraction. The negotiation entailed in this relational process sheds light on the fact that the fieldwork encounter is a political process. The reflexive exercise that enables us to come to this understanding also empowers us to build partnerships rather than extractive, exploitative relations through our research.

I conclude by affirming the mercurial, performative nature of fieldwork conducted 'back home' on the part of the researcher. Coming to terms with various positionalities in the struggle to obtain access is a process of adapting to what works best. Dislocation, disjuncture and alienation from the familiar should be understood not as incidental to the co-creation of knowledge by African researchers studying local phenomena from Western universities, but as birth pains of developing new epistemes with local communities. Knowledge exchange is intrinsically about building learning relationships through a reciprocal exercise. Therefore, being reflexive about why and how we shift between the selves we bring to the field enables us to form more genuine relationships, and brings intellectual humility and honesty about the limitations and quality of our work.

NOTES

1. Asian-Kenyan 52.2%; White Kenyan 24.6%; Black-Kenyan 23.2%.
2. The flower industry contributes approximately 70% to horticulture in terms of export value (2015 calculations, author's own from HCD data) and 1.06% to the national GDP (2018 figures, KFC website). Kenya is the lead exporter of rose cut flowers to the European Union (EU) with a market share of 38% (KFC).
3. For the purposes of segmenting my research, I classified large-scale farms as those over 80 hectares, mid-scale farms between 20 and 80 ha and smallholder farms as anything from a sixteenth of an acre to 3 ha.
4. Sandgren (2012) writes about the "Athomi" (the kikuyu term for the well-educated) which was the generation of African elite who gained economic and social advantages in the colonial and post-colonial administrations due to their ability to read, which was obtained from missionary education.
5. Diane Lewis (1973) writes about how Anthropology as a discipline emerged from the colonial expansion of Europe and therefore anthropologists became agents of empire who established links between Westerners and 'natives'.
6. It is important to note that bureaucratic delays I experienced as a guest researcher are symptomatic of a deeper systemic challenge especially affecting PhD students located in many African Universities. Manyika and Szanton (2001) explain that it takes on average 6–8 years to complete a PhD in most African universities because of inadequate resources and bureaucracy in the approval process, which involves departments, faculties and universities.

REFERENCES

Abrahams-Gessel, S., Denman, C. A., Montano, C. M., Gaziano, T. A., Levitt, N., Rivera-Andrade, A., Munguia Carrrasco, D., Zulu, J., Akter Khanam, M., & Puoane, T. (2015). The Training and Field Work Experiences of Community Health Workers Conducting Non-invasive, Population-based Screening for Cardiovascular Disease in Four Communities in Low and Middle-Income Settings. *Global Heart, 10*(1), 45–54. http://doi.org/10.1016/j.gheart.2014.12.008.

Ali, R. (2015). Rethinking Representation: Negotiating Positionality, Power and Space in the Field. *Gender, Place and Culture, 22*(6), 783–800.

Attia, M., & Edge, J. (2017). Be(com)ing a Reflexive Researcher: A Developmental Approach to Research Methodology. *Open Review of Educational Research, 4*(1), 33–45.

Babcock, B. (1980). Reflexivity: Definitions and Discriminations. *Semiotica, 30*(1/2), 1–14.

Barrientos, S., Knorringa, P., Evers, B., Visser, M., & Opondo, M. (2015). Shifting Regional Dynamics of Global Value Chains: Implications for Economic and Social Upgrading in African Horticulture. *Environment and Planning A, 48*(7), 1266–1283.

Bolger, A. (1997, May 9). Unions Call for Code to Protect Flower Workers. *Financial Times*, p. 4.

Bolo, M. O. (2010). *Learning to Export: Building Farmers' Capabilities Through Partnerships in Kenya's Flower Industry* (Hal Id: hal-00526145). http://hal. archives-ouvertes.fr/docs/00/52/61/45/PDF/Bolo_Learning_to_export. pdf. Accessed January 27, 2018.

Bolo, M. (2012). *Learning and Innovation in Agri-Export Industries.* Saarbrucken, Germany: LAP Lambert Academic Publishing.

Bolo, M., Muthoka, N. M., Washisino, R., Mwai, V., & Kisongwo, D. (2006). Research Priorities for Kenya's Cut-Flower Industry: Farmers' Perspectives. *African Technology Policy Studies Network.* Technopolicy Brief 14. https:// atpsnet.org/wp-content/uploads/2017/05/technopolicy_brief_series_14. pdf. Accessed January 27, 2018.

Bondi, L. (2009). Teaching Reflexivity: Undoing or Reinscribing Habits of Gender? *Journal of Geography in Higher Education, 33*(3), 327–337.

Buxton, A. (2012, January). Linking Smallholders to Modern Markets. *IIED.*

Buxton, A., & Vorley, B. (2012, September). The Ethical Agent: Fresh Flowers in Kenya. *IIED.* http://pubs.iied.org/pdfs/16037IIED.pdf. Accessed January 10, 2018.

Chereni, A. (2000). Positionality and Collaboration During Fieldwork: Insights from Research with Co-nationals Living Abroad. *Forum: Qualitative Social Research Socialforschung, 15*(3). http://www.qualitative-research.net/index. php/fqs/article/view/2058/3716. Accessed January 27, 2018.

Christian Aid. (2008). *Death and Taxes: The True Toll of Tax Dodging.* http://www. christianaid.org.uk/images/deathandtaxes.pdf. Accessed January 20, 2018.

Cousin, G. (2010). Positioning Positionality. In M. Savin-Baden & C. Howell Major (Eds.), *New Approaches to Qualitative Research—Wisdom and Uncertainty* (pp. 9–18). London and New York: Routledge.

Dolan, C. S. (2007). Market Affections: Moral Encounters with Kenyan Fairtrade Flowers. *Ethnos, 72*(2), 239–261.

Dolan, C., & Opondo, M. (2005). Seeking Common Ground: Multi-stakeholder Processes in Kenya's Cut Flower Industry. *Journal of Corporate Citizenship, 18*(12), 87–98.

Dolan, C., Opondo M., & Smith S. (2004). *Gender, Rights and Participation in the Kenya Cut Flower Industry* (Natural Resources Institute Working Paper No. 2768). London: National Resources Institute.

England, K. (1994). Getting Personal: Reflexivity, Positionality, and Feminist Research. *Professional Geographer, 46*(1), 80–89.

Faria, C., & Good, R. Z. (2012). The Importance of Everyday Encounters: Young Scholars Reflect on Fieldwork in Africa. *African Geographical Review, 31*(1), 63–66.

Foley, D. E. (2002). Critical Ethnography: The Reflexive Turn. *International Journal of Qualitative Studies in Education, 15*(4), 469–490.

Geleta, E. B. (2014). The Politics of Identity and Methodology in African Development Ethnography. *Qualitative Research, 14,* 131–146.

Hale, A., & Opondo, M. (2005). Humanising the Cut Flower Chain: Confronting the Realities of Flower Production for Workers in Kenya. *Antipode, 37*(2), 301–323.

Herzfeld, M. (2009). The Cultural Politics of Gesture. *Ethnography, 10*(2), 131–152.

Hughes, A. (2000). Retailers, Knowledges and Changing Commodity Networks: The Case of the Cut Flower Trade. *Geoforum, 31*(2), 175–190.

Jaffee, S., 1992. How Private Enterprise Organized Agricultural Markets in Kenya, *Policy Research Working Paper Series* 823, The World Bank. 347–375.

Jewkes, R., Watts, C., Abrahams, N., Penn-Kekana, L., & Garcia-Moreno, C. (2000). Ethical and Methodological Issues in Conducting Research on Gender-Based Violence in Southern Africa. *Reproductive Health Matters, 8*(15), 93–103.

Kenya Human Rights Commission. (2012). *'Wilting in Bloom': The Irony of Women Labour Rights in the Cut-Flower Sector in Kenya.* Nairobi: Kenya Human Rights Commission.

Kiragu, S., & Warrington, M. (2013). How We Used Moral Imagination to Address Ethical and Methodological Complexities While Conducting Research with Girls in School Against the Odds in Kenya. *Qualitative Research, 13,* 173–189.

Kobayashi, A. (2003). GPC Ten Years On: Is Self-Reflexivity Enough? *Gender, Place and Culture, 10*(4), 345–349.

Leavy, P. (Ed.). (2014). *The Oxford Handbook of Qualitative Research.* Oxford: Oxford University Press.

Lewis, D. (1973). Anthropology and Colonialism. *Current Anthropology, 14*(5), 581–602.

Mandiyanike, D. (2009). The Dilemma of Conducting Research Back in Your Own Country as a Returning Student: Reflections of Research Fieldwork in Zimbabwe. *Area, 41,* 64–71.

Manyika, S., & Szanton, D. (2001). PhD Programmes in African Universities: Current Status and Future Prospects. *A Report to the Rockefeller Foundation.* Berkeley: University of California.

McCorkel, J. A., & Myers, K. (2003). What Difference Does Difference Make? Position and Privilege in the Field. *Qualitative Sociology, 26*(2), 199–231.

Mollinga, P. (2008). Field Research Methodology as Boundary Work: An Introduction. In C. Wall & P. Mollinga (Eds.), *Fieldwork in Difficult Environments. Methodology as Boundary Work in Development Research* (pp. 1–17). Berlin: LIT Verlag.

Mulangu, F. (2016, September). Mapping the Technological Capabilities of Kenyan-Owned Floricultural Firms. *African Center for Economic Transformation.* Presentation at the ASA—UK Annual Conference, University of Cambridge.

Opondo, M. (2006). *Emerging Corporate Social Responsibility in Kenya's Cut Flower Industry.* http://www.unisa.ac.za/contents/colleges/col_econ_man_science/ccc/docs/Opondo.pdf. Accessed December 20, 2017.

Oxfam. (2004). *Trading Away Our Rights: Women Working in Global Supply Chains.* https://policy-practice.oxfam.org.uk/publications/trading-away-our-rights-women-working-in-global-supply-chains-112405. Accessed January 10, 2018.

Patai, D. (1994). Response: When Method Becomes Power. In A. Gitlen (Ed.), *Power and Method* (pp. 61–73). New York: Routledge.

Pillow, W. S. (2003). Confession, Catharsis, or Cure? Rethinking the Uses of Reflexivity as Methodological Power in Qualitative Research. *International Journal of Qualitative Studies in Education, 16,* 175–196.

Reinharz, S. (1997). Who Am I? The Need for a Variety of Selves in the Field. In R. Hertz (Ed.), *Reflexivity and Voice* (pp. 3–20). Thousand Oaks, CA: Sage.

Riisgaard, L. (2009). Global Value Chains, Labour Organization and Private Social Standards: Lessons from East African Cut Flower Industries. *World Development, 37*(2), 326–340.

Riisgaard, L. (2011). Towards More Stringent Sustainability Standards? Trends in the Cut Flower Industry. *Review of African Political Economy, 38*(129), 435–453.

Romero, M., & Stewart, A. (Eds.). (1999). *Women's Untold Stories: Breaking Silence, Talking Back, Voicing Complexity.* New York: Routledge.

Rossman, G. B., & Rallis, S. (1998). *Learning in the Field: An Introduction to Qualitative Research.* London: Sage.

Sandgren, D. P. (2012). *Mau Mau's Children: The Making of Kenya's Postcolonial Elite.* Madison, WI: University of Wisconsin Press.

Savin-Baden, M., & Howell Major, C. (2010). *New Approaches to Qualitative Research—Wisdom and Uncertainty.* London and New York: Routledge.

Siwale, J. (2015). Why Did I Not Prepare for This? The Politics of Negotiating Fieldwork Access, Identity, and Methodology in Researching Microfinance Institutions. *SAGE Open, 5*(2), 1–12.

Srivastava, P. (2006). Reconciling Multiple Researcher Positionalities and Languages in International Research. *Research in Comparative and International Education, 1*(3), 210–222.

Sultana, F. (2007). Reflexivity Positionality and Participatory Ethics: Negotiating Fieldwork Dilemmas in International Research. *ACME: An International E-Journal for Critical Geographies, 6*(3), 374–385.

Taggart, J. M., & Sandstrom, A. R. (2011). Introduction to "Long-Term Fieldwork". *Anthropology and Humanism, 36*(1), 1–6.

Thoen, R., Jaffee, S., Dolan, S., & Ba, F. (2000). *Equatorial Rose: The Kenyan—European Cut Flower Supply Chain*. Washington, DC: World Bank.

Thomson, S., Ansom, A., & Murison, J. (Eds.). (2013). *Emotional and Ethical Challenges for Field Research in Africa: The Story Behind the Findings*. Basingstoke: Palgrave Macmillan.

Wolf, J. (1997, May 10). Report on Flower Industry Unearths Dangers to Workers. *The Guardian*, p. 16.

Wolfe, D. (1996). Situating Feminist Dilemmas in Fieldwork. In D. Wolfe (Ed.), *Feminist Dilemmas in Fieldwork* (pp. 1–55). Boulder, CO: Westview Press.

Zakri, A. H. (2006). Research Universities in the 21st Century: Global Challenges and Local Implications. *Global Keynote Scenario at the UNESCO Forum on Higher Education, Research and Knowledge: Colloquium on Research and Higher Education* 60, 17–39.

CHAPTER 3

Being Familiar, and Yet Strange: Conducting Research as a Hybrid Insider-Outsider in Uganda

Christine van Hooft

Social sciences research involves the study of individuals and communities, and the patterns of behavior that shape different groups of people. In pursuit of new knowledge, researchers undertake field research in which they spend time studying a particular community in order to conduct analysis and draw conclusions about this community. For some researchers, they will be in some way connected personally to the subject group, as an 'insider.' Other researchers will study a group with which no substantial prior contact has been established, as an 'outsider.' Sections of the literature relating to conducting field research have come to recognize that some researchers do not fall into this dichotomy of insiders and outsiders, and instead fall somewhere along a spectrum of insider and outsider.

In preparing for my own fieldwork in Uganda in the first half of 2016, I conducted a literature review of the experiences of field researchers in Uganda and other East African countries, in an effort to prepare for likely challenges and experiences I might face. Having lived in Uganda

C. van Hooft (✉)
Centre of Development Studies, University of Cambridge, Cambridge, UK

© The Author(s) 2019
L. Johnstone (ed.), *The Politics of Conducting Research in Africa*,
https://doi.org/10.1007/978-3-319-95531-5_3

previously, from 2011 to 2013, I was somewhat familiar with the national context. As a former employee of the site at which I proposed to begin my research, the Ministry of Finance, Planning and Economic Development in Kampala, I was also partially familiar with the institutional context in which my research would take place. I was therefore finding myself somewhat stuck between the two categories of researcher proposed by the literature: I was in some ways positioned as an insider to the studied community, but in other ways an outsider.

This chapter proposes a third category of researcher: a hybrid insider-outsider researcher, in which a researcher shares some characteristics of the studied group, but nonetheless is an outsider in regard to other important characteristics. A hybrid insider-outsider may have some familiarity with the subject group based on limited personal experience or experience in the past, but lack sufficient experience to be considered a genuine insider. As the globalization of research and the mobility of researchers increase, an ever-growing number of researchers will experience conducting research as a hybrid insider-outsider. In this chapter, I will detail my experiences as a hybrid insider-outsider researcher, with the goal of complementing the existing literature with the unique insights this positionality can offer.

Positionality: Insiders and Outsiders

In the process of undertaking field research, the social sciences researcher is attempting to locate, analyze, interpret and represent knowledge, acquired through the study of others. An important question for the researcher to ask of themselves is how they are positioned in relation to their research subjects, and how this positionality may affect the collection, interpretation and representation of knowledge they are seeking to undertake. Through a process of reflexivity, the researcher considers how their own position in relation to the subject will affect the outcomes and processes of research (Hellawell 2006, p. 483). By reflecting on their relationship to the studied community, the researcher identifies the effect that the researcher's own beliefs, assumptions and values will have on the research methodology, results and presentation.

One reflexivity mechanism through which a researcher's positionality can be identified is through identifying whether the researcher is an insider or an outsider in relation to the subject community. A significant body of literature exists in defining and exploring these categorizations.

In these discussions, authors offer definitions of insider versus outsider researchers, and there exists a degree of overlap between these definitions. For example, Corbin Dwyer and Buckle (2009, p. 58) describe insiders as those who share a particular attribute with the studied community, such as languages, roles, identities or experiences. Hellawell (2006, p. 484) defines an insider as a researcher who has a priori knowledge of the studied community, as a result of personal knowledge of the community and its members. Hockey (1993, p. 199) indicates that a researcher may be familiar with the location being studied, or may be a part of the community of people being studied. The similarities of these definitions indicate that insider researchers are generally defined narrowly: they are members of the studied community, or share its key attributes. Outsiders, defined in the opposite, are those who are said to be approaching the community of study from beyond its borders, to share no attributes with the community, or have no previous experience of it.

A substantial portion of the literature relating to conducting social research in the field is devoted to assessing whether a researcher who is an 'insider' is better placed for conducting research than an 'outsider.' For example, Corbin Dwyer and Buckle (2009, p. 55) compare their respective experiences of conducting qualitative research in communities to which one researcher related as an insider and one researcher as an outsider. Both insider-researchers and outsider-researchers are thought to have some advantages in being able to conduct research, and so contribute to the body of knowledge on a particular community or topic. Many authors within the ethnographic, anthropological and international development literatures have developed arguments in favor of being either an insider-researcher or outsider-researcher, in terms of the advantages of each position. In favor of being an insider, authors such as Unluer (2012, p. 5) argue that insider-researchers can form a greater level of trust with the studied community due to their existing personal connection to it, have greater familiarity with the community and knowledge of the topic under study, and superior knowledge of the group dynamics of the studied group, in comparison to an outsider-researcher. Paechter (2012, p. 77) adds that an insider-researcher may be more able to access the studied community than an outsider, due to already being familiar to the studied group. The insider-researcher may also benefit from improved rapport and communication with the group, and reduced culture shock (Hockey 1993, p. 199).

While these arguments present some of the advantages of conducting research as an insider, on the other hand, insider-researchers could potentially be affected by disadvantages arising from their closeness to the studied group. These include a loss of objectivity in relation to the group (Unluer 2012, p. 6), interview participants not revealing key information because they assume that it is already known to the researcher (Breen 2007, p. 164), or an insider-researcher overestimating their knowledge or understanding of the group (Corbin Dwyer and Buckle 2009, p. 59). An insider-researcher may resist approaching difficult topics with the studied community for fear of damaging their friendships with group members (Hockey 1993, p. 213). Sherif (2001, p. 437) adds that for an insider-researcher, the boundaries between the researcher and the studied community can be difficult to identify, potentially posing challenges for the insider-researcher to separate themselves from their research with adequate detachment. The insider-researcher may also be at risk of making assumptions or pre-judgments about the research subjects that arise from their familiarity with their context, or may assume that their views of the group are more representative than is in fact the case. There may also be antipathy between the researcher and the studied group, or between the researcher and individuals within the group, potentially leading to the studied community providing incomplete or inaccurate data to the researcher (Hockey 1993, p. 199).

For outsider-researchers, challenges arise from their unfamiliarity to and with the group being studied. These challenges include negotiating the permission to access the studied group (Breen 2007, p. 167), a lack of prior knowledge of the group and of the dynamics within it, and a lack of a pre-existing relationship upon which trust can be based (Unluer 2012, p. 6). The studied community does not regard the outsider-researcher as one of 'their own,' and so may be reluctant to share controversial or damaging information about the community with the researcher. The outsider-researcher may experience practical barriers in conducting their research, such as language barriers or cultural misunderstandings, that are less likely to be faced by an insider (Hockey 1993, p. 199).

On the positive side, the outsider-researcher has some advantages over the insider-researcher. The outsider may be more able to be objective about the studied group than the insider-researcher, and have a greater level of detachment from the community. They are less likely to overestimate their understanding of the material, and less likely to bring prior assumptions about the group into the research (Unluer 2012, p. 6). They do not need to be as concerned about maintaining pre-existing or subsequent relationships with the group, and so are at less risk of self-censoring the topics they choose to discuss with the group (Hockey 1993, p. 199). Overall, as this section has shown, several authors within the literature acknowledge that there are both advantages and disadvantages to being either an insider-researcher or an outsider-researcher.

Insider and Outsider: A Dichotomy or a Spectrum?

Following from this group of authors who discuss the advantages and disadvantages of being an outsider or an insider, are authors who instead argue that the division between insider and outsider is theoretical, and not applicable in the practical application of fieldwork. For these authors, the concepts of insider and outsider should not be considered as dichotomous, but rather as a spectrum along which researchers are located. Corbin Dwyer and Buckle (2009, p. 62) argue that the concept of the insider as opposed to the outsider may be oversimple; there may in fact be a third space for the researcher to occupy. Deutsch (2004, p. 897) notes that any social group contains diversity, so the researcher may experience similarities or differences with different individuals within the group, rather than being an insider or outsider relative to the entire group. Greene (2014, p. 2) describes 'partial insiders,' who share some characteristics of the group, but remain in other ways distant from it. Finally, Ganga and Scott (2006, p. 3) argue that the process of conducting fieldwork can, for someone who thought themselves an insider to a particular group, instead reveal to them the ways in which they are an outsider to the group. Furthermore, the researcher may come to understand aspects or divisions within the community of which they had not previously been aware, despite considering themselves to be an insider relative to the group.

Authors further argue that given that very few researchers are either a complete insider or a complete outsider, researchers are instead located along a continuum. Along this continuum, each researcher is able to draw on some of the advantages of each researcher category. For example, Ganga and Scott (2006, p. 3) argue that a researcher can draw on the ways in which they share more similarities with the group in order to overcome other areas in which they are a relative outsider, such as researching within an age cohort (as an insider) to partially overcome cultural differences (as an outsider). In this way, a researcher can use an aspect that they share with the studied community to form a connection with the studied community, compensating for aspects they do not share with the studied community. Breen (2007, p. 163) explains that by locating herself at a particular point along the insider-outsider spectrum, she was able to draw together the advantages of being both an insider and an outsider, while avoiding the disadvantages of being exclusively one.

For these authors, researchers can be said to be located along a spectrum or a continuum between being an insider and being an outsider, in the sense that the researcher shares characteristics with the studied group, but only to a certain extent. For example, a researcher may share the ethnic background of the studied community, but not a common language, meaning that they are an insider but only to some extent. The imagery of the 'continuum' from insider to outsider implies a sliding scale, where a researcher may be more strongly an insider or more strongly an outsider, depending on the extent to which they share certain characteristics with the studied group.

The imagery of a continuum or spectrum of insider/outsider status creates a useful initial point for understanding the positionality of researchers who are neither complete insiders nor complete outsiders. However, in my own experience, the complications that arose in conducting fieldwork are not fully captured by the 'spectrum' model. In the remainder of this chapter, I propose an expanded definition of the insider-outsider researcher continuum, namely the concept of the hybrid insider-outsider. The hybrid insider-outsider researcher is in some ways a part of the studied community, and an insider to it, but in other ways entirely removed from it—and in addition, this relationship can change over time, as the researcher moves into and out of the studied community and its shared attributes. In the following section, I will relate my own research experience as a former public servant in Uganda, and explain the ways in which the hybrid researcher model frames this experience. My experiences as a hybrid insider-outsider researcher can be useful to researchers who have at some point in time shared the attributes of the studied community, but not all attributes, and who are neither insiders nor outsiders to the community.

THE HYBRID INSIDER-OUTSIDER

Building on the literature described in the preceding section of the chapter, I offer an addition to the concept of the insider-outsider researcher as a continuum or sliding scale: the notion of the hybrid insider-outsider researcher. In this definition, a researcher shares fully some characteristics with the research group, but other characteristics not at all, and these shared attributes may have been shared more strongly at some time periods than in others. In other words, rather than sharing several aspects with the research group to some extent, the researcher shares some characteristics or aspects completely, but in other aspects is a complete outsider, and the researcher may have been an 'insider' to the group to a more concrete extent in the past. For example, a researcher may come from the same professional background as the studied group and fully understand the employment context of the group, but may also be from a separate ethnic group and linguistic background from the studied group. An example of this would be an automotive mechanic from Sweden conducting research with a community of automotive mechanics from Lesotho. While the researcher will be an insider in terms of the group's profession and fully understand the demands and processes of the work being undertaken, in every other respect, the researcher is an outsider to the studied community.

The researcher is thus in some respects an insider-researcher, but in other aspects, an outsider-researcher. This allows the researcher to capture some of the benefits of each of the insider and outsider categorizations, but also brings unique challenges that must be carefully considered by the researcher. In the above hypothetical model, the researcher has the advantage of knowing well what the challenges and demands are of working as a mechanic, and through this knowledge can gain the trust and respect of the studied group. As an outsider in other respects, the researcher has the advantage of being an objective observer of this specific community, and will be at less risk of bringing preconceived assumptions of the group's dynamics into the research. On the other hand, the researcher will face barriers in terms of communication and cultural understanding that would not be faced if they were an 'insider' in this respect as well. As a result of this hybrid status, with insider understanding of some aspects of the community but outsider understanding of other aspects, the knowledge developed by the researcher of this community is multifaceted and complex. The positionality of the researcher relative to the studied community is mixed, and represents an evolving positionality relative to the insider–outsider dichotomy described in the earlier literature.

Conducting Research as a Hybrid Insider-Outsider: A Public Servant in Uganda

My own experience of conducting research as a hybrid insider-outsider researcher arose from conducting doctoral fieldwork in Kampala, Uganda, for the first six months of 2016. My research focuses on the processes of fiscal decentralization and the delivery of public services by government agencies. The quality and efficiency of service delivery are affected to a substantial degree by the strength of the relationships between public servants in different areas and branches of government. My research therefore required that I learn more about the professional experiences and opinions of public servants in government agencies in Kampala, including both central ministries and sectoral agencies.

Throughout this six-month period, I interviewed public servants from the Ministries of Finance, Education and Sports, Health, Local Government, and Public Service. The studied group comprised of public servants at the technical level (for example, 'Economist') to the middle-managerial level (for example, 'Commissioner'), aged from their late-twenties to mid-forties, and all were Ugandan nationals. In common with the studied group, I have myself worked as a public servant, am Anglophone, hold a master's degree, am an economist, and am middle-class. Differently from the studied group, I am an Australian national, a non-resident of Uganda, am not religious, am of European ethnicity, and am unable to converse fluently in any indigenous Ugandan languages. I am also at the lower end of the age group of those interviewed. In the aspects listed above, I can be positioned using the model of a hybrid insider-outsider researcher, in the sense of clearly sharing some characteristics with the studied group, but being in other ways a clear outsider.

Furthermore, my status as an insider in the studied community contains a temporal aspect. This aspect is that several years prior to travelling to Uganda to conduct doctoral research, I lived in Kampala, and worked in the Ministry of Finance. I thus have some familiarity with the contexts of both Uganda and the Ministry, and some familiarity with the interviewees within that Ministry, and it was my hope that this familiarity would provide a strong base from which to begin my research. However, as I lived in Uganda for a relatively short period (two years), and had then been absent from Uganda for a further three years before returning to Uganda for fieldwork, I do not consider myself to be a fully-integrated member of the studied group, and consider myself to be a partial-insider at most.

The complex positionality of myself relative to the studied community in this case posed unique challenges in terms of the care needed in collecting, interpreting and presenting data. Firstly, the aspects in which I am a clear insider and a clear outsider required careful management to ensure that none of the disadvantages of these positionalities described earlier affected the process of research. Secondly, the temporal aspect of having previously been, but no longer, a member of the studied community added a further layer of complexity to my positionality relative to the studied group. Finally, the complexity of conducting research as a partial-insider within the Ministry of Finance itself posed challenges, as my position relative to interviewees in other ministries could be affected by the relationship between those ministries and the Ministry of Finance. Overall, the complexity of my relationship with the studied community necessitated a nuanced and flexible approach. In the remainder of this section, I reflect on the experience of undertaking research as a hybrid inside-outsider, and strategies put in place for successfully negotiating this positionality.

Complete-Insider—Advantages and Disadvantages

The advantages I experienced while conducting fieldwork as a complete insider in some respects, and a partial-insider in other respects, generated certain benefits for my ability to conduct my research. Most significantly, my professional experience as a public servant, albeit in a different national context, proved to be a valuable source of prior knowledge. The similarities in the structure, function and mechanisms of the respective public services of Australia and Uganda allowed me to arrive in Uganda to conduct fieldwork with pre-existing contextual information. For example, I was familiar with the process and timing of the budget cycle, the hierarchy of ministries within government, and the various methods of communication between elected officials and public servants. From a practical perspective, I was aware that an important first step in my research was obtaining written permission to undertake interviews within the Ministry from its most senior public servant, to reassure interview subjects that their senior manager agreed that they could be interviewed by me.

Most importantly, as an insider researcher in terms of being a public servant myself, I was familiar with the main tasks performed by public servants on a daily basis, such as preparing briefings for ministers, consulting with stakeholders within the community and the public service, and conducting data management and research. I was also familiar with the tensions, pressures and expectations faced by public servants, such as demands to facilitate the political objectives of elected leaders even where this necessitates reductions to funding to other priority areas. Given this 'insider' knowledge of the experiences of public servants, I had the advantage of being able to direct my interviews toward some the tensions involved in public service. For example, I was able to discuss with officials in the Ministry of Finance how they handle political pressures that impact the balance of expenditures across sectors, using terminology that was relevant to the professional context of the studied group.

On the other hand, as an insider in respect of being a public servant, there was also the possible disadvantage that I may bring pre-conceived ideas or assumptions into my research. In preparing to undertake fieldwork, I attempted to identify some of the risks that I might need to address, in terms of bringing pre-conceived ideas into the fieldwork process. One of these risks was that my experience as a public servant may lead me to believe that the experiences of all public servants are universal, or that the pressures faced by public servants in Australia were similar to those faced by public servants in Uganda. To the extent possible, I attempted to overcome this problem by reflecting on the assumptions I may have been making at different stages of the research, and asking myself whether these were valid. For example, given that a challenging aspect of the role of a public servant in Australia is working with other departments on joint policy portfolios, I had initially assumed that this challenge would be faced by Ugandan public servants. However, my research revealed that this is a far less common practice in the Ugandan public service than the Australian one, and so is far less of a concern for public servants in Uganda. I also attempted to triangulate and crosscheck my findings where possible, so that each conclusion I have drawn from my research should be based on multiple data points. For example, conclusions I have drawn about the budget process in Uganda are based on similar findings from interviews, documents and budget data itself. In this way, I have attempted to overcome the risk that as an insider to the professional sphere of public service, I have drawn assumptions into my fieldwork that were not warranted or supported by local evidence.

Complete-Outsider—Advantages and Disadvantages

I was, at the time of conducting fieldwork, not a resident of Uganda nor a Ugandan citizen, and in these respects I was a complete outsider relative to the studied community. I had initially expected this separation from the studied community to pose barriers to the research, such as challenges in obtaining sensitive information from interviewees. However, I in fact found this factor to be advantageous in one important way. Specifically, I found that my status as a clear outsider to Uganda itself allowed research participants to place their trust in me, particularly when discussing issues that were politically sensitive. While this may seem counter-intuitive, as it may have been thought that an insider was more likely to be able to gain the trust of the studied community, being completely foreign appeared to generate trust very successfully. This may be because interviewees felt more comfortable discussing sensitive topics with an outsider, because an outsider to Uganda is unable to cause or generate any repercussions for an interviewee who offers controversial information. Research participants may have been more comfortable knowing that the information they provided to me would subsequently depart Uganda with me, and would be anonymized in any future publications. For example, many interviewees reported to me that they were not concerned whether I recorded their name and job title, as they did not perceive that there would be any risk or consequence of my research being connected to them in the future. As a result, research participants seemed to be honest and forthright in their responses, including when discussing sensitive topics or information, and did not appear to hold any reservations about critiquing government institutions or decisions.

Conversely, as a complete outsider to Uganda, I was disadvantaged in a number of ways in the process of conducting fieldwork. A major disadvantage is my relative unfamiliarity with Ugandan indigenous languages, other than basic Luganda (which is primarily spoken in Kampala and in central Uganda). This aspect of being an outsider to the studied community posed clear barriers, such as being limited to interviewing only interviewees with a strong grasp of English (although most public servants work primarily in English). Interviewees occasionally spoke in indigenous languages while being interviewed, often to express an idiom or parable, which meant that I had to interrupt to ask the phrases to be expressed in English; this occasionally interrupted the flow of the interview. More importantly, by not speaking any indigenous languages, I lost some status in the eyes of the interview subjects, as a foreigner's ability to speak indigenous languages is held in high regard in Uganda. My lack of language skill in particular highlighted the way in which I am a clear outsider in Uganda, despite having spent two years living in the country previously.

Partial Insider, Partial Outsider

The complexity of my specific positionality in relation to the studied community posed unusual challenges, but also granted specific benefits, compared to those experienced by a complete-insider or complete-outsider. My previous professional experience in the Ministry of Finance, and lived experience in Kampala, granted some advantages beyond those experienced by an insider into public service generally. For example, I was granted access to the research site (the Ministry) upon arrival in Kampala, on the basis of being remembered by the administration staff and security staff of the Ministry—indeed, I was warmly welcomed. The office administrator from the team in which I had formerly worked began referring to me as 'our returned daughter,' and introduced me to secretaries and administrators within the Ministry who had been hired during the period I had been away from Uganda. Based on this network of secretaries, I was then able to arrange meetings and interviews with senior members of Ministry staff. In some cases, I was familiar to them as a former colleague, and so was granted permission both to interview them directly and to conduct research within their teams. As a result, I conducted interviews with former colleagues across the Ministry, and those contacts then referred me on to other contacts in other Ministries and agencies, allowing the research to proceed with a 'snowball' selection technique for locating interviewees.

As a final advantage of my hybrid insider-outsider status, my previous professional relationship with the studied community meant that interview subjects were able to provide me with smaller amounts of preliminary information, and instead focus on areas of greater complexity. For example, interview subjects were able to pass briefly over explanations of the mechanics of the Ugandan budget process, knowing that I am already familiar with these mechanics, and instead discuss the more complex political-economy factors driving resource-allocation decisions. Compared to my partial insider knowledge of the Ministry's operations, a complete-insider in the Ministry context would likely have had to invest more time in gaining access to the Ministry, in obtaining permission to undertake research within in, and in developing a core level of understanding about the day-to-day operations of the Ministry, before more complex research could begin to be conducted.

On the other hand, my status as a partial-insider posed some disadvantages, in contrast to the advantages described above. Most importantly, my existing familiarity with the Ministry's functions and systems presents a risk that interviewees would bypass important information, in the mistaken assumption that I am already familiar with this information. During several interviews, the interview subject exclaimed that I am already familiar with the material raised by the interview questions, for example responding to questions with, 'But Christine, you know this already!' On occasion, interviewees had to be encouraged to pretend I was not familiar to them, and to tell 'the whole story.' By encouraging research participants to disregard my previous knowledge, I attempted to overcome the risk that interview subjects may have passed over critical information. Nonetheless, compared to a complete outsider to the studied context, it is possible that I may not have received important information, owing to the interviewees' overestimation of my a priori knowledge of the studied context.

A final disadvantage of being a partial-insider, but partial-outsider, in the context of the Ugandan public service is that I may not hold sufficient knowledge of the studied context to be entirely confident that the research subjects have provided me with accurate information. While I do have some background understanding of the specific ministries and broader national context under study, there nonetheless remains a risk that the interview subjects may provide me with information that is either misleading or inaccurate. In order to mitigate this risk, I attempted to base analysis and conclusions on information points that were provided by multiple sources, such as more than one interview, or within interviews as well as databases, or verified in the existing literature. The risk of being provided with incorrect, inaccurate or incomplete information is a greater risk for me as an insider/outsider hybrid researcher than would be the case for a complete-insider researcher, as a complete insider is more likely to have a stronger ability to ascertain the accuracy of provided information. Conversely, the complete-outsider researcher is more likely to observe the risk of their own inability to discern incorrect information, and so take mitigating steps to crosscheck the information provided. For the partial insider-outsider researcher, the risk remains that the researcher's familiarity with the context of the research will lead them to overestimate their ability to identify inaccurate information that has been provided to them.

A final point of reflection for the partial-insider/partial-outsider researcher, who has an incomplete familiarity with both the context and the individuals who are the focus of study, is to ask what assumptions or pre-conceived ideas I might have brought into the research. These assumptions may affect each stage of the research, from the approach to collecting, analyzing to presenting data; my task is to examine how these pre-configured ideas might influence the research process, and how this influence can be managed. For me, these assumptions relate both to the Ugandan political-economy context, and my potential interactions with my own former colleagues. I had expected that the process of persuading interview subjects to participate in the research would be difficult, based on my assumption that interviewees might be reluctant to discuss the sensitivities and political nuances of the resource-allocation processes. This affected the research in that the interviews conducted in the initial stages of the research discussed non-core topics to the research initially, in order to build up to more challenging topics. However, this proved to be both unnecessary and a barrier to concluding interviews on schedule, so this practice was discarded. Furthermore, I had expected that public servants might be reticent to critique the actions of elected leaders, particularly within Cabinet or other senior government positions, but again this proved not to be the case. Overall, I had overestimated the unwillingness of researchers to discuss politically sensitive topics, and so used more time than was necessary during interviews to introduce these topics.

A second risk for my research that was caused by drawing pre-conceived assumptions is the risk of assuming that the research conducted represents a general, rather than specific, position. My familiarity with the political-economy context of Uganda might lead me to erroneously conclude that the findings from my (limited) research are

representative of general opinions in Uganda, or even of all public servants in Uganda. I run the risk of concluding, where the research findings
align with my pre-existing ideas of the research, that these findings are
therefore either 'true' or 'general,' rather than a collection of data and
information from a limited number of sources. For me, it is imperative to
maintain the standpoint that the research conducted occurs within limits
of space and time, and these limits should be reflected in the conclusions
drawn from the research.

Reflecting on the Hybrid Insider-Outsider Experience

Reflecting on my positionality relative to the studied community
reveals the complexity of a researcher who has some lived experience
of the studied group, but nonetheless remains an outsider to it in many
respects. Having had a similar education and professional background
to the studied community, but a different national background, poses
challenges in collecting and representing data. The additional complexity
of having been a part of the studied group, but both briefly and in the
past, further contributes to my evolving positionality relative to the studied community. The literature on the relative experiences of the insider-researcher and outsider-researcher suggests that a researcher can be
located along a spectrum of inclusion relative to the studied group. In
contrast, experiences such as mine indicate that positionality can evolve
to a situation of still greater complexity, where a researcher can share
some attributes of a group but not others, and can move into and out of
the studied group, even before research itself has begun. The situation
of a researcher who has been in the past an insider of the studied group,
but has now returned to being an outsider, warrants separate consideration. This 'hybrid' insider-outsider researcher's positionality evolves over
time, and varies according to the various attributes that they share or do
not share with the studied community.

My partial familiarity with the studied community occurs along two
planes: familiarity with the studied site, and familiarity with the studied people (or, using Hockey's terminology (1993, p. 199), 'places and
peers'). Initially, in terms of data collection, being familiar with the studied site allowed me to capture the advantages of being an 'insider,' such
as access to the research site, despite no longer holding the formal status of an insider. Familiarity with 'place' was also beneficial in managing cultural shock, logistics, and other elements of feeling comfortable

in the physical space of the research. While these advantages were beneficial to me, familiarity with the individuals in the studied group was of more value, in terms of data collection. Personal familiarity, and the sharing of some attributes with the studied community, meant that I was warmly welcomed, allowed me to arrange interviews quickly, and to rapidly re-establish rapport with the interviewees who had previously been known to me. While my membership as an insider of the studied group had expired, and I was now an outsider-researcher relative to the studied group, the re-establishment of this previous insider relationship allowed me to bypass many of the barriers to collecting interview data.

In terms of interpreting and analyzing the collected data, my previous partial experience as an insider in the space of the conducted research allowed me to have a stronger understanding of the context in which the data occur. Compared to a complete outsider researcher, I have an at least partial knowledge of the relevant social, political and economic context, and am able to interpret the data within this context. However, it remains important for me to resist becoming over-reliant on this prior knowledge, and mistake the positionality of a partial-insider as being one of a complete insider. Finally, my status as a hybrid insider-outsider in respect of the individuals participating in the research can be beneficial, but can also present risks when analyzing and interpreting the collected data. Should I wrongly assume that my partial prior knowledge of the context grants me substantial insight into the studied community, I risk assuming that the information I received from interviewees is true, or universal, in ways that may not in fact be substantiated. Having been warmly welcomed back into the research site and studied community, it nonetheless remained important for me as a 'returned daughter' to remain as objective as possible in analyzing and communicating the data collected.

Conclusion

When conducting field research, the social sciences researcher is seeking to collect and interpret information to contribute to the body of knowledge about their topic. In doing so, the researcher engages with individuals within a studied community, and with the context in which that individual resides. The researcher may take a range of positionalities in relation to the studied community, and this positionality may take different forms at different times. The researcher may themselves be a part of the studied community, they may have at one time (but no longer) been a part of the community, they may share some attributes with the studied community but not others, or they may be a complete outsider to the studied community. The positionality of the researcher relative to the community and the individuals they are engaging with for their research will generate opportunities and challenges in the process of collecting, analyzing, and representing data. For the hybrid researcher, sharing some attributes in common with the community, but not others, or perhaps not any longer, can allow the researcher to derive some of the benefits of being both an insider and an outsider relative to the studied community. However, this situation also poses unique risks and challenges to be overcome. For the researcher with an evolving positionality, such as a researcher who has formerly been an insider within the studied community but is now a researcher approaching the community from outside it, the complexity of this relationship introduces a still different set of challenges and opportunities. As the practice of fieldwork becomes more internationalized, with researchers being drawn from a wider range of positionalities relative to their community of study, the importance grows for the researcher of reflexively contemplating their positionality relative to the studied group. In doing so, the researcher is able to identify the challenges and opportunities they are likely to encounter in the process of conducting fieldwork, and the contributions they may be able to make to the body of knowledge in their field.

References

Breen, L. J. (2007). The Researcher 'In the Middle': Negotiating the Insider/Outsider Dichotomy. *The Australian Community Psychologist, 19*(1), 163–174.

Corbin Dwyer, S., & Buckle, J. L. (2009). The Space Between: On Being an Insider-Outsider in Qualitative Research. *International Journal of Qualitative Methods, 8*(1), 54–63.

Deutsch, N. L. (2004). Positionality and the Pen: Reflections on the Process of Becoming a Feminist Researcher and Writer. *Qualitative Enquiry, 10*(6), 885–902.

Ganga, D., & Scott, S. (2006). Cultural 'Insiders' and the Issue of Positionality in Qualitative Migration Research: Moving 'Across' and Moving 'Along' Researcher-Participant Divides. *Forum: Qualitative Social Research, 7*(3), Art 7.

Greene, M. J. (2014). On the Inside Looking In: Methodological Insights and Challenges in Conducting Qualitative Insider Research. *The Qualitative Report, 19*(29), 1–13.

Hellawell, D. (2006). Inside-Out: Analysis of the Insider-Outsider Concept as a Heuristic Device to Develop Reflexivity in Students doing Qualitative Research. *Teaching in Higher Education, 11*(4), 483–494.

Hockey, J. (1993). Research Methods: Researching Peers and Familiar Settings. *Research Papers in Education, 8*(2), 199–225.

Paechter, C. (2012). Researching Sensitive Issues Online: Implications of a Hybrid Insider/Outsider Position in a Retrospective Ethnographic Study. *Qualitative Research, 13*(1), 71–86.

Sherif, B. (2001). The Ambiguity of Boundaries in the Fieldwork Experience: Establishing Rapport and Negotiating Insider/Outsider Status. *Qualitative Inquiry, 7*(4), 436–447.

Unluer, S. (2012). Being an Insider Researcher While Conducting Case Study Research. *The Qualitative Report, 17*(58), 1–14.

CHAPTER 4

Multi-positionality and 'Inbetweenness': Reflections on Ethnographic Fieldwork in Southern Eastern Malawi

Maddy Gupta-Wright

My doctoral studies in medical anthropology began in 2015 and I conducted ethnographic fieldwork in South Eastern Malawi in 2016–2017. Reflecting on my previous training and work as a medical doctor and public health specialist, as well as my master's education in medical anthropology, I became increasingly interested in how my background, different identities, and experiences, shaped, and continue to shape, what I see, and do not see, during my time in the field. I consider this *positionality*, not as an objective, or 'unitary and essentialized "standpoint"' (Ryan 2015, p. 4), but as a way of reflecting on a researcher's multiple states-of-being in the field, and experiences with participants.

In this chapter, I begin by foregrounding the aims and context of my research including the theoretical underpinning of a 'critical biosocial perspective.' I demonstrate how this 'biosocial' concept and my own disciplinary background have bearing on my positionality in the field. Next, I draw on examples from my recent fieldwork, to illustrate ways in which different aspects of my identity, became more or less important within

M. Gupta-Wright (✉)
London School of Hygiene & Tropical Medicine, London, UK

© The Author(s) 2019
L. Johnstone (ed.), *The Politics of Conducting Research in Africa*,
https://doi.org/10.1007/978-3-319-95531-5_4

53

different social spaces, and how this transitioning between, and multiplicity of positions, was at times problematic.

In summary, I hope this chapter can do two things. Firstly, to provide an honest and novel account of fieldwork experience, showing how *multi-positionalities* are constructed from participant's impressions and assumptions, the bi-directional nature of relationships, the social fabric of participants, and from my own ethical and moral quandaries emerging in the field. Secondly, I intend to show how 'in-between-ness' has been a useful way to think about the leaky and transient boundaries of multi-positionalities, rather than reinforcing the fixed and dichotomous idea of 'insiders' and 'outsiders' (Ryan 2015).

THE FIELD SITE AND RESEARCH AIM

My fieldwork involved living in a rural village in the Lulanga area of Mangochi district, South East Malawi amongst a Yao population over a period of fifteen months. Malawi, a narrow landlocked country of Southern Africa with a population of just over 17 million people and a gross national income per capita of $750, is one of the poorest countries in the world (WHO 2013). Mangochi district is one of the largest of 28 districts, and is situated at the southern tip of Lake Malawi. Many in the district, including those who live within the housing settlements of Makanjira and Lulanga on the south east of the lake, define themselves as Yao in ethnicity. Yao people have a distinct history as the 'pioneers of the Arab trading frontier,' and as successful fighters (McCracken 2012, p. 28), although new trade laws during British colonization undermined the Yao's relative wealth, leading to a decrease in their power and success for the Nyasaland[1] economy (McCracken 2012, p. 94).

The aim of my doctoral research was to explore the idea of a *biosocial* perspective, and how it might contribute more productive ways to understand and respond to trachoma, the neglected tropical eye disease. Trachoma, a chronic eye condition caused by recurrent infection with the bacteria *Chlamydia trachomatis*, remains the commonest infectious cause of blindness in the world, and an important public health concern in Malawi, particularly in Mangochi district, where a previously undocumented cluster of trachoma had been suspected.

Trachoma is commonly understood within a narrow, linear, and universal biomedical model, which does not translate to the realities in which it is experienced. Insufficient acknowledgment of trachoma's complexity and local specificity create challenges for the public health response. Trachoma's global elimination policy and public health strategy, surgery, antibiotics, facial cleanliness, environmental hygiene (SAFE) (ITI 2015), is implemented with little attention to the social, political, economic, and historical context in which it is delivered. Assumptions of universal disease experience and rational human responses are being made, and the importance of political ideologies, social relationships, and cultural understandings are ignored. Trachoma exemplifies a need to look beyond the dichotomy of biology and culture, applying a *critical biosocial perspective*, to the understanding of health and disease.

What Do I Mean by *Biosocial*?

My interest in biosocial perspectives originates from observing, first-hand, the shortcomings of the narrow biomedical paradigm underpinning public health policy, and intervention development. Equally inspired by a perceived *biosocial moment*, an intellectual space within the literature, providing a timely opportunity to explore the concept empirically, I wished to contribute to contemporary debates about what *being biosocial* might entail.

The emergence of biosocial anthropology reflects a host of disciplinary shifts: a 'social turn' in the life sciences (Meloni 2014a, p. 595), convergences between evolutionary ecology and sociobiology (Leatherman and Goodman 2011), and a sociological interest in the 'material' and 'embodied' nature of human existence (Meloni 2014a). Prior to this, the early work of medical anthropology was consistently critiqued for its reliance on biomedical constructions of disease, and a 'failure to consider fully or accurately the role of social relations in the origin of health and illness' (Singer 2011, p. 92). Even that which purpose fully recognized biomedicine as *just* one type of culturally constructed medical system, appeared limited by its historic affiliation with the discipline, resulting in an inadequate critique of homogeneously imposed 'Western' categories, concepts and processes (Brown and Inhorn 1990; Lock and Nguyen 2010; Leatherman and Goodman 2011). These shortfalls created the opportunity for a new Critical Medical Anthropology (CMA), which questioned biomedicine's authority, and drew on political-economic approaches, offering much to debates about the nature of the global health industry, institutions and bureaucracies (Pfeiffer and Nichter 2008). In addition, CMA has advanced understandings of social origins of disease, highlighted local specificities, and critiqued concepts of biological determinism, and generalizability in public health. Despite these strengths, CMA has still been charged with periodically ignoring its biosocial roots and, in response, a few scholars returned to the concept of biosocial, posing a variety of different interpretations and uses.

Ingold and Palsson (2013) proposed the most radical interpretation, reflecting on biosocial as not simply the sum of two parts, nor the interaction between them, but these domains as one and the same thing— biosocial, which they define as an analysis of 'a larger series of processes and relationships that exceed the human' (Ingold and Palsson 2013, p. 40). Whilst, the argument for a level playing field for both biological and social phenomena is compelling, their theory involves limited consideration for the interaction between broader political forces, and human experience.

Lock's concept of *local biologies* has been applied to much ethnographic research examining health and disease in local contexts, and is rooted in an anthropological critique of biomedicine (Lock and Nguyen 2010; Meloni 2014b). Lock describes a perpetual interaction of human genes and components of the environmental, economic and social situation of humans. Broad political phenomena, however, feature too little rendering it less appropriate for trachoma, which appears heavily influenced by global health politics, particularly the politics of elimination (Lock and Nguyen 2010).

Farmer and colleagues use biosocial to demonstrate their central quest for equity, calling for a multidisciplinary, re-socializing effort of global health, and a new level of critical thinking (Farmer et al. 2013). Their work supports the application of social theory for intervention through four main areas: the sociology of knowledge, the medicalization of social phenomena, the rationalization of the world, biopower, and structural violence. This attention to both political economy and biological processes is significant; however, it falls short of exploring a more integrated concept of biosocial.

The most promising approach, I have drawn upon for my research, is that of Leatherman and Goodman's Critical Biocultural Synthesis (Leatherman and Goodman 2011). Attempting to combine critical and political-economic, with ecological and human adaptability perspectives (including direct measures of biological status, or examination of biological processes), and borrowing knowledge and skills from fields such as epidemiology, demography, nutritional science, physiology, or pathology,

Leatherman and Goodman's approach has an inherent 'in-between-ness.' They use the term 'critical biocultural *synthesis*,' arguing that *biosocial*, does an injustice to the processual and interactional nature of context, politics and economy (Leatherman and Goodman 2011). I find this approach particularly useful in light of trachoma's deep roots in poverty and marginalization, its clustered distribution exhibited in Malawi, the unusual temporal nature of pathology, and its multiple local complexities in both experience and response.

So, *biosocial* goes beyond the dichotomy of 'diseases,' considered universal 'clinical entities with pathological underpinnings,' and 'illnesses' reflecting patient's perceptions and behaviors (Brown and Inhorn 1990, p. 100). It advances structural and social determinants of disease models (Wilkinson and Marmot 2003), considering conditions as emergent processes of human interactions, resulting from vulnerability and suffering. Biosocial perspectives align with Lock's theory that 'the reality of "normal" biological variation very often falls outside what is deemed normal in biomedicine. Such variation is dependent upon the history of specific populations and the environments and social contexts in which people live' (Lock and Nguyen 2010, p. 53), and these interactions should not be underestimated.

Some of the discomfort with my positionality, and the uncertainty I have experienced, is related to the framing of my research as 'biosocial.' As I have explained, there is no, one, discretely packaged concept of biosocial, and it is clear from its disciplinary origins that this idea requires the researcher to transition back and forth in-between disciplinary ideologies and perspectives. It accepts that the world views being brought together are widely different, but it comes from a place of practical utility; an *alternative* approach, but one which *could* have application.

DISCIPLINARY DILEMMAS

Another aspect of my anxiety around, and interest in, positionality stems from my professional background as a medical doctor. UK medical training, and work as a clinician, did many things to my view of the world, much of which I have reflected on critically since. In particular, concepts framed by the narrow, positivist, and reductionist ideology that underpins the biomedical paradigm.

One philosophy that medical training nurtures, is a sometimes problematic sense of obligation. This sense of duty to respond, to intervene in the lives of others, whether on an individual or population level, is viewed as simultaneously a moral responsibility and an achievable outcome. This focus on impact and intervention serves to reinforce the perception that interpretivist research approaches, without a biomedically informed predefined purpose, unwedded to the principles of objectivity and generalizability, lack value; and the researcher themselves may be charged with being immoral and naval-gazing (Okely 1992).

My decision to study medical anthropology was, in part, precisely to challenge this perspective. I had become increasingly aware of the limited consideration for the context and complexity of public health issues. I had also noted how thoughtful, slow, inductive and critical research, which prioritizes the voices of those unheard and stretches beyond achieving cultural appropriateness in public health, is disregarded. For a short period, I worked on global trachoma policy as a public health professional in a large donor organization. This experience highlighted how dominant biomedical principles and a tendency to ignore context for the sake of intervening at scale, resulted in conclusions that the 'problem' lay with people in the 'communities,' labeled as 'refusers,' 'non-compliers,' or those 'difficult to influence' (Lock and Nguyen 2010, p. 115).

Consequently, I aim for an anthropology *of* rather than *in* global health (Parker and Harper 2006). By this, I mean research that questions the assumptions embedded in policy (including the types and uses of evidence), supports an understanding of the complex local realities of the populations that policy claims to serve, highlights the political nature of health policy development and implementation, and helps to unmask the unforeseen consequences of global health action. My doctoral research, for example, takes a critical perspective of common place public health concepts such as *elimination*, and the *verticality* of disease programs.

At this very fundamental level, my positionality has presented me with a dilemma: how to ensure that my research has utility and legitimacy in global public health spheres, without pandering to the research agendas of positivist ideologies, which narrow the critical lens and reproduce the same assumptions. I want to contribute knowledge toward improvements in the lives of those I research and attend to. But I wish to achieve a careful balance between this application, and a defense of the value of subjectivity, as well as the critical challenge of pervasive and traditional philosophies of public health, where embedded assumptions, and potential harm, may be hidden. At times, I feel that being 'in-between' disciplines and theoretical sources, in order to find a productive biosocial space in which to situate my research, risks diluting perspectives and confusing my arguments. Some of my anxieties about shifting between these different paradigms, and being 'in-between' disciplines, bear relevance for my position and identity in the field, and relationships with research participants.

Setting out to undertake fieldwork, I was acutely aware of the necessity to reflect on many aspects of my own position and identity in the field. I knew it was a crucial process for making sense of data, not least to understand the limits of the lens through which I would make observations, and to challenge my own assumptions throughout my fieldwork. But I was less prepared, and aware, of how my position would actually make me feel about *myself*, how it would shape the way I presented myself in the field, enable different kinds of relationships, and consequently, most profoundly, would *construct* data with research participants.

Navigating Privilege

My fieldwork involved living with a family in a conglomerate of villages, participating in many aspects of everyday Yao life, including attending local meetings, events, and activities, in order to build an understanding of social structures, local politics, and the broader context for health. Amongst the local chief and a village headman, I was instantly ascribed a particular status by being invited to many local political meetings of varying sensitivity. This gave me a unique insight into the social hierarchies, power relations and priorities for these powerful local decision makers.

It is difficult to unravel the reasons for being granted this degree of access with such ease. Of course, in rural Malawi, my white ethnicity expresses wealth and a privileged education, which in this case seemed to overrule other elements of my identity such as gender—no one at these meetings was female, nor is it common for the headmen in this area to be women. Even as I tried to discretely join the back of public meetings in the village, alongside my neighbors and host family, the chief would go to specific efforts to publicly welcome and introduce me. He would occasionally reveal more directly his own agenda for inviting me to events, asking me publicly for financial support for various development activities. I am yet to be able to ascertain how my presence may or may not have impacted on the chief's own status, as I heard many people praise him as a chief for being 'modern,' 'open' and 'collaborative,' allowing 'outsiders in' for the sake of 'development.' He was aware of the nature of my research, but of course had his own expectations for the population he governed, frequently commenting that 'maybe something good will come of this.'

Whilst the position I acquired for the local political meetings was invaluable for access to certain types of information, it was not a position I wanted to maintain when I spent time with families in the village. The inequality and status differences between this 'social elite' and the majority of families are stark, and create a hierarchy which is both different from, as well as in addition to, that which I immediately acquired because of my foreignness. When invited by a village headman to attend a girls' initiation ceremony, I observed how this association with the headman affected my position amongst the mothers of the children in the camp.

It was the headman's wish that he first introduced me to the mothers before entering the camp. He asked me to sit on the raised step, in front of his house, on a new grass mat, separate from his fellow headmen, and directed the mothers to greet me one by one, by kneeling below the step. It was not the way I greeted these women the day before while wandering around the village, nor the way I would the day after. In the camp itself, the women refrained from speaking to, or looking directly at me, but used the ceremony leader, as a kind of gatekeeper. One of the women, a parent of a girl being initiated, seemed bashful, self-conscious and continuously remarked on how 'lucky' the girls were that others in the village would remember this for years, that a *mzungu*[2] attended their ceremony. Other than feeling awkwardly privileged, I did not want them to change anything about the proceedings for the girl's ceremony. On the contrary, according to a member of my host family, who by now had gotten to know me well, the women had been proud to show off their traditions making sure every detail was included. She explained that they had been singing loudly, excited that as I had not taken part in this ceremony myself as a young girl, I was now getting to experience it alongside their own children.

Unique Relationships and Positionalities Over Time

Right at the start of my fieldwork, my first contact with the village was amongst a team of data collectors from a non-governmental organization (NGO) whom I was observing doing a trachoma prevalence survey. On the day of the survey, we were escorted by a village volunteer.

Speaking to her at a later date, she explained how my association with this activity was implicated in the village population's initial perception of me. As she put it:

> We had heard from a man from Salima that an NGO with foreign people had been round taking blood samples from everyone, and that they were doing satanic things – this is what people often think when blood is taken, and these rumors came to me....but because I knew why you were there, and what [the NGO] was doing, I explained this, and these rumors died.

'Rumors' of this nature in rural Malawi, including the very recent fear of 'bloodsuckers' resulting in a series of killings and attacks across the southern region of the country, are not uncommon (BBC News 2002, 2017). These rumors are discussed in the literature most helpfully in terms of social relations, as opposed to a lack of knowledge which makes reference to a simplistic idea of modernization (Geissler and Pool 2006). They may also be interpreted as manifestations of long-endured socioeconomic hardship, unclear origins of wealth, responses to the 'traumatic history of colonialism,' and more recently exacerbated by a rapid growth in the NGO and medical research industry (Geissler and Pool 2006, p. 978). Before I could respond, the lady looked concerned and quickly said:

> ...but no one thinks that of you now, now that they see you have been here a long time and they see you going around in the village and doing things like us. People they have given you a name – it is my name – as we were going around on that day together, so you are my sister.

I was already aware that my association with the NGO might do particular things for my relationships in the village. This may have been due to the sense of status ascribed to those employed through such organizations, or simply because they were not local residents themselves. However, at the time, I had not reflected on how much past relationships with, and rumors about, NGOs as a whole might play into this. Assumptions were made about who I might be, because of my association with a relatively powerful institution known for 'doing' things 'to' people. I was rather taken back by the volunteer's honesty. We had spent considerable time together by then, but I was surprised this had come up in conversation at all. For her to have defended and explained my position to others she knew well was also remarkable. Having her endorsement felt extremely important. She was someone who many people, especially women, respected, listened to, and took their lead from.

This relationship became key to my fieldwork. The mutual trust we established meant that I would go to her to help explain many things in the village, providing an opportunity to comfortably ask the opinion of a woman who occupied a position of authority, and vast local knowledge of the area. The ease at which she spoke to me, understood, but did not overplay, the strangeness of my presence in the village, was fundamental to the construction of my data with regard to health care choices for trachoma and other health challenges. It was also through this particular rapport that I came to foreground the position of the health volunteers in my trachoma story. I learnt of the huge role they play in the program, and how many feel undervalued and under trained.

This example and last quote also indicate that my identity in the village was dependent on the time spent there, and that it was possible to mold positionality with time, by what I did, rather than my more fixed boundaries of identity. For example, most days, together with my host family, I swept the compound, washed plates, fetched water, shopped at the market together, cooked, and went to the fields to farm. I spoke some Chichewa[3] and limited, but day to day, Chiyao[4] in the village, and I dressed as women in the village do, by covering my head, and wearing *chitenje*, the traditional colored material, around my waist. Initial reactions at the novelty of such an 'outsider' being able to 'manage Yao ways' gradually faded, and interactions became more casual, affecting both my own ability to relax, as much as 'lightening' the reception I got from local people.

Language played an important role in my positionality. Despite learning some Chichewa, the Malawian national language, and Chiyao, the local and most commonly spoken tongue, it was essential to employ a translator for fieldwork. I was lucky to find that a neighbor to my host family, was able to speak English, Chichewa and Chiyao. My host family could speak Chichewa, helpful for everyday conversation at the house. Whilst my attempts at limited Chiyao had a huge effect on how people responded to me, excited to be able to use their language to converse, I relied heavily on my translator/research assistant for in-depth conversation, especially during interviews. Employing a local, and popular person, helped people to trust me and accept my presence; however, this reliance upon a young man, of relative high education and opportunity, meant my positionality was shaped to perhaps prevent me access to other groups. Trying to overcome this, I attended meetings and social events alone with the mother and daughter of my host family too, where I could observe in detail and understand some of the dialogue translated from Chiyao to Chichewa.

There were times when the challenging and isolated nature of the fieldwork rendered me guarded or defensive. I have wondered what effect this had on my ability to gain trust, transcend the normal boundaries of social interaction for an 'outsider,' and be afforded insights which are otherwise unseen. Most importantly, I have reflected on whether I was able to be a meaningful participant in daily life in the village, such that I am able to claim authenticity in the data, and that neither my professional nor personal traits, nor limitations, caused me to miss important subtleties in the field. Taking care not to exaggerate the degree of familiarity I did achieve, I am hopeful that progressive informality with informants throughout fieldwork has allowed a richer data on more sensitive topics to be constructed.

An Imagined Community of Biomedics

The most challenging identity I feel I inhabited whilst in the village was that of a medical doctor. I had never introduced myself as such, and within the context of my life in the UK, I identify as a public health practitioner and a training anthropologist, but no longer as a practicing medical doctor. Neither was it my intended role at the field site. However, as a white woman, from abroad, studying an eye disease, the immediate assumption *was* that I *could* treat eye health problems, and people would stop me in the village and arrive at my family's house to get advice and treatment. This presented me with a moral predicament—how to manage people's expectations, whether I should or should not intervene, examine, and give advice, knowing that whilst I have not worked as a medical doctor for the last five years, the closest other qualified doctor is seventy kilometers away in a private hospital.

This 'access' to research participants with eye health problems presented me with another conundrum. It was invaluable for my research to be able to examine them for trachoma (which I am trained to do, and which was always an intended research activity), but if there was no sign of trachoma, and I suspected something else was wrong, I had no pathways through which to refer them for treatment. Not only was I *not* linked into the Malawian health system, I had no certainty that treatments for these conditions would *actually* be available. In these scenarios, I was only able to advise them to attend the private Christian health center in the village, the government facility in a town 20 km away, or the district hospital 120 km away. These options all seemed unsatisfactory, given that the people asking me for help, were either seeking to avoid these consultation fees or travel costs, or asking for a second opinion, since treatment received from one of these places had not provided relief. Despite explaining my position explicitly from the outset, I felt constantly in danger of providing false hope to those seeking help. I was not equipped to take the role of diagnostician, instead, only that of a trachoma 'screener' or 'health adviser.'

To a degree, my concern originated from an un-preferred practice in biomedicine whereby to be diagnosed without provision of treatment is viewed as less just or moral. Whilst my own perception of my role was dictated by limits in my knowledge and skills, I was surprised that most people remained keen to continue being advised despite the lack of potential medicine. I had already witnessed at the health center how important the receipt of a substance for a 'treatment' was to people. People had become deeply dissatisfied when they were merely provided with information by the nurse or medical assistant, despite having paid the consultation fee. This 'demand' was in turn encouraging the staff to default to using unnecessary antibiotics or painkillers so that the patient received *something*. Such expectations were different of me, perhaps since I was agreeing to listen, examine, and advise them for free, with most people appearing to find an explanation for their symptoms in itself a therapeutic process. There were others who seemed dissatisfied and confused by information in the absence of treatment, which challenged to me to think of the ethics of intervening at all, especially when I suspected the person's quest for appropriate help would probably be futile.

At the health center, and observing the health surveillance assistants at various health events, I found my belonging to this 'imagined community of biomedics' both a help and a hindrance. It allowed me access to discussions between health workers, which I may otherwise not have interpreted with ease, due to the medical jargon, references to medical technology, and a mutual understanding of some of the day to day resource limitations that they faced. This position also granted me ways of participating that helped me to see different perspectives.

Being professionally able to assist the health surveillance assistants (HSAs)[5] with vaccinations in the village (knowing what kit to hand them and when, for example), allowed me to speak more informally with them whilst undertaking their day-to-day activities and provided 'access' to them as participants. However, I often felt a sense of guilt knowing that these participants are in part involved in the model of infectious disease control which I had set out to critique. It was not unusual, especially at the beginning, to sense a 'wariness' from the healthcare workers at the health center, as if they felt their personal medical practice was being scrutinized. The nurse, for example, during a clinic, asked me, smiling nervously, 'So what do you think? What would you do?' She was seeing a patient whose symptoms, in her opinion, did not fit an obvious formulaic diagnostic pattern, for whom, she felt, the lines were blurred. Whilst she knew my background, and was aware of the caveats I placed around my limited medical knowledge and expertise, she seemed to want to operate on the basis of a consensus, and saw me as someone 'qualified' to support her decision-making. Similarly, HSAs, when asked about their role in finding patients with trachoma for an NGO mobile surgical clinic, were quick to deny their involvement in the diagnostic process as a way of relieving them from anticipated critique:

...oh no we don't diagnose... we just bring anyone who has an eye problem because we are not trained to pick up trachoma, we leave that to... [mentioning the name of the NGO].

My position in this scenario is that of a 'medical expert' of trachoma, or senior medical colleague/ophthalmologist, rather than a researcher. This is despite the NGO in question remaining the most equipped with the skills for trachoma assessment, despite the rhetoric around healthcare capacity building and the development of sustainable skills in the health system.

From a conversation with a sinanga[6] in the village, it was clearer how my association with biomedicine played a role in constructing data. He had agreed to speak to me at his home, but did not want to be recorded since he was concerned that 'some people at the hospital don't understand my work' and it would 'cause trouble for him.' I reiterated that I had no direct connection with the health center and that no one would hear the anonymized recording, but he maintained his point of view on the issue. Some of the data generated from the discussion represent his fear that I had other connections to governmental authority and that my role there was to police his activity. He spent considerable time showing me his membership card to the *Malawi Traditional Healer's Association*, printed on which was a list of legal acts, written in English, by which, he told me, all members were governed. Although he talked freely about specific clients he had treated, his answers to my questions referring to these scenarios were peppered with statements justifying his position as a healer relative to doctors at the hospital. As he put this:

> The difference between doctors and what I do is that I can also treat people with problems caused by witchcraft and problems such as the son being imprisoned in south Africa [he had been telling me about how one of his clients had sought help to release his son from prison for an invalid visa]. Doctors at the hospitals don't know how to treat these problems.

SHIFTING AND COMPETING RESPONSIBILITIES

In addition to concerns of representation and the ethics of medical practice discussed so far, I became perturbed by the shifting and competing responsibilities I had by the end of the fifteen months toward many different types of research participants. Some were recipients of trachoma interventions who, perhaps because of my attention to their stories and lives, saw me as a kind of 'spokesperson.' One group of women, who had recently had surgery to correct the painful deformity of the eyelid, explained how they had not been visited by the team for 'follow up' after their operation. As a result, they had experienced some untreated and painful complications, for which medical care was at least 120 km away and costly, where the nearest ophthalmologist was based. Assuming I had a link to the NGO, they came to me to ask for help in making their 'case' for follow-up to be rescheduled in the village. One of the more confident women, with whom I had spent some time over the past few months told me:

> This is not something I wanted, but we were forced to do it, and then they haven't come like they said they would…it is like we did our bit but they are not doing theirs – they fail to come to check us…I can feel the scratching and so I don't want to open my eye as the pain gets worse, but we are worried about these wires that are scratching as we still can't do anything at the house or garden and this is the busiest time of year. Maybe you can

tell them to come back. They won't listen to us you see I went to [THE HSA] and told him but still there is nothing, and we are here still suffering with these wires in our eyes.

They viewed me as part of the same system, as one of 'them,' but at the same time expected me to be able to resolve this problem of their being missed out as a kind of impartial bystander. This was not just their perception, however, but also my expectation of myself. I wanted to think it possible to adopt a kind of activist-anthropologist position in this scenario. Unable to resist the opportunity to redress some of the power imbalances for these women, by honoring their request, I spoke to an existing contact at the NGO, querying why there had been such a delay in reviewing these women. He told me of an absolute lack of funds, and consequently, a sequence of logistical barriers which served to justify why they, and the district surgeon, contrary to the global policy protocol, had not been back to the area. One of the surgeons commented:

> The follow-up is so important....but you know that time I failed because I...I stopped on the way there were a lot of rains, there are a lot of water moving towards the...the road, so I felt with the motorbike I won't pass... yeah and the other thing was an issue to do communications sometimes there was break of communication. You know the network that side so I try to tell maybe err...tell [his colleague at the NGO] to say I have failed....I cannot proceed so maybe you share the message maybe you use the text you tell the senior HSA. So if you think err...I did it deliberate no, no you are wrong! ...but if you have the drugs if you have maybe the...the resources now, I'm very...even I've been trying maybe to talk to [his colleague at the NGO], 'when am I going to see those cases'. You understand how the money works.

In this moment, he needed an ally in me, and his knowledge of my background meant that he knew I had been on his 'side of the fence' before in the position of someone whose responsibility it was to make a lot happen with very little money. His NGO colleague tried a similar tactic: 'And what about you, can't you explain to the [funders] that we don't have the money to run extra follow up visits?' he asked, shifting the responsibility for a solution onto me momentarily. He saw me at this time as someone who could transcend the next level of hierarchy in the system, and speak directly with the international funders. Whilst

I had sought explanation for the women in the village whose care had been neglected, I then came to empathize with this surgeon who, using his own initiative, with no additional funding for fuel had attempted to attend the follow-up appointments, starting the 120-km drive to the field. I understood the logistical challenges with the journey and the season, and I felt guilty for not feeling equipped to be able to do what they requested and ask for more money on their behalf. Despite having never been connected to the funders, my white and foreign status evoked assumptions of disposable wealth and influence over the donors for the program.

As well as both the women and the surgeon seeing me as their personal advocate, the HSA, who I had also approached on behalf of these women, responded: 'Ahhh you see these are troublesome women..... they came yesterday and shouted at me...so you must tell them it is not my fault!' This time, the HSA judged me as closer in position to him as a healthcare professional than to a resident in the village, and hence expected me to be able to champion *his* perspective over that of the women themselves.

My competing and multiple positionalities were also demonstrated during a meeting between the funding representative and two NGOs involved in trachoma at my field site. This scenario ignited feelings of disloyalty, being in-between these multiple positionalities, and clouded my interpretation of the moral standpoints of each of the informants. One of the NGO workers, an experienced epidemiologist, a confident and skeptical critic of international donors, their restrictive funding, 'ulterior motives and hidden agendas,' had conducted a survey in the region, following a suspicion that there were many more people in the area with active infection than were previously documented. I had taken a role in one of the survey teams for this exercise as an important participant observation opportunity, to understand the diagnostic process and workings of a survey team, at a large scale. The survey had shown that in fact there were larger numbers of people than known with signs of *trichiasis*, the eyelid deformity that in ten to twenty years' time might render them sightless.

In my position, as a part of the survey team, I was seen as an ally to the epidemiologist, who, during this particular discussion, was trying to make a case for the 'people left behind.' As he put it: '...Maddy has been finding more anyway, she will tell you about the location and how there are many neglected areas, difficult-to-reach people...'. The other NGO had been responsible for conducting the surgery for trichiasis in the area and had recently withdrawn their mobile clinic services in response to concluding that they had met the target number of operations. The funding representative had been informed of this 'achievement' and agreed to cease operations, stopping funding. I had worked closely with this NGO representative too, documenting his perspective on the trachoma policy. As we left the meeting, he caught me alone to comment: 'You see Maddy, what is wrong with these people? You have seen how they are refusing things and living still with lack of hygiene...so you know.' Shortly before the meeting it had been the funding representative who had invited me along, expecting me to be able to 'bring some clarity to situation' having been 'an observer' in the area. She had told me that she was not sure why the new survey had been done in the first place, nor how it was that she had been told they had already finished the surgery, when the survey showed this was not the reality.

Each of these representatives operate in a hierarchical system for the national trachoma program in Malawi and consequently assume particular power relations. I had developed relationships with each throughout my fieldwork in order to understand the many perspectives on the trachoma policy. Each had a reason to ask for my support, comradery and approval, based on how they perceived my identity, but these were mutually exclusive perspectives. This had implications for how, and when, I portrayed my own opinion on these issues and it made me question whether I had, in the quest for 'data,' been misleading and secretive. Some of the positionalities I inhabited were imposed and some were those that I had worked hard to adopt in order to establish trust and rapport and make my research work. Much of that brought me discomfort since, although I was not falsifying identities, I would, consciously or subconsciously, emphasize aspects of myself for particular participants. I saw this as part of demonstrating appropriate conduct with different kinds of people, yet it also at times afforded me great advantages. These multiple 'performances,' referring to Goffman, allowed specific access and authority which ultimately enhanced my fieldwork experience. I worked hard to maintain rapport with people in many layers of my fieldwork, taking time to think about the perspective of research participants whenever I would be about to engage them (Goffman 1990).

CONCLUSIONS

As an early career anthropologist, to dwell heavily on the self for reflexivity is, of course, not unusual. In an attempt, to strike a tricky balance between a helpful process of 'self-critical sympathetic introspection' (England 1994, p. 244), and 'a form of self-indulgent narcissism' (Ryan 2015, p. 2), my interest in positionality, has reached beyond analytical scrutiny, or its role as a methodological tool, and instead toward a more uncomfortable reflexivity, fore-fronting power relations, and my own fractured and competing sympathies (Pillow 2003). Reflecting in these different ways on my positionality in the field has brought to light its fluidity and complex origins. I have provided many examples of ways in which my *multi-positionalities*, with their dynamic and shifting boundaries, were developed, have bearing on, and were informed by, my day-to-day experiences in the field, challenging any fixed ideas of researcher positionality, and supporting the concept of *in-between-ness* as helpful in reflexivity. I have also explored how my multiple identities suited different social spaces, and themselves constructed data of a particular nature.

I first demonstrated how my affiliations and experience with biomedicine, public health principles, and anthropological critique shaped my aspiration to conduct research of this nature, and how each continues to influence my interpretation of fieldwork. I have discussed how my roots in these mixed disciplines lead me to strive for a balance between utility and original, critical thought, whilst reconciling my own insecurities, and navigating a productive space in which to contribute new knowledge. Shifting the focus from the fieldworker to the topic of research, I have shown how 'biosocial' has shaped my awareness of my own positionalities and my degree of comfort being *in-between*. This unique positionality, allows me to reflect on, and benefit from both the revealing lenses, and the 'blind spots,' of the disciplines of biomedicine and critical anthropology.

Reflecting on my own relative privilege, and the shifting and competing nature of multi-positionalities, I have considered the morality of a kind of performed positionality in different fieldwork settings, with different research participants, and how this relates to issues of representation, leads me to question my own legitimacy in the field, and conjures feelings of mixed loyalties to different kinds of participants. Referring to unique relationships, I have demonstrated how the multi-positionalities I inhabited during fieldwork, were loaded with 'baggage'—the past and present conduct of those with whom I felt, and was felt to be associated.

That said, I argue that positionalities are not only shaped by the more 'fixed' experiences, ideologies, and heritage, but by motives, assumptions and expectations of both the researcher and research participants, all dynamic in time and context.

I have discussed the origins of these positionalities, how they changed over time, and overlapped; each having consequences for the kinds of data collected, the quality of the data, and the way in which it will subsequently be interpreted. Despite the challenges that navigating multi-positionalities presents, I have found being *in-between* highly generative of some important ideas emerging from my data. I am exploring biomedical and epidemiological terms and technologies at great depth, asking what they do *in* and *on* people's lives, and what unintended consequences may prevail. For example, when considering the powerful notion of *elimination*, my understanding of how it satisfies principles of utilitarian action in public health, demands 'gold standards' and targets, and injects urgency, and momentum, will be particularly helpful in its critique. I question the appropriateness of its verticality, its potential to repackage, or perpetuate inequalities, and the risk that it may unhelpfully enhance existing social and political hierarchies.

Having an understanding of the biomedical framing of trachoma, its pathology, transmission, and diagnosis, gives me a unique position from which to consider the social construction of the disease within the biomedical cultural system, the process of negotiating diagnosis, and the construction of trachoma relative to other aspects of health and misfortune at my field site.

Reflecting on multi-positionalities during fieldwork and the emotions they evoke is helping me to interpret my field notes, and the conclusions I draw. This degree of honest reflexivity, and attention to multiple informants' perspectives, will, I hope, allow me to contribute new ideas in the discipline of critical biosocial anthropology, and our understanding of trachoma in Malawi.

NOTES

1. The former name of Malawi, 1911–1964, during the period of British Colonial rule.
2. Bantu language term used widely in East Africa to refer to a white person, dating back to the eighteenth century.
3. Malawi's national language; of the Chewa ethnic group.

4. The language of the Yao ethnic group; the dominant language at my field site.
5. The term used for Malawi's paid, community public health workers.
6. The commonly used term in Chichewa and Chiyao for 'traditional healer' or 'witchdoctor'.

REFERENCES

BBC News. (2002). *Vampires' Strike Malawi Villages*. http://news.bbc.co.uk/1/hi/world/africa/2602461.stm. Accessed December 15, 2017.
BBC News. (2017). *Malawi Cracks Down on 'Vampire' Lynch Mobs*. http://www.bbc.co.uk/news/world-africa-41692944. Accessed December 10, 2017.
Brown, P. J., & Inhorn, M. (1990). The Anthropology of Infectious Disease. *Annual Review of Anthropology, 19*, 89–117.
England, K. (1994). Getting Personal: Refexivity, Positionality, and Feminist Research. *Professional Geographer, 46*(1), 80–89.
Farmer, P., Kim, J. Y., Kleinman, A., & Basilico, M. (2013). *Reimaging Global Health*. Berkeley and Los Angeles: University of California Press.
Geissler, P. W., & Pool, R. (2006). Editorial: Popular Concerns About Medical Research Projects in Sub-Saharan Africa—A Critical Voice in Debates About Medical Research Ethics. *Tropical Medicine & International Health, 11*(7), 975–982.
Goffman, E. (1990). *The Presentation of Self in Everyday Life*. London: Penguin.
Ingold, T., & Palsson, G. (2013). *Biosocial Becomings: Integrating Social and Biological Anthropology*. Cambridge: Cambridge University Press.
ITI. (2015). *The SAFE Strategy*. http://trachoma.org/safe-strategy. Accessed February 21, 2015.
Leatherman, T., & Goodman, A. H. (2011). Critical Biocultural Approaches in Medical Anthropology. In M. Singer & P. Erickson (Eds.), *A Companion to Medical Anthropology* (pp. 29–48). Oxford: Blackwell.
Lock, M., & Nguyen, V. K. (2010). *An Anthropology of Biomedicine*. Oxford: Blackwell.
McCracken, J. (2012). *A History of Malawi 1859–1966*. Woodbridge: James Currey.
Meloni, M. (2014a). How Biology Became Social, And What It Means for Social Theory. *The Sociological Review, 62*(3), 593–614.
Meloni, M. (2014b). Remaking Local Biologies in an Epigenetic Time. *Somatosphere*. http://somatosphere.net/2014/08/remaking-local-biologies-in-an-epigenetic-time.html. Accessed February 25, 2016.
Okely, J. (1992). Anthropology and Autobiography. Participatory Experience and Embodied Knowledge. In J. Okely & H. Callaway (Eds.), *Anthropology and Autobiography: ASA Monographs 29* (pp. 1–28). London and New York: Routledge.

Parker, M., & Harper, I. (2006). The Anthropology of Public Health. *Journal of Biosocial Science, 38,* 1–5.

Pfeiffer, J., & Nichter, M. (2008). What Can Critical Medical Anthropology Contribute to Global Health? A Health Systems Perspective. *Medical Anthropology Quarterly, 22*(4), 410–415.

Pillow, W. S. (2003). Confession, Catharsis, or Cure? Rethinking the Uses of Reflexivity as Methodological Power in Qualitative Research. *International Journal of Qualitative Studies in Education, 16,* 175–196.

Ryan, L. (2015). "Inside" and "Outside" of What or Where? Researching Migration Through Multi-positionalities. *Forum: Qualitative Social Research Socialforschung, 16*(2). http://www.qualitative-research.net/index.php/fqs/article/view/2333/3785. Accessed January 20, 2018.

Singer, M. (2011). The Development of Critical Medical Anthropology: Implications for Biological Anthropology. In A. H. Goodman & T. Leatherman (Eds.), *Building a New Biocultural Synthesis: Political-Economic Perspectives on Human Biology* (pp. 93–126). Ann Arbor: The University of Michigan Press.

WHO. (2013). *Country Profile Malawi.* http://www.who.int/countries/mwi/en/. Accessed February 21, 2016.

Wilkinson, R., & Marmot, M. (2003). *Social Determinants of Health the Solid Facts* (2nd ed.). Copenhagen: World Health Organization Europe.

CHAPTER 5

Landscapes of Desire: The Effect of Gender, Sexualized Identity, and Flirting on Data Production in Rwanda and Zimbabwe

Lyn Johnstone

This chapter explores the effect of gender and sexualized identity on data production. It begins from a critical feminist epistemology which calls for a recognition of the ways in which gendered power relations shape the research process (McDowell 1992; Rose 1997; Ackerly et al. 2006). Students in the field may be unprepared for how their gender and sexuality shape and limit interactions with different groups of research subjects as, until recently, much of the focus in the literature on positionality was fixed around issues of the researcher's privileged position, positioning the lens on differences of race and class (Gilbert 1994). Feminist scholars argue, however, that gender, and by extension sexuality, has a profound influence on the research process. As they see it, gender can fundamentally shape every stage of a research project from the methods we employ and the analytical categories we choose, to the questions we ask, the ways in which we interact with our research subjects, and the ways in which we gather, as well as interpret, the data we collect (Nast 1994; Mattingly and Falconer-Al-Hindi 1995; Sundberg 2003).

L. Johnstone (✉)
Royal Holloway, University of London, Egham, UK

© The Author(s) 2019
L. Johnstone (ed.), *The Politics of Conducting Research in Africa*,
https://doi.org/10.1007/978-3-319-95531-5_5

The idea that gender can shape and influence the research process was first brought home to me during the fieldwork for my doctoral research project during which I conducted a series of interviews in Rwanda and Zimbabwe. My research focused on the continuing relevance of the Commonwealth to African states and used the metaphor of the organization as a family to explore relationships between Britain and Zimbabwe—which withdrew from the organization in 2003; and Britain and Rwanda—which joined the organization in 2009. My goal, simply put, was to gain African perspectives on the effect, if any, that Commonwealth membership had on these states by interviewing politicians, academics, journalists, and civil society representatives and getting a feel for whether they thought the Commonwealth was still relevant.

In preparation for fieldwork, I immersed myself in as many stories and experiences that other researchers were willing to share, either in person or between the pages of books. These ranged from the more serious issues around research permits, censorship, and the political aspects of conducting research in Rwanda with its increasingly draconian attitude to speech freedoms, and Zimbabwe with its continuingly strained relationship with Britain and the West, to the logistics of when to go, where to stay, and whether I would have access to ATMs in Harare. None of my preparation took into account the fact that I was female. Partly because, despite not believing myself to be a detached and neutral researcher with the ability to perform what Haraway (1988, p. 582) has referred to as the 'god trick,' I was rather naïvely under the impression that the political theme and focus of my research inhabited a gender-neutral space and that neutrality would stretch to envelop the researcher in its gender-neutral cloak. Reflecting on my fieldwork since returning from the field, it seems apparent in hindsight that I did not account for gender in the planning stages of my trip because I had not yet become entangled in the day-to-day realities of conducting fieldwork that scholars such as Parr (1996) have described as a process involving a great deal of mess.

Many International Relations researchers, as well as geographers and anthropologists, have written on the messiness of fieldwork, particularly in the early stages where uncertainty and bewilderment are made all the more painful by the destabilizing aspects that accompany the challenges of navigating a field imbued with political relations where researchers come face to face with different ideologies and political viewpoints that challenge our image of the world (Agar 2006; Jacoby 2006).

These feelings of bewilderment and uncertainty surfaced during the first few interviews that I conducted in Rwanda as I came face to face with ideas and opinions that challenged the way I understood many of the issues under my research lens. Reflecting on her own fieldwork experience as an International Relations scholar conducting interviews in Zimbabwe, Gallagher (2016, p. 446) refers to these feelings as 'catastrophic encounters'; a concept she adapts from Kristeva's notion that encounters between strangers have a 'violent, catastrophic' quality brought about when the dichotomies we have constructed of self and other are exposed by solid encounters in the field. As Gallagher (2016, p. 446) sees it 'coming face to face with...uncontrolled reality' such as one might experience in an interview situation 'shakes not only our feeling of understanding the world, but of understanding ourselves.'

The confused feeling described by Gallagher here demarcates my introduction to, and subsequent reflection on, the field site as a gendered space and my position as a researcher within it. The gendered introduction to which I refer came early in my fieldwork experience in Rwanda. Having successfully conducted my first interview with a youth leader only two days before, I began my second interview with a trade unionist with the relatively confident attitude that the questions I had designed had the potential to generate interesting data from interviewees. Having established my credentials and gotten through the formalities of consent, the discussion proceeded in a manner similar to that of the previous interview, until, that is, at about the halfway point in our two-hour conversation, my interviewee suggested that if I wanted to talk about the Commonwealth some more we could go out for coffee and discuss my research in a more 'casual' setting. The manner in which this invitation was delivered was quite different to the more formal conversation that had preceded it, and I was unsure of my interviewee's intentions. Any kind of stepping away from the more formal interviewer persona that I had tried to construct since arriving in the field left me questioning my skills as a researcher.

What I am describing here is one aspect of the catastrophic encounter of Gallagher's description above. Through this one casual interjection by my interviewee my position in the research encounter seemed to change rather dramatically as coming face to face with this uncontrolled reality turned what I thought was my understanding of myself as a researcher somewhat upside down. One of the reasons for this was that, before entering the field, my assumptions of what made a good researcher incorporated objective, rational, disembodied, and emotionless ideas, suggesting that, while I subscribed to a post-positivist ontology, my understanding of conducting fieldwork had nevertheless inherited aspects of the positivist tradition which forefronts the idea of the 'distant asexual researcher' (Diprose et al. 2013, p. 296). As I was working through my initial discomfort and embarrassment upon receiving my interviewee's coffee request, a confusing thought emerged. I wondered whether my response to the interviewee's invitation would affect the data collection process, or indeed the constitution of data I was attempting to collect.

By thinking in this way, I felt dependent on the way in which my interviewee constructed me and wondered if declining the interviewee's invitation would end his willingness to be interviewed. Despite my discomfort, I politely turned down the invitation, managing both the boundaries of the interview and any feelings of embarrassment and respect without compromising the ethical line between interviewer and interviewee. But while I had successfully navigated an awkward and uncomfortable hurdle on the one hand, I found myself unable to shake the feeling of having failed somehow as a researcher on the other. This feeling was complicated further when the interviewee's style of answering my questions developed into what can only be described as flirtatious. Taking into consideration my inability to let go of my assumptions of what a good researcher should be, my reaction to the interviewee's flirtation surprised me. Rather than continue to be uncomfortable I found myself relaxing much more into the interview and returning the flirtation. This consisted of mild, flirtatious banter that accompanied my responses to the trade unionist's answers. Even as I realized that flirting was potentially opening a door to data production, I felt a little uncertain about doing so partly because it did not fit my idea of what a researcher did and partly because I was behaving in a more playful, sexualized, and therefore less formal way than I had expected.

There are many reasons why International Relations researchers and other scholars might not wish to talk about these so-called flirtatious or sexualized aspects of fieldwork. Perhaps the most obvious of these is that there is a certain amount of squeamishness that continues to permeate academic convention limiting focus on sex, sexuality, and desire in their many forms (Bell 1995). To some extent, as Cupples (2002, p. 382) writing on desire in the field observes, the reluctance to talk about these aspects of fieldwork demonstrates a continuance of the ongoing myth of the researcher as detached and objective. This observation goes some way toward explaining the slow progress in this area over the past two decades since Binnie (1997, p. 225), writing on the need to incorporate sexual embodiment into the research process for political as well as epistemological reasons, observed 20 years ago that, for the most part, there is a tendency in the academy for scholars to skirt around the edges of sex and sexuality preferring to theorize in the abstract and discuss sex in a more intellectualized and disembodied form.

In spite of this squeamishness however, there are at least two reasons which suggest that a greater attention to the sexualized aspects of fieldwork might be beneficial to our research when reflecting on positionality. The first of these, as I noted at the beginning of this chapter, is that it is impossible to escape our gender and sexualized identity in the field (Morton 1995). This means that when we enter the field, we enter as members of groups about which our host communities already have preconceptions and theories and therefore our research can potentially be affected by stereotypical understandings of who we are (Cupples 2002; Gallagher 2016). The second reason, leading on from the first, is that we not only position ourselves in the field but are also positioned too by our research subjects. Caplan (1993) connects this point to sexuality when she argues that even if we disregard the impact of our sexualities on our research, or believe the political angle of our research project acts as a kind of detached and objective academic cloak, we continue to be sexually positioned by those whom we research. As Cupples (2002, p. 383) has aptly pointed out, in the field our sexualized identities are constructed for us, 'we might be viewed as wives, mothers, desirable foreign women, potential sexual partners and these views impinge on the research process in ways that cannot always be predicted,' but do not have to be ignored.

This appeared to be the case in my interview with the trade unionist and being constructed by research participants in this manner was initially a difficult concept for me to comprehend. However, once I had gotten around the dominant idea of the researcher as disembodied and emotionless, instead of defaulting to the setting of somehow failing as a researcher, I wondered what kind of effect different kinds of flirting might have on data production. What happens to the quality and quantity of data production, for example, when a researcher reciprocates the flirtation directed at them? Are there situations when flirtatious banter might be used as a way to balance power relations during interview encounters, break the ice, or help us navigate our way to a conciliatory end in the more challenging phases of interviews? Conversely, are there instances when flirtation might actually impede data production? It is questions such as these that have the potential to take the literature on gender and sexualized identity in new and interesting directions, and it is this that I want to explore in this chapter.

Within the rich body of literature on positionality and reflexivity, feminist scholars have challenged the ways in which we engage with gender and its role in the complexity of relations in fieldwork (see for example Haraway 1988; Gibson-Graham 1994; Rose 1997; Chattopadhyay 2013). But very little attention has been given to sexuality beyond dramatic events which endangered or severely unsettled the researcher or the research project (Moreno 1995; Grenz 2005). While not discounting the many important works on the subject of sexual harassment in fieldwork (see Clark and Grant 2015), the point of this chapter is not to focus on the vulnerability of the female researcher alone in the field, but to generate new insights on different dynamics during the research process and illustrate that these dynamics might have an effect on the type as well as the amount of data we produce and collect. In drawing attention to the possibilities as well as the pitfalls of flirting as a technique and form of data production, I am suggesting that researchers might find this exploration of flirting helpful and gain useful insights into the gendered behavior engaged in by themselves and their research participants. At the very least I hope that this chapter can facilitate further discussion in the area of negotiating our subject positions and help researchers step away from the idea that we need to separate ourselves from the mythical illusion that a researcher and their research have no interdependence and we need to be something radically different than ourselves in the field.

In the discussion that follows, I offer and explore examples of my own experience with flirtatious research encounters ranging from explicitly sexualized flirtation directed by research participants to examples of less explicitly sexualized everyday flirtatious banter between me, as interviewer, and my interviewees. I look closely at the ways in which the flirtatious elements of the encounters are manifested and how power and agency are balanced or manipulated by both parties before concluding with some observations about the effects of flirting on data production. Before exploring my own encounters in the field, however, I want first to look at others in the literature, who have written similarly on flirting or sexualized attention and the data collection process and attempt to pin down what I mean when I use the term 'flirting.'

THE FIELD OF DESIRE AND DESIRE IN THE FIELD

Between January and March 2015, I conducted research in Kigali and Harare, the respective capital cities of Rwanda and Zimbabwe, working mostly alone with the exception of a one-day period when I worked with a gatekeeper to hold focus group discussions. Unlike many field researchers for whom the need to cultivate relationships with key informants is crucial to developing a rapport with a wider range of participants with a view to facilitating immersion into communities (Gilchrist 1999), my work was based on in-depth semi-structured elite interviews which I arranged with interviewees through a process of cold-calling, to begin with, followed by word-of-mouth recommendations.

As I noted earlier in the chapter, before heading to the field I had tried to immerse myself in the stories told by other researchers, as these stories, and the challenges that their authors conveyed through them, helped me in some ways to navigate my way along a path that was unfamiliar to me. Once in the field, however, I found that the literature I had previously sought out addressed what had been my pre-fieldwork concerns around access to interviewees (*How would I contact potential research participants?*) and amount of data to be collected (*How many interviews would I need to conduct?*). While these questions remained relevant, the literature from which I had sought assurances offered few answers to my concerns, following my Rwandan interviewee's mid-interview coffee invitation, about what to do when an interviewee brings flirtatious and sexualized behavior into an interview or research interaction.

My search for answers led me to the work of feminist scholars writing on positionality and reflexivity in fieldwork and the research process. Reflecting on my own issues with gendered positionality that had come to light, a handful of writers stood out whose experiences I read with great interest. The most helpful voices in this literature belonged to those writers who stepped away from conventional reflections on women's experiences of interviewing other women to focus the analytical lens more closely on the constantly changing subject positions and power relations which occurred during women's experiences of interviewing men. Female scholars who have written on these experiences have reported such issues as power struggles, heterosexual tension and male domination, which often led to the researcher being on the receiving end of expressions of sexism, misogyny, and inappropriate attention and requests for sexual favors (Arendell 1997; Grenz 2005; Diprose et al. 2013). While these examples all provide valuable insights into sexualized identity and sexualized identity construction, with the exception of Newton (1993), Bell (1995, 2007), Binnie (1997), Valentine (2002), and Cupples (2002) who call for the inclusion of sexual emotions (lust, desire, and intimacy) between the researcher and researched, few of these experiences expand the reflexive lens to consider the researcher's agency or embodiment in the sexualized encounter.

Since returning from the field and completing my doctoral research, new literature has begun to emerge that reflects on how sexuality might be used as an instrument for data collection. One example that stands out above all others is an article by Kaspar and Landolt (2016) whose fieldwork experiences while conducting research on the appropriation and production of urban public spaces in Zurich led the authors to reflect on issues around, and ramifications of, flirting in the field. Like my own fieldwork experience, Kaspar and Landolt (2016, p. 107) did not set out with the aim of examining the effect of what they refer to as 'innocuous sexualizations of research encounters' on the constitution of data. Rather the authors' decision to reflect on the process of data production in such sexualized research encounters came only after they had been on the receiving end of such encounters while attempting to conduct interviews with young people and park dwellers in situ. Describing their reaction to the flirtatious, sexualized behavior of their research participants, Kaspar and Landolt (2016, p. 115) note that they found the contradictory emotions that the encounters aroused in the researchers provided 'exemplary accounts of the fluid, ever-changing character of positionalities,' and they believe that these flirtatious interactions had a considerable impact on the contingency of data collection.

This seems an appropriate juncture to address the question of what exactly is meant by flirtation in this context. In their article, Kaspar and Landolt (2016, p. 108) define the practice as a 'communicative and embodied social interaction that adds a sexual component to a mostly one-to-one interaction, in which sexual attraction to the interlocutor is expressed.' While I largely agree with this definition, and this is certainly the case in at least one of the examples from my own experience, which I analyze below, what seems to be missing from Kaspar and Landolt's discussion is any kind of expansion or further definitional discussion on their claim that there are 'countless shades of flirting' (2016, p. 108). Definitions of flirting, for example, might include implicit warm flirtatious banter between two parties, who, as the Oxford English Dictionary (2018) defines it, 'play at courtship...without serious intentions' as an easy way to build rapport. They might also include more explicitly sexualized language or actions on the part of one party that go unreciprocated by the other. These two very different shades of flirting sit at opposite ends of a spectrum that we might describe as ranging from playful encounters to sexual harassment, but how do we pin down or draw lines between the numerous shades of flirtatious behavior in between?

This is not an easy question to answer. One clear reason for this, as my own research encounters will show, is that, what might begin as playful, might just as quickly escalate to something more resembling harassment, and what might start as sexualized might just as easily change into something different along the way. Departing from Kaspar and Landolt, my usage expands the scope of analysis to explore countless other shades of flirting and the difficulties of drawing lines between these different kinds.

Following my experience with the coffee invitation from my Rwandan interviewee, flirtation appeared to become a technique that seemed to be ever present in my interviews. Although this was present in many of the interviews I conducted in Rwanda, it appeared to play much more of a role during interviews in Zimbabwe. This might simply have been down to the fact that I conducted more interviews in Zimbabwe and therefore had more chances to reflexively analyze positionality; alternatively, it might be because the Rwandan leg of the fieldwork had given me ample time to come to terms with the catastrophic process and decentering of my own research assumptions involved in interviewing. Either way, my experiences with flirting and data collection in Zimbabwe were far more frequent than during any other part of my three months in the field.

Drawing on examples from my fieldwork experience in Zimbabwe below, I describe the key elements of flirting in three interview encounters. I illustrate how techniques of flirting entered the interaction, whether, and in what ways, they were reciprocated, and how I dealt with the more explicitly sexualized forms of flirting that came along. In the following section, I will then attempt to analyze these in more detail paying attention to issues of power and agency before discussing the effects that these encounters might have had on data production.

'Can You Tell Me Why Zimbabwe Left the Commonwealth...'

The first example is an interview with a Zanu-PF politician. I had made contact with his office at the suggestion of a member of the opposition party whom I had interviewed earlier in my fieldwork in Harare. After several cancellations, a number of discussions on the telephone, and one trip to his office, where I spent an afternoon getting to know his secretary while I waited in vain for the politician to return from a meeting, we finally met, on the politician's suggestion, in the gardens of the Bronte Hotel just outside the center of Harare. Arriving early to the meeting, I waited in the gardens. As the politician arrived, he approached the table, looked me slowly up and down and declared: 'Yes, you look like a research student!'. I was unsure whether this observation had any subtext other than the fact that, because of the last-minute arrangements of the interview, I had not had very much time to pay attention to the rather casual way that I was dressed. The comment was not what I had envisioned would be the opening gambit in my first ever meeting with a Zanu-PF politician, but I was nervous about our meeting, and I found myself laughing.

As the politician sat down and the interview began, I opened with my usual question: Why did Zimbabwe leave the Commonwealth? Despite knowing the answer quite well, I had included this question as my opener in all interviews as it not only produced interesting and nuanced answers from interviewees, but also became an interesting way to observe the different ways that my interviewees and I performed gender. Without exception, the male research participants I interviewed used their answer as an opportunity to 'teach' me about Zimbabwean politics and history. In this particular encounter, however, the politician's soliloquy took a more sexualized turn as he began to talk about colonialism being very much about rape, as he put it: 'the British colonization of Africa was like consensual rape. It happens and you have a couple of children as a result and then you think, well I might as well make the most of this family situation now.' For the purposes of data production, this encounter reflects on a similar experience by England (1994, p. 86) who has written on the contradictory position of listening to the stories of research participants 'while also thinking how their words will make a great quote for my paper.' While the politician's words certainly fell into this category, I experienced this act, following his opening comment on my appearance, as testing the boundaries of the flirtatious game and although there was nothing more in the way of flirtation, other than friendly banter, for the remainder of the interview, I confess that I was glad when it was over.

'I Personally Have No Problem with Homosexuality...'

My second example involves an interview with a young journalist. I had made contact with the journalist at the suggestion of a university professor I had interviewed the week before and had set up the meeting by email. The meeting took place at his office in the central business district of Harare. As I arrived the journalist came out to meet me in the foyer and led me to a meeting room where, despite a large glass table with many chairs taking up considerable space in the middle of the room, we sat close to each other at one end. We began our conversation in a flirtatious manner with my interviewee injecting laughter as well as jokes into his answers and me responding in a similar manner. As the interview progressed, the discussion turned to human rights in the Commonwealth and a recent statement by the, then, British Prime Minister David Cameron about the possibility of Britain withdrawing aid to Commonwealth member states that continued to criminalize homosexuality.

Up until this time our conversation had been permeated with friendly flirtation, but on the mention of homosexuality, my interviewee's demeanor changed from laughter and flirtation to more of a whisper noting: 'You guys shouldn't push it on us, we've got our own history...I personally have no problem with homosexuality, I think it's a condition that can be cured, but we still have to recognize their rights.' I was surprised and slightly panicked by the change in persona. There was a pause and then the flirtatious laughter began again, but this time with more vigor.

'I Wish I Could Come Up to Your Hotel Room...'

The third example, one of the more interesting illustrations of the complexity of relations in fieldwork and also one of the most challenging in terms of reflexive analysis, was a research encounter that happened right at the end of my time in the field. Taking a few days off to see Zimbabwe beyond the downtown area and suburbs of Harare, I joined my host family on a road trip to Bulawayo, a city in the south of the country.

Arriving in Bulawayo I parted company with my hosts and booked myself into a hotel on the road to the Motopos National Park with the intention of doing some sightseeing early the next morning. While checking into the hotel, I struck up a conversation with a prominent local politician based in a neighboring city who was in Bulawayo for a conference and I wasted no time in enquiring if he would consent to an interview. The politician agreed and we made arrangements to meet later in the hotel restaurant and discuss politics over dinner.

Later, in the hotel restaurant, as the interview began we chatted casually about Britain and Zimbabwe and the interviewee told me details of his work and life. Occasionally, a question about marriage or children would be directed my way, but nothing that seemed to suggest that the interview would progress to anything beyond the friendly flirtation that entered the conversation from time to time usually accompanied by a joke from the interviewee about some aspect of married life. A little while into the encounter, the interviewee received a phone call on his mobile phone. After talking for four or five minutes he hung up and returned to our conversation apologizing for the interruption with the explanation that, 'that was my girlfriend, but don't let that put you off, I would still like to come up to your hotel room.' I was surprised and a little taken aback at the politician's brazenness, particularly so soon after talking to his girlfriend on the phone, but was relieved when he appeared to accept that I was more interested in the interview. Returning from the field, I was reluctant to analyze this interview believing it not to contain anything in the way of what I considered to be 'serious' or 'valuable' data. The following section of the chapter will show that I was wrong on both accounts.

EXPLORING FLIRTING IN THE FIELD: POSITIONALITY, PERFORMANCE, PRODUCTION

One of the most striking features of the encounters I have described here is the way in which flirtation could change from a tool which broke the ice to something which defused or even raised tensions, more likely than not within the same encounter. In my first interview for example, mild flirtation relieved the tensions between the research participant and the researcher and effectively improved the atmosphere. The politician's joke that I looked like a research student broke the ice and I appreciated the flirtatious banter on one level for the acceptance that it seemed to bring. By beginning the encounter with a joke about my appearance, the interviewee opened the door to further interaction of this friendly, playful kind. Yet flirtation also raised tensions as our different rationales collided. What I thought would be an awkward and uncomfortable interview brought about by the politics and history of Britain and Zimbabwe, turned out to be an awkward and uncomfortable interview brought about by awkward and uncomfortable flirtation. As a result I felt uneasy, insecure, and in some moments even vulnerable as the discussion turned to anger and the interviewee's descriptions of sexual violence added layers to my feelings of unease.

Why, then, did I go along with this flirtation? Haraway's (1988) explanation of positioning is useful in providing something in the way of an explanation here. Writing on the potential power dynamics that can operate in research relationships, Haraway directs our attention to the varying levels of micro-politics which occur during these encounters arguing that power relations have an influence on our interactions in the field. Considering Haraway's notion of positioning in relation to my encounter above, I was of course acquainted with the existing dominant paradigms that position me, a white western researcher, as the more powerful in the interview encounter, but less so with the complexities that gender could add to the mix. Thus, while I might have had more power as a white researcher in this context, it is reasonable to infer that as a woman I had less. Reflecting on this complexity now that my fieldwork is over, it is conceivable that the politician was using maleness to redress the power imbalance and in the course of engaging with flirtation, I played an active role in enabling this rebalancing.

Attention to gender in the particular workings of power in fieldwork encounters raises questions about the implications that reciprocating flirting had on agency; specifically my own in this encounter. I have already discussed the contradictions and complexities that underlie flirtatious interview encounters which, while uncomfortable, nevertheless produced interesting and unexpected data; however, my reciprocation of the Zanu-PF politician's flirtation actually made the awkward encounter more comfortable at times. Such an observation has ambiguous effects, where I want to suggest that my reciprocal flirtation was an expression of agency on my part, rather I find myself concluding, at least in the first example I have outlined above, that it was more of an abdication. But as

I grapple with the extent of my own participation in the production of knowledge that this realization brings, I am further struck by the extent to which performance played a role in the encounter. The notion of performativity developed by Butler (1990) is particularly useful with regard to examining the ways in which performance might intersect with the notion of sexualized identity and flirting in the field. Butler emphasizes the necessity to take account of the material body alongside the dynamic of performativity in conceptualizing gender. As she puts it, there is no core identity that precedes the one we perform, no 'natural body' that pre-exists its cultural inscription (Butler 1990, p. 25). This means that gender is not something that one *is*, but rather something that one *does*—an act, or as Butler (1990, p. 25) puts this, 'a set of repeated acts within a highly rigid regulatory frame.' Butler is not suggesting that the subject is free to choose which gender he or she is going to enact here, rather she suggests that by repeating or performing gendered acts the subject is stabilizing gender as an institution.

This emphasis on gender as a performative act is continued in my interview with the young journalist in Harare. The reciprocated laughter at jokes or comments made, the interviewee's willingness to 'teach' me about Zimbabwean politics and history through lengthy answers to my questions, all point to Butler's observation that both my interviewee and I were 'doing, displaying, asserting, narrating, performing, mobilizing, maneuvering' the literal, physical, and discursive activities or norms associated with our respective genders (Martin 2003, p. 354). In reiterating these norms my position as a researcher was far removed from the objective, emotionless role that had influenced my feelings of failure earlier in my fieldwork. Any previous naivety on my part about the interdependence between researchers and their research had disappeared as I came to understand the effect these gendered performances might have on the production of data.

It did not escape me that interviews with men were easier for me, involving more eye contact and body language. Returning to the audio transcripts each evening after conducting my interviews I was able to pinpoint where each of us—the female interviewer and the male interviewee—had performed our ascribed gender roles. My male interviewees teaching me about some small aspect of history or political culture I had usually already acquired extensive knowledge about through years of research. At first I was annoyed at the idea of being 'taught' by these men, but the realization that each retelling of the story brought more nuance and soon gave way to mild flirtatious gestures of surprise and encouragement for the interviewee to elaborate more. These performances seemed to have a positive effect on the production of meaningful data and in ways similar to those described by Kaspar and Landolt (2016, p. 115), I engaged in play which I felt was 'safe and beneficiary to my goals.'

The complex layers of paradox and performance were further illuminated as my interview with the young journalist progressed to a discussion of human rights and homosexuality. What I have described above as friendly, flirtatious behavior directed my way by my research participant appeared to be accelerated by the explicit content of the interview question. There is nothing unusual about an interviewee responding in different ways to different interview questions, and nothing unusual about changes in mood as an interview progresses. What is particularly interesting for the purposes of this analysis of flirting and performance, however, is the speed in which my interviewee's demeanor changed from friendly and flirtatious, to serious and cold, and back to flirtatious all within the space of a few seconds. The more homophobic the journalist's comments, the more performed his masculinity and flirtatious behavior became. Equally illuminating was how dramatically my position as a researcher seemed to change with my interviewee's demeanor. Within a split-second I had moved from unthreatening to threatening, and then quickly back to unthreatening. In the middle of this situation, a confusing thought emerged. I wondered whether it would create a distance between us if I showed any kind of, even subconscious, reaction as I did not want to jeopardize the chance to elicit further meaningful data. Flirting marked a conciliatory end to a challenging phase that saw both interviewer and interviewee negotiating our subject positions. And yet, as much as I reciprocated the friendly flirtatious banter for the data it seemed to produce, I was happy when my interview with the journalist was over. Flirtation had relieved the tension in an uncomfortable moment in the interview and hence improved the atmosphere, but it also marked the end of what could have been my interviewee letting go of any preconceived notions of what he might have thought I wanted to hear. Thus, while I am not convinced that friendly flirtation inhibited more aggressive and honest conversation from my interviewee, I cannot say for certain that it did not.

In the final encounter, flirtation also appeared to inhibit more honest conversation, but in a much more sexualized manner. While researchers concerned with power and gender relations may find it interesting to analyze the trajectory of flirtation throughout the encounter, along with my interviewee's explicit invitation to have sex, what is more interesting with regards to my discussion of gender and sexualized identity in the field is my own role in this encounter. Reflecting on Rose's (1997, p. 316) observation that female researchers are situated, not by what they know, but what they uncertainly perform, I want to suggest that in my eagerness for data production I had not considered how agreeing to conduct this interview over dinner might have sounded to my interviewee. Reflecting on the encounter later I wondered whether this eagerness, along with the location of the interview—a hotel where I was sleeping—had additionally added an extra complexity to the encounter. I make this observation based on the speed with which my interviewee accepted my non-availability and how fast I moved from the position of 'a potentially available woman, who was even frightened that she would be harassed, to a non-available object of desire' (Kaspar and Landolt 2016, p. 113). Once flirtation had been removed from the table, our conversation settled into a trade-off of a completely different kind. In the course of the conversation that followed, the politician informed me that he had seized the opportunity during our chance meeting earlier in the day to arrange our interview dinner with the view to eliciting my advice on how leftwing political groups in Britain might be able to 'help' opposition candidates in Zimbabwe. I have no way of knowing whether this was the politician's way of covering any embarrassment but any tension brought about through flirting appeared to quickly dissolve.

All three of these encounters say interesting things about flirting in the field and its effect on positionality, but what can we make of the effect of flirting on data production? When the inconstant, generative content of flirting varies so widely and its form manifests so diversely, how does one go about figuring out the effect of flirting on the amount or type of data one collects? This is a far from simple question and I am, quite frankly, unsure about the answer. Returning to the three encounters, I have described in this section, as well as my coffee invitation by the trade unionist in Rwanda, with an eye to the production of data, leads me to conclude that the more playful, friendly, and flirtatious the interaction, the more lengthy the data production. This does not mean, of course, that a longer interview means more valuable or usable data; however, playful and flirtatious banter effectively created an atmosphere where the research participant was more willing to expand on an answer.

While this observation might simply be a reflection of McDowell's (1988, p. 167) assertion that female researchers are often perceived by male interviewees as 'unthreatening' and more 'supplicant' compared to older, more established male academics, making interviewees more willing to reveal information, my conclusion nevertheless is that reciprocated mild flirtatious interaction, at times, helped facilitate this exchange of information. This observation does not negate the value of the data that were produced during my more uncomfortable explicitly sexualized flirtatious encounters, on the contrary, although I was often relieved when the interview was over, these encounters were much more complex and although they produced less data, they nevertheless revealed more about how positionalities can shift in the course of interactions. Additionally these interactions, although uncomfortable, also contained interesting and at times pleasurable moments, both of which could facilitate as well as impede data production.

CONCLUSION

One of the most reassuring aspects of fieldwork for a novice researcher is finding similar experiences to our own in the literature which provide guidance while out in the field. In this chapter, I have focused on sexualized identity and flirtation and how they are articulated and performed in fieldwork encounters because the current representation of these practices in the literature did not fit with my own experiences during fieldwork. As I have noted, before commencing my fieldwork my assumptions of what made a good researcher incorporated objective, rational, disembodied, and emotionless ideas 'inherited from the positivist tradition of the distant asexual researcher' (Diprose et al. 2013, p. 296). Despite designing my research around a post-positivist epistemology, I described earlier in the chapter a naivety on my part, in early fieldwork encounters, to fully appreciate the interdependence between myself and my research. Since returning to what I would describe as my more uncomfortable encounters with gendered and sexualized positionality in the field, I have come to realize that I was strongly influenced by the squeamishness of academia and it was only when I started to reflect on the emotions and uncertainties caused by these flirting episodes that I realized I had entered the field imagining myself and my research participants as non-sexual.

One of the more thorny questions for me while researching this chapter has been why so many accounts of sexualized identity and gendered positionality have so far largely ignored the female researcher's agency in these practices of flirtation. My search for answers to this inevitably took me back to the squeamishness I have described above, but it also gave me time to reflect on what Kaspar and Landolt (2016, p. 115) have referred to as 'the conflicting rationales of professional obligation and personal (dis)pleasure.' Female researchers can often find themselves in a position of dependence on their research informants to meet the need to produce data. I have described in the chapter how my own obsession with conducting 'one more interview' led to an interview over dinner in a hotel restaurant and my discomfort of being on the receiving end of some explicitly sexualized flirting. The more squeamish reader might question the ethics of reciprocating friendly flirtatious banter that might inevitably lead to encounters such as this. To frame the discussion in such a way, however, would be to enlist our entire understanding of flirtatious interaction entirely in the service of sex or sexual harassment.

As I noted in my definitional discussion earlier in the chapter, there are countless shades of flirting. As a corrective to the more one-sided illustrations of sexualized identity in fieldwork encounters, that risk (re)producing Western and orientalist notions of the other, I have attempted to show in the chapter that flirtation can be structured and initiated by female researchers as well as by their male research participants. I have swung back and forth in the chapter between discussions of flirtation, which involve playful banter on the part of both the researcher and the research participant, and more explicitly sexualized flirting encountered by the researcher where research participants attempt to test the boundaries of the interview. I have done this in order to give an idea of the different shades of flirtation which researchers might encounter in the field, and I have tried to show that these can be both comfortable or uncomfortable encounters as well as something in between.

I cannot claim definitively that I was able to collect more data through this practice—my accounts demonstrate that flirtatious behavior on the part of either the interviewer or interviewee could both facilitate data collection and impede it—but once I had accepted that we cannot account for or control the ways in which our research participants position us in our fieldwork encounters and that being positioned in gendered ways was somehow a failure on my part as a researcher, I found that when used alongside the explicit content of the interview questions flirtation, owing to its playful character, can be a powerful way in which we develop knowledge about the fluidity of our subject positions and come to embrace the messy process of fieldwork.

REFERENCES

Ackerly, B., Stern, M., & True, J. (Eds.). (2006). *Feminist Methodologies for International Relations*. Cambridge: Cambridge University Press.

Agar, M. (2006). An Ethnography by Any Other Name. *Forum: Qualitative Social Research Socialforschung, 7*(4). http://www.qualitative-research.net/index.php/fqs/article/view/177. Accessed December 15, 2017.

Arendell, T. (1997). Reflections on the Researcher-Researched Relationship: A Woman Interviewing Men. *Qualitative Sociology, 20,* 341–365.

Bell, D. (1995). [Screw]ing Geography (Censor's Version). *Environment and Planning D: Society and Space, 13,* 127–131.

Bell, D. (2007). Fucking Geography, Again. In K. Browne, J. Lim, & G. Brown (Eds.), *Geographies of Sexualities: Theory, Practices and Politics* (pp. 81–88). Farnham: Ashgate.

Binnie, J. (1997). Coming out of Geography: Towards a Queer Epistemology? *Environment and Planning D: Society and Space, 15,* 223–237.

Butler, J. (1990). *Gender Trouble*. London: Routledge.

Caplan, P. (1993). Learning Gender: Fieldwork in a Tanzanian Coastal Village, 1965–85. In D. Bell, P. Caplan, & W. J. Karim (Eds.), *Gendered Fields: Women, Men and Ethnography* (pp. 168–181). London: Routledge.

Chattopadhyay, S. (2013). Getting Personal While Narrating the "Field": A Researchers Journey to the Villages of the Narmada Valley. *Gender, Place and Culture: A Journal of Feminist Geography, 20*(2), 137–159.

Clark, I., & Grant, A. (2015). Sexuality and Danger in the Field: Starting an Uncomfortable Conversation. *Journal of the Anthropological Society of Oxford, 7*(1), 1–14.

Cupples, J. (2002). The Field as a Landscape of Desire: Sex and Sexuality in Geographical Fieldwork. *Area, 34*(4), 382–390.

Diprose, G., Thomas, A. C., & Rushton, R. (2013). Desiring More: Complicating Understandings of Sexuality in Research Processes. *Area, 45*(3), 292–298.

England, K. (1994). Getting Personal: Refexivity, Positionality, and Feminist Research. *Professional Geographer, 46*(1), 80–89.

Gallagher, J. (2016). Interviews as Catastrophic Encounters: An Object Relations Methodology for IR Research. *International Studies Perspectives, 17*(4), 445–461.

Gibson-Graham, J. K. (1994). "Stuffed If I Know!": Reflections on Post-modern Feminist Social Research. *Gender, Place and Culture, 1*, 205–224.

Gilbert, M. R. (1994). The Politics of Location: Doing Feminist Research "At Home". *Professional Geographer, 46*, 90–96.

Gilchrist, V. J. (1999). Key Informant Interviews. In B. F. Crabtree & W. L. Miller (Eds.), *Doing Qualitative Research* (pp. 70–89). Thousand Oaks, CA: Sage.

Grenz, S. (2005). Intersections of Sex and Power in Research on Prostitution: A Female Researcher Interviewing Male Heterosexual Clients. *Signs, 30*(4), 2091–2113.

Haraway, D. J. (1988). Situated Knowledges: The Science Question in Feminism and the Privilege of Partial Perspective. *Feminist Studies, 14*(3), 575–599.

Jacoby, T. (2006). From the Trenches: Dilemmas of Feminist IR Fieldwork. In B. Ackerly, M. Stern, & J. True (Eds.), *Feminist Methodologies for International Relations* (pp. 153–173). Cambridge: Cambridge University Press.

Kaspar, H., & Landolt, S. (2016). Flirting in the Field: Shifting Positionalities and Power Relations in Innocuous Sexualisations of Research Encounters. *Gender, Place and Culture, 23*(1), 107–119.

Martin, P. Y. (2003). "Said and Done" Versus "Saying and Doing": Gendering Practices, Practicing Gender at Work. *Gender and Society, 17*(3), 342–366.

Mattingly, D., & Falconer-Al-Hindi, K. (1995). Should Women Count? A Context for the Debate. *Professional Geographer, 47*, 27–35.

McDowell, L. (1988). Coming in From the Dark Feminist Research in Geography. In J. Eyles (Ed.), *Research in Human Geography* (pp. 154–173). Oxford: Blackwell.

McDowell, L. (1992). Doing Gender: Feminism, Feminists and Research Methods in Human Geography. *Transactions. Institute of British Geographers, 17*, 399–416.

Moreno, E. (1995). Rape in the Field: Reflections From a Survivor. In D. Kulick & M. Wilson (Eds.), *Taboo: Sex, Identity and Erotic Subjectivity in Immersed Anthropological Fieldwork* (pp. 219–250). London and New York: Routledge.

Morton, H. (1995). My Chastity Belt: Avoiding Seduction in Tonga. In D. Kulick & M. Wilson (Eds.), *Taboo: Sex, Identity and Erotic Subjectivity in Anthropological Fieldwork* (pp. 168–185). London: Routledge.

Nast, H. J. (1994). Opening Remarks on "Women in the Field". *Professional Geographer, 46*, 54–66.

Newton, E. (1993). My Best Informant's Dress: The Erotic Equation in Fieldwork. *Cultural Anthropology, 8*, 3–23.

Parr, H. (1996). Mental Health, Ethnography and the Body: Implications for Geographical Research. Paper Presented at a Conference on Feminist Methodologies, Nottingham.

Rose, G. (1997). Situating Knowledges: Positionality, Reflexivities and Other Tactics. *Progress in Human Geography, 21*(3), 305–320.

Sundberg, J. (2003). Masculinist Epistemologies and the Politics of Fieldwork in Latin Americanist Geography. *The Professional Geographer, 55*(2), 180–190.

Valentine, G. (2002). People Like Us: Negotiating Sameness and Difference in the Research Process. In P. Moss (Ed.), *Feminist Geography in Practice: Research and Methods* (pp. 116–126). Oxford: Blackwell.

CHAPTER 6

Fieldwork and Emotions: Positionality, Method Choices, and a Radio Program in South Sudan

Kerstin Tomiak

In International Relations research, emotions have traditionally been a poor relation to the prevalent understanding of good research being objective and rational. This might be a consequence of the discipline's traditional use of the state as the unit of analysis and its mainly quantitative research tradition. While disciplines like sociology and anthropology increasingly acknowledge the importance of emotions in research (see, e.g., Dickson-Swift et al. 2009; Davies 2010; Clarke and Knights 2015), International Relations still lag behind. This is all the more remarkable since the discipline's ethnographic turn brought with it an interest in experience, interpretive methodologies and the politics of knowledge production, as well as an increased attention to fieldwork (Nordstrom and Robben 1995; Siriam et al. 2009; Autesserre 2014, 2017; Bliesemann de Guevara and Kostic 2017).

This chapter contributes to the literature on conducting fieldwork by shedding light on the importance of acknowledging the effects of emotions on our research. It argues that the emotions a researcher

K. Tomiak (✉)
Hebrew University of Jerusalem, Jerusalem, Israel

© The Author(s) 2019
L. Johnstone (ed.), *The Politics of Conducting Research in Africa*,
https://doi.org/10.1007/978-3-319-95531-5_6

experiences in the field have a profound effect, not only on the researcher's well-being, but also on their methodological choices. The chapter argues that emotions are best understood as part of a researcher's positionality. Positionality is about the researcher's self and how this influences the research. While, more often than not, the main focus in the scholarly literature on positionality is on class, ethnicity, and gender, I argue that it is not *only* these parts of a researcher's self that have an impact, rather the experiences made in the field, and equally significantly, the emotions that these experiences trigger, play an important and often overlooked part in a researcher's positionality also.

I develop my argument through a discussion of my fieldwork experience in South Sudan. In 2012, I was sent to the country by a small NGO for a media project, a community radio station that was to broadcast in the refugee camps of Jamam and Gendressa in the country's Upper Nile state. At the time, I was a journalist with the experience of training in conflict zones, but I had no experience of conducting research on an in-depth scale. Although not formally fieldwork, this first stay shaped my picture of South Sudan. The emotions I experienced while carrying out the project had a profound influence on my later doctoral fieldwork and it is this observation that led me to the understanding that a researcher's emotions shape knowledge production. Before turning to the interviews and an analysis of my emotional reactions to research participants, I review methodological debates about emotions in and around the field of International Relations studies, identifying where my own contribution to these debates takes place.

The Field of Emotions in Research

Up until the late 1990s, among the central and more traditional categories in the study of International Relations 'emotions had occupied the role of a strange uncle who is invited to all family reunions but often sits isolated at the coffee table' (Clément and Sangar 2018, p. 3). This is because, as a number of scholars have aptly pointed out, while there was no shortage of emotions running through some of the most influential International Relations paradigms, for example, 'fear' in realism (Freyberg-Inan 2006) and 'mutual sympathy' in liberalism (D'Aoust 2014), analyzing these concepts as emotions or, further still, granting emotions status as legitimate research objects was a practice rarely carried out until the early 2000s (Hutchison and Bleiker 2008).

Although it goes beyond the scope of this chapter to provide any kind of history of the scholarship on emotions in International Relations, as much of this is focused on explaining why emotions matter conceptually, since the 2000s the research on emotions in the study of world politics has advanced to a point where, as Hutchison and Bleiker (2014, p. 492) have observed, 'a growing number of International Relations scholars now see emotions as an intrinsic part of the social realm and thus also of world politics.'

But, while emotions have permeated the study of International Relations conceptually, their acknowledgment in social science methodology, as I noted earlier, has severely lagged behind (Clément and Sangar 2018). Much of the slow development in this area stems from a certain amount of reluctance in the academy to let go of the idea that a researcher ought to be objective, rational, and above all emotionless and detached from their object of enquiry (Davies 2010; Jackson 2011). It is expectations like these that have led many researchers to confess that they have felt a certain amount of pressure to rein in their emotions when conducting fieldwork and disregard them once again at the writing up stage. Feminist scholars have argued that subscribing to this kind of empiricist or positivist epistemology more often than not means that researchers 'veil' or 'repress' the different concepts and conditions that make observation possible (Gregory 2000, p. 206). Rejecting the positivist tradition, these scholars have called for the recognition of the ways in which our positionalities fundamentally shape every stage of the research project including the methods we employ to gather and interpret data (Nast 1994; Mattingly and Falconer-Al-Hindi 1995). Much current scholarship on positionality and fieldwork has responded to this call to retrieve subjectivity from the margins to give it a more central place in methodological debates, but few among these studies have given any serious attention to emotions in the field.

Recently, however, new scholarship has begun to appear which attempts to bring emotions in. Of particular interest to this chapter is the work of a number of scholars who are taking the literature in new and interesting directions. Writing on the psychology of anthropological fieldwork experience, these scholars have astutely observed that while literature on positionality has explored the varying ways that a researcher's identity, personal history, gender, ethnicity, and class affect how they interact with and are positioned by their research participants, it has relatively ignored the researcher's 'states of being' (Davies 2010, p. 1).

Reflecting on their own fieldwork experiences and the emotions that they evoked, some authors have called on scholars to question the role of emotion in their own research process.

Seear and McLean's (2008) work is an example of this. Drawing on their personal experiences with illness and homosexuality respectively, the authors discuss how, in spite of their closeness to their research topics, they tried as much as they could to maintain a professional and emotional distance between themselves and their research participants. This had an emotional toll on the authors who argue that they feared that if they had not conformed to the positivist tradition which demands that a researcher be neutral and objective, and therefore lacking in emotion, they would have jeopardized the validity of their research (see also Oakley 1981; Reger 2001; Rager 2005). Following the observations of Seear and McLean, other scholars, such as Crapanzano (2010) and Jackson (2010), have recognized the valuable insights that paying attention to one's emotions can provide on the extent to which emotions affect positionality.

My commentary aims to supplement these efforts. I too look at links between the researcher's emotional reactions to fieldwork encounters and how these affect positionality and method choice, but I do so by considering an element that is currently underdeveloped in the literature on emotions in the field. This is the notion of emotional labor. Writing on the commodification of human feelings in the customer service industry, and drawing on the work of flight attendants to make her point, Hochchild, in her influential emotional labor thesis the *Managed Heart* (1983), observed that the cost of performing emotional labor was as harmful as that of physical and mental labor. As Hochchild (1983, p. 7) sees this, emotional labor is the work that includes the suppression of one's feelings and emotions, 'in order to sustain the outward countenance that produces the proper state of mind in others.'

Drawing on my experience conducting research in South Sudan in 2012, I explore my own experience with emotional labor and show how the environment in the refugee camps and the stories I was told by research participants forced me to manage my feelings. I then go on to explore how the experience changed my stance on methods and impacted my later method choices. Despite the growing interest in emotional aspects of fieldwork, remarkably little attention has been paid to the intersection of these two areas. I argue that emotions affect the way we conduct research. As Finlay (2002, p. 532) states, 'reflexive analysis in research encompasses continual evaluation of subjective responses, inter-subjective dynamics, and the research process itself.' It thus puts the focus on being aware of how we construct knowledge, and this should not be limited to data gathering and analysis; rather the reflexive process should start before, with questions about why we have made the decision to gather a particular type of data.

This is still hardly specified in the literature in any detail. Researchers rarely acknowledge issues around professional expectations, personal choice or the potentially debilitating impact of emotionality in the research process. Method choice 'cannot be made in the abstract' (Alveson and Sköldberg 2009, p. 350), and emotions play an important role. In this chapter, I argue that the emotions we experience during research can change our positionality; this in turn affects our future selves as researchers and therefore our research. While not necessarily bad or problematic this needs to be understood and acknowledged, in not doing so we run the risk of reflexivity not truly being taken seriously. My own contribution to this emerging research, then, questions not only what impact emotions can have on the research process but additionally whether emotions experienced in situ affect only the study at hand. In other words, do the emotional reactions we have as researchers stay within the bounds of the research project, or are their effects long-term, potentially impacting future research projects?

To find answers to these questions, and to show the impact of the emotions I experienced during my fieldwork, I draw on my field notes and diary entries that I kept while in the field. During this time I conducted interviews and held informal chats with inhabitants of the refugee camps. Most interviews were not recorded; instead, I took notes. The reason for this was that possibilities for interviewing usually occurred spontaneously, and, more often than not, in these situations I had no, or no functioning, voice recorder with me. In some cases batteries died unexpectedly, while in others participants said they would feel more comfortable if I did not record. The field notes capture the chats and informal interviews I held with the refugees. As I was conducting them in English, either directly with an interview partner or through a translator, they were written in English. My diary was a personal document where I recorded the feelings I experienced during my work. I looked for common themes in the field notes and interviews and traced my feelings in the diary. Compared with each other, the two sets of documents show how 'violence' was an overarching theme in the interviews, how this impacted on me, and the emotions I experienced.

The use of personal diaries in research is not unproblematic. There is a fine line between what Delamont (2009, p. 58) refers to as 'autoethnographic self-obsession' and reflexive writing on a social setting or phenomenon. I use my diary here to illustrate that emotions have an impact on research and a researcher's positionality. In this sense, I consider the use of my personal diary justified. Starting with a brief description of the environment and the difficulties in reaching it, I will now give an account of the project I was working for and the research I was conducting. Following this, I show how violence emerged as an overarching theme and the effect this had on me, in particular how this had an effect on and changed my positionality in the field.

The Environment

In September 2012, I flew with the United Nations Humanitarian Air Service (UNHAS) from Juba, the capital of South Sudan in Central Equatoria, to Malakal, the capital of Upper Nile state, and continued from there by helicopter to Maban in the north of South Sudan. What sounds like a relatively easy and straightforward journey was in fact an ordeal. Planes were overbooked and rescheduled. For days, I would drive to Juba Airport, where a crowd of people pushed into the building hoping to get on a plane. When my turn finally came, a two-hour flight took me to Malakal, where I then connected with the helicopter which took me further north. As the helicopter touched down in Maban, there were only trees, bushes, and a sandy trail as far as the eye could see. After a two-hour jeep ride, sometimes through puddles that resembled small lakes, I finally reached the camp—a handful of Tukuls built to house the NGO staff, a little outside the tiny hamlet of Jamam to the one side, and the refugee camp to the other. Local staff had prepared food for our arrival. I switched my mobile on, but there was no reception. It was then that I began to feel quite lost.

The refugee camps in Upper Nile state in South Sudan were constructed in response to the conflict in South Kordofan and Blue Nile state that started in 2011. Following the outbreak of violent conflict, which was accompanied by aerial bombings, military attacks against the civilian population, and large-scale human rights abuses, people fled their homes in vast numbers. In 2011, approximately 25,000 refugees arrived in Maban County and a further 35,000 came in May 2012 (Tiller and Healy 2013). By 2013, estimates claim that roughly 80,000 people from South Kordofan had fled to South Sudan, and more than 160,000 of the population of Blue Nile had left for the refugee camps in Ethiopia and South Sudan's Upper Nile state (James 2015).

Refugees arrived in South Sudan weak, dehydrated, and malnourished, and death rates in the camps were high. Maban County is a swamp that is dry only during the dry season. In the rainy season, huge parts are flooded. It is a harsh environment for the population and even worse for vulnerable refugees. Initially, the host population in Maban was willing to embrace and help the refugees; but when more people arrived, tensions over scarce resources rose to the surface (see Hutton 2013). To address the situation, an NGO planned a small community radio station as part of the humanitarian response, and this was the project for which I was hired.

The aims of the station were to communicate with the refugee population and keep them informed on such things as food distribution schedules, administrative needs, and the availability and frequency of medics in the camp. Despite these clear aims, however, the question of what precisely the refugees, people who had fled their home country, who had left everything behind, and had experienced massive violence, would want and need from a radio program, had not been adequately addressed. The project, or at least my part of it, did not include a research component. It was a short-term consultancy of only two months, and my main contribution was planning the actual station, contacting companies to purchase the necessary equipment, and drafting the broadcast schedule and program guidelines.

Despite my limited time, I wanted to investigate the needs and wants of the refugee population regarding a radio program. I thus talked, mostly with the help of a translator, with hired local workers of the NGOs, visited elder meetings and food distributions, and chatted during long walks through the camps with their inhabitants. Truth be told, this was not only done to deliver a meaningful program. Knowing that I would start my doctoral research afterward and that it might be on South Sudan, this research on the side was a welcome opportunity to familiarize myself with the country and to hone my research skills.

THE RESEARCH

I had no systematically planned and executed research design. For a number of reasons, I had decided on interviews and informal chats as the methods for collecting data for the project. At the time I understood myself more as a qualitative researcher, and I was comfortable with the interview situation. Further, I saw interviews as a chance to let participants talk for themselves (Czarniawska 2014; Schaffer 2015). As I wanted to investigate what the people wanted from the radio program, a survey offering categories such as 'News,' 'Health,' and 'Sport' would have been an appropriate method. At first, however, I did not see this as a viable option. This was because, I was not certain that, if I went along the survey path, I would be able to distribute enough questionnaires to get meaningful answers. Collecting a representative sample would have been problematic, if not impossible given the situation on the ground. A questionnaire would have required translation, and I would have needed a local interviewer for a longer period. As the whole thing was unofficial, I had neither the staff nor the resources for either. Borrowing a translator for ad hoc walks and interview sessions was fine, but asking them to work as surveyors was a different issue altogether.

Deciding on categories to include in a potential questionnaire was also tricky. I had only limited knowledge of the religion, values, and customs of the people in the refugee camp, and drawing up a questionnaire with closed questions could easily lead to confusion. Schaffer (2016, p. 10) points to the necessity to 'elucidate shared meanings' as concepts cannot be seen as universal, but need to be negotiated and translated. This holds true for a project such as this where both the researched and the researcher come from very different backgrounds. Before I could ask meaningful questions about radio programs, I needed to make sure that there was a common ground of understanding. Finally, I needed to understand if there were specifics in communication style, or cultural or religious rules governing who or what could be heard on air. I needed a clear idea of what people desired, and I wanted to know how a radio program would need to be presented to be of relevance to its listeners. Interviews were thus an appropriate method, as the main point was to understand (Silverman 2013).

Choosing interview participants was a relatively unstructured process. Put simply, I talked to everyone who was willing to talk to me. More often than not, as I noted earlier, these exchanges happened spontaneously often while walking through the camp, attending food distribution, or at meetings between elders and NGO staff working in the area. On these walks, I was always accompanied by one of my South Sudanese colleagues and employees of my NGO. In total, I conducted twelve interviews or chats as they are perhaps better described. Two of these were recorded, and during the other ten I jotted answers down in my notebook. Seven were with male refugees and five with females. Only two were conducted in English. Three of the male refugees were elders, and four of the females were young girls, approximately between fourteen and sixteen years old.

A COMMON THEME: EXPERIENCING VIOLENCE

The following extracts reveal the extent to which violence and the discussion of violent incidences were an omnipresent theme in the interviews I conducted. In every interview and conversation, remarks were made to either experienced or conducted violence. The first interview started as follows:

> *Kerstin*: Can you tell me what you would want from a radio station? What kind of programs would you find helpful for people here in the refugee camps?
>
> *J*: Yes. Thank you. My name is J. I was a child soldier. I don't know how old I was when they took me and trained me. I was in the war. Fighting in the war a long time.[1]

In the diary, I noted my confusion about his opening remarks:

> A strange thing, I ask him about what program he would think good or ok, he answered with a childhood account. Is this a cultural thing, part of an introduction? I did not really know how to react to that, so I asked again about preferences for a radio program.[2]

These openings later proved a common theme. I asked about preferences for a radio program, the question was answered with a reference to violence and the experienced dire circumstances. An older woman said that soldiers had attacked her in her home. A young boy talked about constant hunger. Comparing the notes from the chats with my personal diary revealed the change in my emotions and reactions to these statements.

The longer I stayed in the camp, the more the diary indicated a sense of increasing uneasiness and concern.

Two weeks after the initial interview and confusion I talked to two girls who said that what they wanted most was to go back to school and, if that could not happen, the next best option was a program on education. Following this initial and comfortingly non-violent remark, the girls said that they wished for this because they had stopped going to school a long time before they had fled with their families to South Sudan, because of the bombing. This bombing, they said, went on while they fled. They then went on to describe how they had been targeted and had hidden in the bush. In the diary I noted:

> I truly have no idea how to react to statements like this. How does one react to such a statement? 'I was nearly killed a couple of times, now I want to go to school.' What is a good way to respond?[3]

Again, ten days later, at an elders' meeting in Gendrassa, a male respondent started our interview with the response that he had lost his wife while fleeing:

> *Man*: (talks in foreign language)
>
> *Translator*: He says he is from Blue Nile. He lost his wife while fleeing.
>
> *Kerstin*: What do you mean 'lost'?
>
> *Translator*: (talks to interviewee, who answers). Lost her. He says, there were men, and he could hear them. Hear his wife. And then he lost her. He had to run. In the bush.
>
> *Kerstin*: Ok.[4]

It is quite telling that, at this point, I did not question further what was meant, but instead brought the conversation back to focus on radio programs. I asked my translator when we were back at the camp what the man had meant, and the diary entry shows my discomfort clearly:

> I have no idea how to react to this. I asked the translator later, when we were back in our office, what the guy had meant. She died? Yes, he said, maybe she died. What do you mean, maybe? She got lost? No, he answered. He could hear her. What does that mean? And after a minute or so of silence, my translator looked up but still not looking at me he said:

Hear her screaming. I still don't know what exactly happened, but I don't think I want to know.[5]

The features of emotional labor, trying to manage my feelings while at the same time attempting to react in a manner that I felt appropriate for a researcher, show clearly throughout my field diary entries. What made this experience particularly draining emotionally was the fact that I did not know how to react appropriately when listening to an account of personal suffering. My identity as a researcher was at odds with my identity as a human being. This schism in my professional and personal reactions is especially salient in the extract above and played a role in my decision not to probe further into what my interviewee had meant when he said that he had 'lost' his wife. In the diary, I mention that I did not ask this because I was afraid of the answer. This talk had taken place toward the end of my stay in the camp, and the diary entry ends with the thought that: 'I really don't think I want to go on doing this.'[6]

Throughout the field notes I made on my chats with the refugees in the camps, I noted that when I asked what radio programs were wanted, my participants answered with a reference to the circumstances of fleeing from Sudan. The diary entries show that the more I listened to these stories of oppression, of murder, bombs and flights, the more they impacted me emotionally. I was in no way prepared for these stories, and this did not get better by typing my notes and thus effectively re-living the chats.

Following an especially dreadful day, I decided to quantify. Instead of reading and trying to make sense of the experience, I started counting. I merely skimmed the notes for answers to my question about the radio program and I counted notions of 'News,' 'Health,' and the like. As I had already experienced these conversations, I had a general idea of which parts of the texts I wanted to avoid, and I became relatively successful in sidestepping them. I had nowhere near enough material for meaningful statistical analysis, but at this point I did not care about this. I urgently needed distance from the material, and my attempts at categorization and calculation provided this.

I had not foreseen what answers I would get to the relatively harmless question, 'What radio program would you like to listen to?' but, however, I phrased the question, I was met with accounts of suffering. My main difficulty was that I could not reconcile my feelings, which were a painful mix of compassion, outrage, and horror, with the need to react professionally. Controlling my voice and facial expression became more and more difficult, and finally I found myself looking to the ground or into the distance when asking my questions, and this avoidance felt like I was rebuking my interviewees, which ultimately made me feel worse.

Consequences and Conclusions

I spent just about six weeks in the refugee camps in South Sudan. This was not a particularly prolonged period, but it was long enough to develop the urgently felt need to create distance between myself and the stories that the refugees told me. This distance was achieved in some way in my subsequent decision to apply techniques of quantification to the data that I had collected. Counting the responses that my interviewees gave around the issue of radio programming and effectively blending out everything else made handling the data much easier.

Based on this experience, in this chapter, I argued three intertwined points with regards to the importance of emotions in research. First, emotions are frowned upon in traditional research. They are understood as tainting data and thus thought to weaken research findings. To avoid this, researchers are expected to hold back their emotions and display an objective state of mind toward their participants. This, and this is my second point, turns research into an emotional labor. The importance of this concept for researchers has only recently been acknowledged in the literature on fieldwork, and mostly in the fields of health-related research with a feminist perspective. In this literature, the effects that conducting emotionally draining research can have on the researcher have been clearly described. However, as the number of novice researchers that conduct fieldwork in emotional demanding and potentially dangerous settings is on the rise in the field of International Relations, the importance of acknowledging emotions and their possible effects seems increasingly important for International Relations departments where doctoral research students are preparing for the field.

This brings me to my third point. Not only is it important to acknowledge emotions in the field for the researcher's well-being, but it is important for research results, also. Contrary to the idea that emotions weaken results by adding elements of a researcher's personality, it might be argued that they, in fact, strengthen results too. Emotions are part of the researcher's positionality. Other than a researcher's class, gender or ethnicity emotions make for a more fluid part of identity. Still, this makes them no less powerful, up to the point where they can change a research design, as they did when I was in South Sudan, where I switched to quantification solely because of the emotions I was experiencing. While there is nothing wrong with choosing a quantitative method, the reasons behind method choice need to be acknowledged because specific methods provide particular answers. Based on the answers I got from the interviews I conducted, my final recommendations for the radio program included both a school program and a storytelling program. If I had only carried out a questionnaire, I probably would not have included these two elements, simply because I did not think about them. For the refugees I talked to, these two programs were meaningful and important. On the other hand, if a survey had been planned from the beginning it would have perhaps been more representative. It is not at all impossible, but rather likely, that I overestimated the importance of some categories based on my original conservative sample. At any rate, the method chosen has an impact on the findings.

A more long-term consequence of my experience in the refugee camps became clear when I was offered another consultancy in South Sudan. This consultancy came with a research component, and I advocated strongly for a survey rather than focus groups. Scientifically and practically, a survey was as, or probably even more, justifiable as focus groups or interviews would have been, but it was my former experience that made me urgently want to carry out a survey. Also, when the time came to design the research for my doctoral research project, I was adamant that it would be quantitative. These choices were not made on the grounds of the research question or a particular worldview, but based on my earlier experience in the refugee camps.

It could be argued that despite my claim that my personal preferences changed from qualitative to quantitative methods, my methodological position continues to oscillate since those days in South Sudan. I am using my diary and field notes here, and while my doctoral research has a quantitative component, it also includes an interview part and a portion based on ethnographic observation. My new found preference for quantitative research, then, did not stick.

Are the influence and effects of emotions on knowledge production overestimated? I do not think so. Some years have passed since my first experience in South Sudan, and it is only because of this passing of time, that I was willing to engage with the material I gathered in the refugee camps again. During my doctoral research project, it took a gently nudging supervisor and a prolonged stay in South Sudan's capital Juba to be ready to talk to people again, and when conducting interviews, I was more on my watch than before. It is no exaggeration to say that the experience in the refugee camps made me a more careful interviewer and shaped my interview style. My positionality, in this way, has indeed changed and it did so based on emotional experiences. It is not an exaggeration to say that we develop as researchers during our careers and based on the experiences we make. Emotions are a part of these experiences, and they can have a profound effect on our well-being, but also, indeed, on our results. In this way, traditional research is right; where it is wrong is with the idea that frowning upon emotions will silence them. Emotions are part of the human experience and, as such, they are naturally present and play a part when conducting research. They cannot be silenced, they have lasting effects, and it is for this reason that we, as researchers, need to acknowledge their effect on the research we conduct as well as the methods we choose to conduct it.

NOTES

1. Field notes, September 16, 2012.
2. Diary, September 16, 2012. Translated from German.
3. Diary, September 30, 2012. Translated from German.
4. Field notes, October 10, 2012.
5. Diary, October 10, 2012. Translated from German.
6. Diary, October 10, 2012. Translated from German.

REFERENCES

Alveson, M., & Sköldberg, K. (2009). *Reflexive Methodologies. New Vistas for Qualitative Research* (2nd ed.). London: Sage.

Autesserre, S. (2014). *Peaceland. Conflict Resolution and the Everyday Politics of International Intervention*. Cambridge: Cambridge University Press.

Autesserre, S. (2017). International Peacebuilding and Local Success: Assumptions and Effectiveness. *International Studies Review, 19*(1), 1–19.

Bliesemann de Guevara, B., & Kostic, R. (2017). Knowledge Production In/About Conflict and Intervention: Finding "Fact", Telling "Truth". *Journal of Intervention and Statebuilding, 11*(1), 1–20.

Clarke, C., & Knights, D. (2015). Negotiating Identities: Fluidity, Diversity and Researcher Emotions. In C. Clarke, M. Broussine, & L. Watts (Eds.),

Researching with Feeling: The Emotional Aspects of Social and Organizational Research (pp. 35–50). London: Routledge.

Clément, M., & Sangar, E. (2018). Introduction: Methodological Challenges and Opportunities for the Study of Emotions. In M. Clément & E. Sangar (Eds.), *Researching Emotions in International Relations: Methodological Perspectives on the Emotional Turn* (pp. 1–30). Cham: Springer.

Crapanzano, V. (2010). "At the Heart of the Discipline": Critical Reflections on Fieldwork. In J. Davies & D. Spencer (Eds.), *Emotions in the Field: The Psychology and Anthropology of Fieldwork Experience* (pp. 55–78). Stanford, CA: Stanford University Press.

Czarniawska, B. (2014). *Social Science Research: From Field to Desk*. London: Sage.

D'Aoust, A. M. (2014). Ties That Bind? Engaging Emotions, Governmentality and Neoliberalism: Introduction to the Special Issue. *Global Society, 28*(3), 267–276.

Davies, J. (2010). Introduction: Emotions in the Field. In J. Davies & D. Spencer (Eds.), *Emotions in the Field: The Psychology and Anthropology of Fieldwork Experience* (pp. 1–32). Stanford, CA: Stanford University Press.

Delamont, S. (2009). The Only Honest Thing: Autoethnography, Reflexivity and Small Crises in Fieldwork. *Ethnography and Education, 4*(1), 51–63.

Dickson-Swift, V., James, E. L., Kippen, S., & Liamputtong, P. (2009). Researching Sensitive Topics: Qualitative Research and Emotion Work. *Qualitative Research, 9*(11), 61–79.

Finlay, J., (2002). "Outing" the Researcher: The Provenance, Process, and Practice of Reflexivity. *Qualitative Health Research, 12*(4), 531–545.

Freyberg-Inan, A. (2006). Rational Paranoia and Enlightened Machismo: The Strange Psychological Foundations of Realism. *Journal of International Relations and Development, 9*(3), 247–268.

Gregory, D. (2000). Empiricism. In R. J. Johnston, D. Gregory, G. Pratt, & M. Watts (Eds.), *The Dictionary of Human Geography* (pp. 205–206). Malden, MA: Blackwell Publishers Ltd.

Hochschild, A. R. (1983). *The Managed Heart: Commercialization of Human Feeling*. Berkeley: University of California Press.

Hutchison, E., & Bleiker, R. (2008). Emotional Reconciliation: Reconstructing Identity and Community After Trauma. *European Journal of Social Theory, 11*(3), 385–403.

Hutchison, E., & Bleiker, R. (2014). Theorizing Emotions in World Politics. *International Theory, 6*, 491–514.

Hutton, L. (2013). Displacement, Disharmony and Disillusion. Understanding Host-Refugee Tensions in Maban County, South Sudan. *Danish Demining Group*. https://reliefweb.int/report/south-sudan-republic/

displacement-disharmony-and-disillusion-understanding-host-refugee. Accessed October 29, 2017.

Jackson, M. (2010). From Anxiety to Method in Anthropological Fieldwork: An Appraisal of George Devereux's Enduring Ideas. In J. Davies & D. Spencer (Eds.), *Emotions in the Field: The Psychology and Anthropology of Fieldwork Experience* (pp. 35–45). Redwood City, CA: Stanford University Press.

Jackson, P. T. (2011). *The Conduct of Inquiry in International Relations: Philosophy of Science and Its Implications for the Study of World Politics.* Abingdon: Routledge.

James, W. (2015). Perspectives on the Blue Nile. In S. Totten & A. Grzyb (Eds.), *Conflict in the Nuba Mountains: From Genocide by Attrition to the Contemporary Crisis in Sudan.* New York: Routledge.

Mattingly, D., & Falconer-Al-Hindi, K. (1995). Should Women Count? A Context for the Debate. *Professional Geographer, 47,* 27–35.

Nast, H. J. (1994). Opening Remarks on "Women in the Field". *Professional Geographer, 46,* 54–66.

Nordstrom, C., & Robben, A. (Eds.). (1995). *Fieldwork Under Fire: Contemporary Studies of Violence and Survival.* London: University of California Press.

Oakley, A. (1981). Interviewing Women: A Contradiction in Terms. In H. Roberts (Ed.), *Doing Feminist Research.* London: Routledge.

Rager, K. (2005). Compassion, Stress and the Qualitative Researcher. *Qualitative Health Research, 15*(3), 423–430.

Reger, J. (2001). Emotions, Objectivity and Voice: An Analysis of a "Failed" Participant Observation. *Women's Studies International Forum, 24*(5), 605–616.

Schaffer, F. C. (2015). Ordinary Language Interviewing. In D. Yanow & P. Schwartz-Shea (Eds.), *Interpretation and Method: Empirical Research Methods and the Interpretive Turn.* Abingdon: Routledge.

Schaffer, F. C. (2016). *Elucidating Social Sciences Concepts: An Interpretivist Guide.* London: Routledge.

Seear, K., & McLean, K. (2008, December). Breaking the Silence: The Role of Emotional Labor in Qualitative Research. In *The Australian Sociological Association (TASA) Annual Conference Proceedings.* Melbourne: University of Melbourne.

Silverman, D. (2013). *Doing Qualitative Research* (4th ed.). London: Sage.

Siriam, C. L., King, J., Martin-Ortega, O., & Herman, J. (Eds.). (2009). *Surviving Field Research: Working in Violent and Difficult Situations.* London: Routledge.

Tiller, S., & Healy, S. (2013). Have We Lost the Ability to Respond to Refugee Crises? The Maban Response. *Humanitarian Exchange*, 57. Humanitarian Practice Network at ODI. http://odihpn.org/magazine/have-we-lost-the-ability-to-respond-to-refugee-crises-the-maban-response/. Accessed May 21, 2016.

CHAPTER 7

Researching Diaspora Citizenship: Reflections on Issues of Positionality and Access from a Zimbabwean Researching Zimbabweans in South Africa

Langton Miriyoga

Much of the scholarly literature on fieldwork and positionality examines the challenges and ethical dilemmas that researchers face at every stage of their research from conceptualizing to conducting, to analyzing and writing up. But as some scholars have pointed out, this literature is dominated by writers who are mostly British, European, or American resulting in, as Mandiyanike (2009, p. 64) has observed, a 'discernible paucity of published material' by scholars from the 'third world' carrying out research at home. Those 'third world' researchers who have published, among them Ite (1997), Tevera (1999), Mullings (1999), Smith (1999), Visser (2000), and Mandiyanike (2009), offer insights into the challenges faced by researchers from the global South returning home, but few of these scholars have focused on the challenges a researcher might face when the 'home' to which they are returning is located in the diaspora. This chapter addresses this gap in the literature.

L. Miriyoga (✉)
Royal Holloway, University of London, Egham, UK

© The Author(s) 2019
L. Johnstone (ed.), *The Politics of Conducting Research in Africa*,
https://doi.org/10.1007/978-3-319-95531-5_7

My doctoral research examined the ways in which migration reconfigures senses of belonging. As a migrant myself who moved from Zimbabwe to South Africa to escape political and economic instability and violence, I have a vested interested in exploring the experiences of Zimbabwean migrants living in South Africa as well as the UK, where I recently completed my doctoral studies. There is a significant population of Zimbabwean migrants living in South Africa who, because of the situation they find themselves in, as well as xenophobia in South Africa, are exposed to hardships, discrimination, and violence. My research aimed to give a voice to this vulnerable and marginalized population.

In February 2015, I travelled from London to South Africa armed with what I believed to be a robust methodological framework coupled with a set of preconceptions about how the research process would unfold. I somewhat naively anticipated that being a Zimbabwean with experience living in South Africa would make the process of fieldwork straightforward. But that was far from what actually transpired. What I had originally believed would be an easy task, based on my identity as a member of the Zimbabwean diaspora, actually turned out to be a much messier and more time-consuming project than I had initially contemplated. It rather turned out to be an arduous and, in many ways, eye-opening exercise that raised questions about the ways in which positionality can impede data collection, as I will show in each of the following sections of this chapter which discuss the pitfalls of organizing and conducting a qualitative research on the experiences of vulnerable and marginalized migrants from the perspective of an insider.

My goal in this chapter is to provide an account of the positionality and access challenges I faced conducting fieldwork in South Africa. Much of what I understood about fieldwork before entering the field I had derived from research methods textbooks and a number of research workshops which attempted to bring these textbooks to life. While these books provided something in the way of grounding in what to expect in the field, missing were the voices of indigenous researchers reflecting on the ethical and emotional challenges of conducting research back home. In what follows, I draw extensively on my own experiences in the field in order to reflect on and make visible the potential challenges, risks, and opportunities faced by researchers returning 'home.' In sharing these experiences, I hope that the chapter can provide guidance for researchers—from African states and beyond—who are based in western academic institutions and are planning to carry out fieldwork in their home countries or on communities with which they share an identity.

NEGOTIATING ACCESS: PRACTICAL CHALLENGES AND STRATEGIES

One of the major challenges reflected in the literature on conducting fieldwork is that of identifying research participants (Hall 2008; Liamputtong 2007; Denscombe 2010). As researchers, we need to pay particular attention to generating suitable samples and recruitment methods; however, identifying a suitable sample of research participants based on a sampling framework is far from a straightforward process, particularly when the population that you are attempting to research is marginalized and vulnerable (Shepherd et al. 2010, p. 288).

As a result, the first thing I did when I arrived in the field was to try to make access to research participants easier. I was aware that I needed assistance in locating research participants and took steps to facilitate this by holding a consultative meeting with PASSOP, a refugee rights group in South Africa. My reasons behind this were twofold. Firstly, it was important to make PASSOP aware of what I was trying to achieve in my research, as open and honest communication would help to convince them of the value of my project therefore facilitating their assistance. Secondly, a consultative meeting with a civil society organization such as PASSOP would help me to identify 'hidden' migrants as well as give me an update on any recent developments affecting the Zimbabwean diaspora living in the country (Parrado et al. 2005; Bloch 2007).

The term 'hidden' when used in the context of migrant populations is used interchangeably to refer to vulnerable or hard-to-reach groups of people (Melrose 2002; Benoit et al. 2005; Liamputtong 2007). These hidden groups, in the case of my research, are the Zimbabwean diaspora, many of whom are exiled in South Africa because of political instability in their home country. Locating these 'hidden' migrants was important for the direction of my research as I wanted to get away from the tendency of researchers, policymakers, and practitioners, when studying diaspora groups, to focus their attention on problems experienced in urban areas by those with valid and secure immigration statuses (Lipton 1977; Polzer 2012). Overcoming this entrenched spatial bias was a desirable goal in my own study because, with the exception of Polzer (2012), very little scholarly research exists on the lived experiences of Zimbabweans living and working on the farms around the Cape Winelands in the Western Cape Province of South Africa. By gaining access to these Zimbabweans, I would be able to give a voice to the experiences of less educated and often undocumented Zimbabweans from rural backgrounds living in South Africa. Ultimately, however, accessing these groups proved too challenging given the time and financial constraints imposed on my research, and like many doctoral researchers who have experienced similar constraints, I found myself having to rethink my access approach.

My new approach involved shifting the focus back to urban areas with a view to finding participants for my study. Gaps in the literature here suggested a dearth in the study of Zimbabwean migrants living in black townships in South Africa, as these areas tended to be less accessible for researchers because of, among other factors, the prevalence of crime (Jacobsen and Landau 2003; Polzer 2012). With this in mind, I made deliberate efforts to incorporate these segments of the Zimbabwean population, devising strategies to penetrate those places considered inaccessible by other researchers and practitioners. But these efforts were accompanied by their own set of challenges, the greatest of which was personal safety.

Before moving to the UK to begin my doctoral studies in 2013, I lived for a number of years in the South African townships of Langa, Khayelitsha, and Lower Crossroads. During this time I was victim to a number of muggings as well as the target of petty crime. These experiences complicated my fieldwork by effectively feeding into the anxieties that I was already experiencing as a novice researcher on his first foray into the field, and this made working in the townships much more challenging. Given my anxieties around these issues of personal safety, as well as the difficulties associated with getting Zimbabweans to come forward voluntarily and share with me their experiences of migrant life, I set out to reduce some of these fieldwork challenges.

One way I did this was through collaboration with civil society organizations such as the aforementioned PASSOP who provided me with unrestrained access to a pool of Zimbabwean migrants coming to their offices for support. Collaboration with groups like PASSOP not only made it easier to interact with participants in a relatively safe environment, but also opened up whole networks of Zimbabwean migrants through access to contact databases used when mobilizing immigrants for protests and campaigns. But while collaboration with PASSOP helped me to mitigate challenges of access to research participants in Cape Town, as well as overcome some of my fears about personal safety, the Johannesburg leg of my research trip presented a different set of access and safety challenges, the political and violent nature of which stretched to the limits any previously successful approach I had developed to gain access to the hidden population at the heart of my research.

The challenges to which I am referring were outbreaks of xenophobic violence across South Africa that coincided with my fieldwork in April 2015. Zimbabweans, as well as other African foreign nationals, living in South Africa have been subjected to xenophobic attacks and mass deportation over the last decade (Crush 2008). These were particularly violent in 2008, and again in 2015, where acts of violence killed several people and displaced thousands more (Smith 2015). As a result, it was largely unsafe to engage in public spaces in cities, and this, combined with the near invisibility of the immigrant community, threatened to derail the Johannesburg leg of my trip. With the help of intermediaries, however, I managed to navigate areas such as Vosloorus, parts of which are notorious for petty crime and violence, without any problems. Additionally, working with intermediaries not only helped in identifying participants, but seemed to alleviate some of the fear, anxiety, and suspicion that can often exist between researchers and research participants (Bloch 2007; Polzer 2012).

I find it important to take a moment to pause here and reflect on how taking part in my research might intersect with the notion of being vulnerable for the research population in this instance. What I mean by this is that for some potential research participants marginalization and intimidation by the state—both in Zimbabwe and in South Africa—had become so internalized and entrenched that fear and suspicion made them very wary of agreeing to take part in a research project that, down the line, had the potential to improve their day to day lives (Raftopolous and Savage 2004; Kilgore 2011).

For those who were willing to take part in the project, internalized and entrenched fear and suspicion also threatened to militate against the quality of our encounters. Some research participants, for example, feared for their own lives and the lives of their relatives back in Zimbabwe if they were to speak negatively against the Zimbabwean state. This was compounded by the belief, often shared among the Zimbabwean 'diaspora,' that the Zimbabwean government deploys intelligence operatives in countries where its citizens are hosted to spy on their activities (Pasura 2014). This was brought home to me through an encounter with a small group of Zimbabweans in the Vosloorus township who openly displayed their suspicion that I was a Zimbabwean state agent.

In the face of such suspicion and vulnerability a question arises as to how one can build trust with marginalized groups in the field. This is not an easy question to answer, however my affiliation with PASSOP, a group well known for being critical to the Zimbabwean government, as well as my decision to work with intermediaries, was invaluable in gaining the confidence of participants. The following section on ethical issues fleshes out some of further challenges I faced and the tactics I used to build trust in more detail.

ETHICAL ISSUES

Ethics constitute an important consideration when carrying out research with vulnerable research participants (Gregory 2003). Firstly, participation has to be negotiated and consent needs to be sought on the basis of accurate information about the research and its implications (Babbie 2013). This is not always a straightforward process. Participation in research is always accompanied by some degree of risk for vulnerable and marginalized participants (King and Horrocks 2010; Babbie 2013). In the case of my own research project, it was important to ensure no harm or backlash would confront participants either during or after their involvement in the study, but uncertainty regarding how signed consent documents would be used, lack of adequate confidence in the process and mistrust on the part of the participants, meant that the process of gaining written formal consent was not possible. Faced with the dilemma of how to gain consent, I made the decision to seek permission verbally, providing assurance that anonymity and confidentiality would be guaranteed. One of the ways we agreed this could be achieved was by ensuring that no names and residential addresses were written on interview schedules or in my notes, and that I would use forenames and pseudonyms in my records of interviews and discussions, and any subsequent publications of my work.

My research touched on highly sensitive, personal issues that encroached on both the private and personal lives of my participants. In addition to informed consent, which protected participants through anonymity and privacy, it was equally important to avoid, or at the very least to minimize, any stress, trauma, and anxiety that participants might experience both during research encounters and afterward (Hall 2008; Denscombe 2014). This required greater sensitivity on my part to the way research encounters were designed and managed. Although some of the issues we discussed had the potential to revisit emotional trauma for those who participated, I made every effort to be sensitive, taking care not to ask questions in ways that would cause distress or open up old wounds. Additionally, I set up debriefing sessions after interviews and group discussions following such sensitive and emotional conversations with participants. It was not only my participants who benefitted from these sessions; as a migrant with experience living in South Africa, I found that some of my research encounters triggered painful memories of my own.

REFLECTIONS ON SUBJECTIVITY AND BIAS

Scholars subscribing to a positivist epistemology traditionally believe that good empirical research is conducted by an objective, emotionally detached, and unbiased researcher; however, when one conducts their research in contexts where the researched population experience injustice, suffering, and oppression, it becomes difficult for research to be totally dispassionate and objective (Dwyer and Limb 2001; Letherby et al. 2013; Harding 2015). As my own experiences reveal, emotional engagement can be a useful tool in generating good research, especially when researching lived experiences of marginalized and vulnerable groups in society (Zuckerman 1991; Ellis and Flaherty 1992; Davies 2001). What this reveals, however, as I noted at the beginning of the chapter, is that a researcher's own subjectivities and biases permeate the entire research process—from the questions asked to how answers are generated, and how the researcher makes sense of those results. It is crucial, therefore, to acknowledge and be honest about those subjectivities and biases, as they are not easy to escape (Rabinowitz and Weseen 2001)—and this is what I am going to do here.

My passion toward my research and the researched population emanate from my own past experiences in Cape Town. As a Zimbabwean migrant who had lived in South Africa for more than five years prior to beginning my doctoral research, the intimacy of my emotional connection with the researched community is without question. Having been directly affected by some of the issues that form the subject of this research, specifically the struggle for legal status and recognition as well as different forms of discrimination that continue to be experienced once legal status is achieved, I found it impossible to detach myself emotionally. This was nothing new. As I pointed out earlier, one of the main reasons that I embarked on a study of Zimbabwean migrants living in South Africa was as a result of my own feelings about the discrimination and hostility I had experienced as a migrant myself. I felt passionate about exposing these experiences in some way and one way to do this was through research of this nature. This attachment to both the people and their experiences goes some way toward explaining the strong empathy I felt and displayed toward my research participants; their personal stories invoked strong emotions and painful memories of my own past struggles as a migrant in South Africa.

The outbreak of xenophobic violence in Durban and Johannesburg during my stay, coupled with attacks on Somali informal traders in Cape Town around the same time, further compounded my empathy toward the research population and feelings of anger toward the South African government and people. Additionally, during my time conducting research in Philippi, one of the larger townships in Cape Town, I also witnessed an incident involving a Zimbabwean woman whose house was broken into by armed men who assaulted her and stole some of her belongings during the night. Although the matter was reported to the South African police immediately after the incident, police officers arrived at the scene some eight hours later. These events were particularly upsetting and I found myself growing more and more cynical toward the South African way of life. I felt that Zimbabweans were being subjected to exclusion and were no longer welcome in South Africa, and this impression helped to justify my feelings of empathy toward my research participants.

All of these things speak to a level of subjectivity running through my research which, as critics might argue, could easily have filtered into my reading of my participants' perceptions of the same or similar phenomenon. While it would be disingenuous for me to argue that this was not the case, I nevertheless believe that some of these aspects of my subjectivities placed me at a better vantage point from which to view what Zimbabweans were going through at the time, perhaps in ways that socially and emotionally distant researchers would not have realized. Encountering many of the issues that research participants faced myself meant that I could more easily grasp the agonies and understand the trauma that some of the participants shared with me during interviews and focus group discussions. This meant that I was more inclined to listen passionately and empathetically.

POWER DYNAMICS AND POSITIONALITY

My research is built partly on a commitment to a transformative epistemological and methodological framework, with a particular emphasis on the relationship between the researcher and the researched, aimed at empowering the latter (Mertens 2009; Mertens and Ginsberg 2009; Kara 2015). I share the assumption that this transformative paradigm and related methodologies prove useful in societies characterized by structural imbalances in power relations among different categories of society among other forms of injustices operating in those societies (Finley 2008). This assumption explains the particular attention I paid to the dynamic interaction between myself, as the researcher, and the participants who took part in my research; and how they related with each other during the process.

Upon entrance to the field, I was aware that power dynamics could play out in subtle ways, both among the researched themselves and also between the research participants and the researcher. With this in mind, I repeatedly asked myself how my research participants would view me as a Zimbabwean and as a researcher. I was of course cognizant of the existing dominant paradigms that portray the researcher as more powerful (Patai 1991; Sidaway 1992; Lal 1996), but much of the scholarly literature that focuses on power dynamics in the field is, as Mandiyanike (2009, p. 64) observes, written from a 'British, European and/or American angle.' How would the fact that I am Zimbabwean, with experiences similar to my research population, affect symbolic and actual constellations of power in the field?

Encounters with female participants were a challenge in this area. Female migrants tend to be under-represented and their voices not often heard in social research (Polzer 2012). During the planning phase of my fieldwork, I had anticipated a gender bias in the way participants took part and expressed themselves in the study. When fieldwork commenced, I was briefed by PASSOP activists about the tendency of most Zimbabwean women to not freely take part in research. In many instances this was the because of suspicion on the part of husbands who would not allow a male researcher to sit down with their wives in private to have a confidential conversation. Although I did not experience such incidences, I made efforts to inject gender-sensitivity into all stages of my research process as a critical way of guarding against and detecting any such forms of disempowerment (Eichler 1988; Bailey 2008). One of the ways in which I did this was to identify, with the help of one of my female colleagues at PASSOP, a 'safe space' in which female participants would feel comfortable enough to share their stories and experiences. Our solution was to invite participants to PASSOP offices for interviews thus ensuring respondents were in a safe, comfortable environment.

Anxieties around power and positioning complicated almost every aspect of my research encounters. At the beginning of interviews or focus groups, for example, I was unsure about whether to introduce myself comprehensively in terms of who I was and my own personal achievements. On the one hand, I thought introducing myself in this way would not only have been ethical, but also a gesture of openness toward the participants about who I was. On the other hand however, a comprehensive introduction might have resulted in some participants positioning me as well-to-do, successful, and powerful; a perception which had the potential to perpetuate a sense of disempowerment and disadvantage among those participants who, for example, may have had to abandon their own ambitions due to their own situation and settlement in South Africa.

The fact that I was pursuing doctoral studies in the UK represented a fault line in my relationship with the migrants whose lives I was researching (Fanow and Cook 1991; Miller and Glassner 1997). While, some developed a sense of admiration and pride in me as a Zimbabwean who had come a long way from being an asylum seeker in South Africa to a doctoral student in the UK, others appeared envious toward me for the same reasons. At times this envy led to requests from my participants for financial benefits for their participation in the study. Those who asked were under the impression that, as I was in the UK, I must have been earning a lot of money, and I therefore had the capacity to help them out.

While power dynamics, such as these, played out and complicated my encounters with research participants in different ways, anxiety around questions of how my positioning in relation to these actual constellations of power would impact upon my research findings added a further layer of complexity to my encounters (Harding 1987; Bhavnani 1988; Minh-ha 1989; Williams 1996). Would the way my research participants positioned me affect the nature of the information they were inclined to share? There was a risk that participants might feel they had to tell me what they thought would please me, or alternatively provide me with distorted stories of their experiences. In extreme cases, I feared that they would withhold information or withdraw from participating in any meaningful conversation, thinking perhaps that I was exploiting them and their experiences for my own benefit.

At times power balances played out among the research participants themselves. On occasion, I observed that some participants were dominating discussions and presenting their experiences in general terms during focus group discussions. I began posing mildly critical questions to the dominant speakers as a way of counterbalancing their dominance. Dealing with such issues was not always easy. While some encounters were marked by dominant participants, others were marked by silence. This was often the result of internalized structural, systemic and historical victimhood causing a sense of powerlessness among some participants. The silence of research participants could never be addressed during the actual encounter itself and, as I have discussed in earlier sections of the chapter, could often be compounded by a lack of trust in the research process and the researcher.

All of these things speak to the subtle power dynamics that exist between researcher and researched. And yet, while I largely agree with the dominant paradigm that suggests that my academic knowledge and professional experience allocated me significant power over my research participants, it is also critical to understand that my participants, in actual fact, held a significant amount of power of their own. Writing on the asymmetrical power dynamics in research relationships, some feminist scholars have begun to challenge the portrayal of power dynamics in the field as one-way relationships. As these scholars see it, a researcher's need to produce meaningful data can, to some extent, rebalance the power dynamics of research encounters effectively placing the researcher in the dependent position thus giving the research participants more power (Cerwonka and Malkki 2007; Billo and Hiemstra 2013). In the case of my own research participants, they were the ones living in risky parts of townships, struggling to access public services, experiencing life as 'illegal' immigrants and, by virtue of their experiential knowledge of their own day-to-day lives, they held the key to information I was seeking to explore. In an effort to empower my participants, I went out of my way to stress this to them often pointing this out at the beginning of focus group sessions.

How my research participants saw me played an important role in achieving my aim of understanding participants' everyday life experiences using citizenship lenses. This ties with an idea of research as a relational process in which the researcher transacts with the researched during research encounters, thus shaping emerging knowledge (Smith 1999; Visser 2000; Dwyer and Limb 2001; Finley 2008). As I pointed out at the beginning of this chapter, before entering the field I had assumed that my insider status as a Zimbabwean migrant would grant me easier access to research participants, but I quickly learned that this was not the case. I saw myself as an insider, but did this mean that my research participants saw me this way too?

Reflecting on this question since returning from the field, there were certainly elements of my identity which shaped my positionality and perhaps positioned me more strongly in the eyes of my research participants as an 'insider.' These included my ethnicity and history as a black Zimbabwean who had lived in South Africa for more than four years, had shared familiar experiences and issues with immigration documentation, spoke fluent Shona, had experienced xenophobia and other forms of discrimination, and had worked with PASSOP advocating for migrant rights. Many of these elements of my own identity and experience overlapped significantly with the identity and daily experiences of the research participants I encountered in Cape Town, where I had lived for over four years, effectively positioning me as an insider.

Scholarship on positionality has long been interested in the question of how a researcher might gain access to more privileged or balanced viewpoints in their fieldwork encounters (Mullings 1999). Much of this scholarship has traditionally been concerned with the boundaries of researchers as insiders or outsiders. The binary implied in the insider/outsider debates has, until recently, been dominated by rigid assumptions of the insider as advantaged because they are able to use their knowledge of the group to gain more intimate insight and opinion (Abu-Lughod 1988; Hill-Collins 1990). But there are difficulties with this way of thinking. More recent scholarship has begun to problematize this dichotomous thinking arguing instead that this understanding 'seeks to freeze positionalities in place' (Mullings 1999, p. 340).

Reflecting on positionality and the pitfalls of dualistic thinking, some writers have observed the difficulties of conducting research on populations with backgrounds similar to the researcher in one way or another (Beoku-Betts 1994; Acker 2001; Merriam et al. 2001). This is an interesting observation, and I have deliberately chosen to end this section in this way so as to raise one final point. One of the most important realizations that comes from this discussion of positionality is that, as a researcher, I can never fully know whether my being black, being Zimbabwean, and being a migrant, helped position me in way that enabled me to gain an intimate view in the participants' daily life experiences, compared to any other researcher with a different identity. It is possible that my 'insider' status may have actually prevented some participants from speaking truthfully about their experiences. As researchers experiencing similar issues have found out, vulnerable groups especially can be more likely to trust those who are perceived as not directly implicated in local issues and communities (Liamputtong 2007). The reasoning behind this observation is that an outside researcher not directly implicated in the community being researched might be perceived as less likely to impose value judgment on participants' experiences. In the case of my own research, my participants may have been too ashamed or shy to speak out for fear that I might share their experiences with other Zimbabweans.

Conclusion

In this chapter, I have attempted to shed some light on the challenges of carrying out fieldwork when the researcher and researched share an identity and common culture. Along the way I have used the terminology common to the literature, that of conducting research 'back home,' yet my experience and the experiences of my research participants do not fit comfortably into this description. This is because, as I have made it clear throughout, returning home to conduct fieldwork did not involve returning to my birth country of Zimbabwe, but rather to the place where I have lived since leaving the country I call home. Drawing on his own experiences of conducting research in his home country, Mandiyanike (2009, p. 70) observes that 'returning home for fieldwork invoked a sense of belonging' for the researcher. But, as should be apparent in the anxieties that have permeated my discussion here, conducting fieldwork in a place that troubles the idea of home complicates the idea of belonging adding additional layers of complexity to the research process by raising questions about bias, subjectivity, and positionality.

In writing about these experience and anxieties here, I have tried to paint a picture of these complex layers and the ways in which all three compounded almost every encounter I experienced in the field. I have discussed the problems I faced and the battles I fought with myself over the issue of bias, when I myself have memories and experience similar to those being described by my research participants about their marginalized status in a country often hostile to their very existence; I have outlined my cognizance about the role that power can play in encounters of this kind; and I have discussed ethical dilemmas that I confronted. By drawing attention to my challenges in these areas, I am not suggesting that the fieldwork encounters of non-African/other researchers escape the issues of bias, subjectivity, and positionality, but rather that 'third world' scholars returning 'home' to conduct fieldwork face the additional complexities and contradictions of conducting research on their fellow countrymen and women.

One of the most reassuring aspects of fieldwork is finding similar experiences to our own in the literature, as Johnstone in this volume observes. Thus while there continues to be a 'paucity' of African scholars writing on their experiences in the field, it stands to reason that 'third world' researchers planning their first fieldwork encounters will continue to consult the experiences of British, European, and/or American scholars discussing their professional responsibilities to distant others (Mandiyanike 2009, p. 64). Rather a lot of this literature continues to be occupied with the debate over epistemology. This is a debate which claims to have moved on from positivist ideas of the researcher as objective and dispassionate, yet continues to set aside valuable space in discussions of encounters in the field to justify and discuss why and how they have left positivism behind.

My experiences alone demonstrate the difficulties associated with this conception of research, particularly when researching in the context of different forms of social injustices. But as my references were mostly from western scholars writing in western textbooks, when I first headed to the field I found that many of my preconceived notions of what fieldwork would entail were based on the experiences of outsiders. I quickly found that biases and subjectivities were unavoidable in my research and, while we can spend a long time discussing how reflexivity has moved fieldwork out of the realm of the positivist researcher, what is more important, I believe, is to hammer the message home that as a researcher returning home to conduct fieldwork, there is no escape from bias and subjectivity and we need to be sure to write these into our practice.

Although we will never find a strategic blueprint for dealing with challenges in the field, given the diversity of field experiences and researchers themselves, I do hope that my experiences discussed in this chapter can suggest a number of lessons for those African researchers planning to conduct research on their fellow countrymen and women. At the very least, I hope that my experience has made two things clear. Firstly, while it is important to plan and design research before setting off to the field, having a thoroughly conceived methodological framework based on conventional research methods derived from western textbooks may not be adequate due to the complexities of the field. Secondly, unforeseen challenges relating to the practicalities of doing research will always emerge. These will inevitably challenge your preconceived notions of what fieldwork entails and will challenge your ability to adapt and be innovative.

REFERENCES

Abu-Lughod, J. L. (1988). Fieldwork of a Dutiful Daughter. In C. Altorki & C. F. El-Solh (Eds.), *Arab Women in the Field: Studying Your Own Society* (pp. 139–161). New York: Syracuse University Press.

Acker, S. (2001). In/Out/Side: Positioning the Researcher in Feminist Qualitative Research (1). *Resources for Feminist Research, 28*(1–2), 189–210.

Babbie, E. (2013). *The Practice of Social Research* (14th ed.). Boston, MA: Cengage Learning.

Bailey, K. (2008). *Methods of Social Research* (4th ed.). New York: The Free Press.

Benoit, C., Jansson, M., Millar, A., & Phillips, R. (2005). Community-Academic Research on Hard-To-Reach Populations: Benefits and Challenges. *Qualitative Health Research, 15*(2), 263–282.

Beoku-Betts, J. (1994). When Black is Not Enough: Doing Fieldwork Amongst Gullah Women. *The National Women's Studies Association Journal, 6*(3), 413–433.

Bhavnani, K. (1988). Empowerment and Social Research: Some Comments. *Interdisciplinary Journal for the Study of Discourse, 8*(1–2), 41–50.

Billo, E., & Hiemstra, N. (2013). Mediating Messiness: Expanding Ideas of Flexibility, Reflexivity, and Embodiment in Fieldwork. *Gender, Place and Culture, 20*(3), 313–328.

Bloch, A. (2007). Methodological Challenges for National and Multi-sited Comparative Survey Research. *Journal of Refugee Studies, 20*(2), 230–247.

Cerwonka, A., & Malkki, L. H. (2007). *Improvising Theory: Process and Temporality in Ethnographic Fieldwork.* Chicago: Chicago University Press.

Crush, J. (2008). South Africa: Policy in the Face of Xenophobia, Migration Policy Institute. Available at https://www.migrationpolicy.org/article/south-africa-policy-face-xenophobia. Accessed January 15, 2018.

Davies, S. (2001). Philosophical Perspectives on Music's Expressiveness. In P. A. Juslin & J. A. Slobada (Eds.), *Music and Emotion: Theory and Research* (pp. 23–44). Oxford: Oxford University Press.

Denscombe, M. (2010). *Ground Rules for Social Research: Guidelines for Good Practice*. Berkshire: Open University Press.

Denscombe, M. (2014). *The Good Research Guide: For Small-Scale Social Research Projects* (5th ed.). Maindenhead: Open University Press.

Dwyer, C., & Limb, M. (Eds.). (2001). *Qualitative Methodologies for Geographers: Issues and Debates*. London: Arnold.

Eichler, M. (1988). *Non-Sexist Research Methods: A Practical Guide*. London and New York: Routledge.

Ellis, C., & Flaherty, M. (1992). An Agenda for the Interpretation of Lived Experience. In C. Ellis & M. Flaherty (Eds.), *Investigating Subjectivity: Research on Lived Experience* (pp. 1–16). London: Sage.

Fanow, M. M., & Cook, J. A. (1991). Back to the Future: A Look at the Second Wave of Feminist Epistemology and Methodology. In M. M. Fanow & J. A. Cook (Eds.), *Beyond Methodology: Feminist Scholarship As Lived Research* (pp. 1–15). Bloomington: Indiana University Press.

Finley, S. (2008). Arts-based Research. In G. Knowles & A. Cole (Eds.), *Handbook of the Arts in Qualitative Research: Perspectives, Methodologies, Examples and Issues*. Los Angeles, CA: Sage.

Gregory, I. (2003). *Ethics in Research*. London: Continuum Publications.

Hall, R. (2008). *Applied Social Research: Planning, Designing and Conducting Real-World Research*. South Yarra: Palgrave Macmillan.

Harding, S. (1987). *Whose Science, Whose Knowledge? Thinking from Women's Lives*. Ithaca, NY: Cornell University Press.

Harding, S. (2015). *Objectivity and Diversity: Another Logic of Scientific Research*. Chicago and London: The University of Chicago Press.

Hill-Collins, P. (1990). *Black Feminist Thought: Knowledge, Consciousness, and the Politics of Empowerment*. Boston: Unwin Hyman.

Ite, U. (1997). Home, Abroad, Home: The Challenges of Postgraduate Fieldwork "at home". In E. Robson & K. Willis (Eds.), *Postgraduate Fieldwork in Developing Areas: A Rough Guide* (pp. 75–84). London: RGS-IBS.

Jacobsen, K., & Landau, L. B. (2003). Dual Imperative in Refugee Research: Some Methodological and Ethical Considerations in Social Science Research on Forced Migration. *Disasters, 27*(3), 185–206.

Kara, H. (2015). *Creative Research Methods in the Social Sciences: A Practical Guide*. Bristol: Policy Press.

Kilgore, J. (2011). *We Are All Zimbabweans Now: A Novel.* Athens: Ohio University Press.

King, N., & Horrocks, C. (2010). *Interviews in Qualitative Research.* London: Sage.

Lal, J. (1996). Situating Locations: The Politics of Self, Identity, and "Other" in Loving and Writing the Text. In D. Wolf (Ed.), *Feminist Dilemmas in Fieldwork* (pp. 185–214). Boulder, CO: Westview Press.

Letherby, G., Scott, J., & Williams, M. (2013). *Objectivity and Subjectivity in Social Research.* Thousand Oaks, CA: Sage.

Liamputtong, P. (2007). *Researching the Vulnerable: A Guide to Sensitive Research Methods.* London: Sage.

Lipton, M. (1977). *Why Poor People Stay Poor: Urban Bias in World Development.* London: Temple Smith.

Melrose, M. (2002). Labour Pains. *International Journal Social Research Methodology, 5*(4), 333–351.

Merriam, S. B., Johnson-Bailey, J., Lee, M.-Y., Kee, Y., Ntseane, G., & Muhamad, M. (2001). Power and Positionality: Negotiating Insider/Outsider Status Within and Across Cultures. *International Journal of Lifelong Education, 20*(5), 405–416.

Mertens, D. M. (2009). *Transformative Research and Evaluation.* New York: Guilford Press.

Mertens, D. M., & Ginsberg, P. E. (2009). Frontiers in Social Research Ethics: Fertile Ground for Evoluton. In P. E. Ginsberg & D. M. Mertens (Eds.), *The Handbook of Social Research Ethics* (pp. 580–613). Thousand Oaks, CA: Sage.

Miller, J., & Glassner, B. (1997). The 'Inside' and the 'Outside': Finding Realities in Interviews. In D. Silverman (Ed.), *Qualitative Research: Theory, Method and Practice* (pp. 99–112). London: Sage.

Minh-ha, T. (1989). *Woman, Native, Other: Writing Post-coloniality and Feminism.* Bloomington: Indiana University Press.

Mandiyanike, D. (2009). The Dilemma of Conducting Research Back in Your Own Country as a Returning Student—Reflections of Research Fieldwork in Zimbabwe. *Area, 41*(1), 64–71.

Mullings, B. (1999). Insider or Outsider, Both or Neither: Some Dilemmas of Interviewing in a Cross-Cultural Setting. *Geoforum, 30,* 337–350.

Parrado, E., Flippen, C. A., & Metzger McQuiston, C. (2005). Migration and Relationship Power Among Mexican Women. *Demography, 42,* 347–372.

Pasura, D. (2014). *African Transnational Diasporas: Fractured Communities and Plural Identities of Zimbabweans in Britain.* London: Palgrave Macmillan.

Patai, D. (1991). US Academic and Third World Women: Is Ethical Research Possible? In S. Gluck Berger & D. Patai (Eds.), *Women's Words: The Feminist Practice of Oral History* (pp. 137–153). London: Routledge.

Polzer, T. (2012). Together Apart: Migration, Integration and Spatialized Identities in South African Border Villages. *Geoforum, 43*(3), 561–572.

Rabinowitz, V., & Weseen, S. (2001). Power, Politics, and the Qualitative/Quantitative Debates in Psychology. In D. L. Tolman & M. Brydon-Miller (Eds.), *Qualitative Studies in Psychology: From Subjects to Subjectivities: A Handbook of Interpretive and Participatory Methods* (pp. 12–28). New York: New York University Press.

Raftopolous, B., & Savage, T. (Eds.). (2004). *Zimbabwe: Injustice and Political Reconciliation*. Cape Town: Institute for Justice and Reconciliation.

Shepherd, G., Parsonage, M., & Scharf, T. (2010). Social Inclusion: Research and Evidence-Based Practice. In J. Boardman, A. Currie, H. Killaspy, & G. Mezey (Eds.), *Social Inclusion and Mental Health* (pp. 279–294). London: Royal College of Psychiatrists.

Sidaway, J. (1992). In Other Worlds: On the Politics of Research by "First World" Geographers in the "Third World". *Area, 24*(4), 403–408.

Smith, L. T. (1999). *Decolonising Methodologies: Research and Indigenous Peoples*. London: Zed.

Smith, D. (2015). Johannesburg's Foreign Shop Owners Close Up Early Amid Threats of Violence, *The Guardian*. Available at https://www.theguardian.com/world/2015/apr/15/johannesburg-threats-violence-foreign-shop-owners-close-early. Accessed January 10, 2018.

Tevera, D. (1999). Do They Need Ivy in Africa? Ruminations of an African Geographer Trained Abroad. In D. Simon & A. Narman (Eds.), *Development as Theory and Practice* (pp. 134–145). Harlow: Addison Wesley and Longman.

Visser, G. (2000). In Other Worlds: On the Politics of Research in a Transforming South Africa. *Area, 32*, 231–235.

Williams, B. (1996). Skinfolk, Not Kinfolk: Comparative Reflections of the Identity of Participant Observation in Two Field Situations. In D. Wolf (Ed.), *Feminist Dilemmas in Fieldwork*. Boulder, CO: Westview Press.

Zuckerman, A. (1991). *Doing Political Science: An Introduction to Political Analysis*. Boulder, CO: Westview Press.

CHAPTER 8

Gatekeeping Success in the Namibian CBNRM Program

Carolin H. Stamm

In late 2012, a few months after enrolling as a doctoral student in Tourism and Development studies, I embarked on a three-month field trip to southern Africa. My destination was the Kavango-Zambezi Transfrontier Conservation Area (KAZA TFCA), a cross-border protected area combining various national parks and tourism hotspots such as the Okavango Delta and the Victoria Falls in the Kavango and Zambezi river basins across Angola, Botswana, Namibia, Zimbabwe, and Zambia. Officially launched in March 2012, KAZA is a story of superlatives. Roughly the size of France, it is the largest cross-border conservation area in the world, uniting five countries, three of which, Angola, Namibia, and Zambia, were directly involved in the South African Border War lasting over 20 years until the end of apartheid. Home to approximately two million people and the largest contiguous African elephant population in the world, KAZA aims to combine comprehensive community engagement, conservation and tourism, the latter of which is intended to be 'the vehicle for socio-economic development in the region' (Peace Parks Foundation 2017).

C. H. Stamm (✉)
SRH University of Applied Sciences Berlin, Berlin, Germany

© The Author(s) 2019
L. Johnstone (ed.), *The Politics of Conducting Research in Africa*,
https://doi.org/10.1007/978-3-319-95531-5_8

133

My interest in KAZA was the role of intermediaries (state and non-state actors as well as private investors) as 'development brokers' for facilitating community-based tourism enterprise-building in the KAZA region. I wanted to understand how the external facilitation of tourism development, traditionally a foreign, white-owned industry in southern Africa,[1] impacts on the long-term viability of community-based tourism ventures and how it enables or obstructs local governance structures for robust community institutions.

Upon my departure to the field, I was optimistic and ambitious. This was because, owing to an existing key contact at KAZA's principal donor agency, as well as a number of lead contacts in the region, I assured myself that my networking skills would produce the required connections to the movers and shakers within KAZA. A number of interviews with development intermediaries generated valuable insights, although these were not necessarily conducive to my research endeavor. 'What *is* KAZA?' was a question I commonly encountered. Those who were familiar with the conservation area told me that it was 'too politically charged!' and 'too young a project to be evaluated.' 'TFCA? We call it RIBS: Romantic international bullshitting stories' commented a senior consultant for integrated conservation and development projects.

The negativity toward KAZA on the ground came as a surprise and I was keen to learn how those working within KAZA would respond to this. Unfortunately, however, my curiosity was never satisfied as my enquiries to the KAZA Secretariat went unanswered. What had begun as optimism gave way to feelings of naivety and, as I waited in vain for a response from the Secretariat, two things started to become clear to me: First, gaining top-level access to research subjects might actually be an unrealistic aim, and second, there was something of a negative attitude toward KAZA at the micro level that I might never be able to overcome. Out of these two realizations a question arose: How would I ever be able to conduct research if I could not gain access to the very people that were the focus of my research? The answer to this question came to me during a two-week stay in Windhoek where, as one door appeared to close on me, another research opportunity presented itself.

While staying in Windhoek, I introduced myself to several national and international NGOs and their rural community clients—the target beneficiaries of the Namibian national community-based natural resource management (CBNRM) program. Participation and decentralization are core principles of CBNRM where the state devolves user rights and decision-making powers over wildlife resources to local communities (Jones 2010). Forming CBOs, accountable and representative local level units (Ribot 2002), is the precondition for rural area residents to benefit from their natural resources. The first four Namibian conservancies[2] were registered in 1998. Since then, the CBNRM program has progressively expanded to 42 conservancies in 2005 and 83 in 2017 (NACSO 2017). NGOs have played a fundamental role in facilitating CBO development; the national CBNRM policy explicitly recognizes them as 'key partners [...] helping to create or strengthen community based structures and building management capacities and linking communities to funding sources' (Ministry of Environment and Tourism (MET) 2013, pp. 14–15).

This 'new door' opened by means of an invitation to attend a two-day workshop in Windhoek, organized by two leading NGOs, to enhance the relationship between conservancies and their tourism joint-venture partners from the private sector. This event turned out to be a networking paradise producing 'high-quality connections' (Dutton and Dukerich 2006, p. 25) to a number of key NGO figures, one of whom provided the requisite support letter for my research permit application. Equally importantly, the workshop enabled me to connect more 'naturally' to the individuals holding pivotal conservancy positions, such as manager and chairperson, who permanently live in the rural areas. These were the people who, for me, were the hardest to reach. Not quite aware of it then, I had established the links to key figures who would be the instrumental enablers of a further three-month fieldwork period, which I conducted one year later.

With these new and valuable connections under my belt, my revised research project investigated the social interaction between the NGOs as implementers and CBOs as consumers of rural development projects in Namibia, with the aim of answering two questions: What were the implications of substantial NGO support for CBO development? And, how did CBO members perceive and negotiate on-going 'free' NGO support? Other studies suggest that continuous support by external development agents (albeit unintentionally) creates dependency on such services. Hence, the point of departure for my research from the existing literature was that there is a causal relationship between scope and intensity of external NGO facilitation and the robustness and long-term viability of CBOs. Largely absent in the literature, however, was the conceptualization of dependency as a two-way relationship where NGOs rely on successful project outcomes to justify and secure their own continued relevance in rural development endeavors.

Based on a qualitative-inductive approach, a case study methodology was chosen as it is both exploratory and explanatory in nature (Silverman 2010; Easton 2010). Advocates of actor-oriented perspectives of development (Long 2001; Mosse 2005) argue that rural development practice is the product of social interaction and 'must be looked at relationally' (Long 2001, p. 19). For empirical research, this implied close engagement with actors. The multiple sources of data collected consisted of in-depth interviews, ethnographic data based on 'passive unobtrusive observation' (Robson 1993, p. 159) logged as field notes and case-specific documents shared by CBO and NGO representatives.

I purposely chose two cases studies for my fieldwork, both referred to as 'success stories' in the corresponding CBNRM literature, as they represented fundamentally different ways in which their NGO support was structured. The first conservancy case study was located in Kunene Region in north-western Namibia. This case was unique as it featured the only conservancy which had adopted an approach where support services were 'mixed and matched' from several different NGOs. Thus, rather than having one constant supporting NGO, the Kunene CBO had a dynamic NGO forum delivering services to them. The second case was a CBO located in the north-eastern Zambezi Region (formerly Caprivi). The Zambezi case embodied a typical case as it was representative of the vast majority of Namibian conservancies which have received constant support from one stable 'mother NGO' since inception.

Silvermann (2010, p. 203) distinguishes two kinds of research settings, 'open or public' versus 'closed or private'; conservancies resemble the latter. They are membership-based organizations, clearly confined to geographical boundaries and often to particular ethnic groups. A majority of these are located in the rural north of Namibia, home to the poorest and most deprived regions countrywide (Government of the Republic of Namibia 2015). Being white, female, and German made me an obvious outsider, therefore gaining and maintaining access to the two CBOs I had chosen as case studies would have been impossible without an ally in the conservancy. And while expatriate NGO networks seemed more easily accessible here, their protectiveness of their role as key CBNRM program implementers required a more subtle negotiation of access.

This chapter discusses the challenges I faced in negotiating this access. Specifically, it illustrates how research that heavily relies on fieldwork is profoundly influenced by the opportunities and constraints encountered during data collection which lie, more often than not, in the hands of gatekeepers.

Defined as 'culture brokers' (Jezewski 1993, p. 79), 'switchmen' (Clark 2010, p. 487) or, more generally, 'intermediaries' (De Laine 2000), gatekeepers have received considerable attention in the literature on fieldwork and methodology due to their powers to enable, as well as obstruct, a researcher's access to the people, institutions, and settings which hold the knowledge that researchers desire (see, for example, Mulhall 2003; Wolcott 2005; Shaw 2008; Kitchin and Tate 2013). One problem with the many accounts of gatekeepers in this literature, however, is that while they provide useful insights into the powers that gatekeepers can wield over access in the field, the actual process of negotiating this access is often underdescribed (Grant 2017). The lack of real attention to this rather significant bargaining procedure has given the impression that 'negotiating access is unproblematic' (Grant 2017, p. 2). Campbell et al. (2006, p. 103) note that once access is achieved 'dealings with the gatekeeper are rarely mentioned,' perhaps because, as Wanat (2008) diagnoses, access and continued cooperation with the gatekeeper are mostly treated as one process instead of being distinguished as two different methodological aspects. Reeves (2010, p. 315) laments that, due to the fixation on access, the manner in which 'researchers leave study populations or sites is rarely explored.'

Echoing these criticisms of largely unidirectional portrayals of the gatekeeper as 'a static and instrumental figure to be gotten past' (Crowhurst 2013, p. 463), in this chapter, I reflect on the genealogy of my fieldwork by emphasizing the reciprocity of the research encounter with CBO and NGO members facilitating access to, and safeguarding the reputation of, their institutions. The chapter addresses three main areas: (1) How access to individual CBOs and the NGO scene was negotiated; (2) how these relationships evolved during the two fieldwork periods; and (3) how this interaction influenced empirical research outcomes. Although both groups represented civil society organizations, their governance structures, political agenda, and corresponding interests were intrinsically different. Accordingly, gaining and maintaining access followed a different logic. The chapter therefore contains two separate sections where CBOs as 'closed' membership-based organizations are discussed first, followed by the Namibian NGO scene.

In focusing on the above issues, the chapter makes a contribution to the (re)conceptualization of the gatekeeper–researcher relationship by acknowledging the connection between methodological approaches of entering and remaining in the field (Bondy 2013) and how this process shapes empirical research findings. Ultimately, it is argued that the manner in which access to knowledge is negotiated should not be divorced from the results it generates. A more critical evaluation of the role of gatekeepers in the data collection process, subsequent analysis, and formulation of empirical findings enables a more honest reflection of how knowledge is co-created.

ENTRANCE AND CONTINUED ACCESS TO CONSERVANCIES

Gaining access to research settings presents a challenge that is 'unique to each study' (Wanat 2008, p. 192). Regarding my own research, building relationships with CBO members was of paramount importance in order to physically carry out the research. As mentioned above, when I (re-)entered the field for actual data collection during the second fieldwork period, I drew heavily on the connections I had already established, during the previous field trip, with a number of CBO representatives, their tourism joint-venture partners and designated support NGOs. As such, the preliminary field visit acted as a critical catalyst for relationship building. Without this visit, it seems unlikely that I would have been able to spend extended periods of time in the rural areas.

As it happened, the negotiation of my continued access took place 'without any explicit discussion occurring' (Grant 2017, p. 2). Here, a number of factors positively impacted the relationship with my research subjects—above all, the fact that I had visited the communal conservancy areas and spent time with individual CBO members during my previous fieldtrip, which contributed to a shared 'understanding of expectations of behavior' (Bondy 2013). Grant (2017, p. 2), writing on the process and challenges of conducting fieldwork, cautions that 'communication that requests too much too soon from participants' may result in non-access. Not forcing my research agenda upon my hosts, for example through excessive requests for interviews, seems to have been conducive to the relaxed and friendly nature of my on-site stays and, as a result, my hosts invited me to stay longer than I would have had the courage to ask. Apart from gaining access to the people and procedures intrinsically related to the workings of the CBO, staying onsite also allowed for what Miles and Huberman (1984, p. 42) have referred to as 'working a bit at the peripheries.' In the case of my research, this translated into gathering a wide range of opinions from community members who were not directly involved with the conservancy, but were very much influenced by its developments.

I deliberately chose the respective CBO managers as my point of entry to data collection. Managers function as the key link between the management committee governing a CBO, comparable to a board of directors, and the paid employees running the conservancy on a day-to-day basis. They also act as principal contact for any dealings with their joint-venture partner and support NGO. As such, they closely resemble gatekeepers, defined by Tushman and Katz (1980, p. 1071) as 'key individuals who are both strongly connected to internal colleagues and strongly linked to external domains.' Both staying with and shadowing the daily schedules of these managers enabled me to observe routines at the conservancy office and obtain access to the administration and documentation of the CBO. Furthermore, by shadowing, I was able to attend crucial events such as the annual game quota audit by the ministry, and NGO-delivered capacity building and planning meetings. Observing these key activities considerably aided my understanding and helped me to conceptualize CBO–NGO interaction as a number of themes emerged. Not being affiliated with a certain NGO (for example through sponsorship of research) likely prevented bias of association (Stevens 2001) and potentially a situation where I would have been seen as 'with' a particular NGO (Campbell et al. 2006, p. 116). Another positive side-effect of staying with the managers in the village, as opposed to being based in faraway tourist lodges, was continued access, which positioned me to be physically and institutionally close to the conservancy office and to observe everyday routines to comprehend the workings and the social fabric of the CBO (Gummesson 2000).

The costs associated with engaging in research are often absorbed by its participants. Hence, issues surrounding financial compensation of gatekeepers and interviewees are well-acknowledged, especially in the constellation of Westerners conducting research in developing countries (Scott et al. 2006). There was no monetary exchange with my hosts—I did not offer, nor did they ask. The question remains: *Why* did my hosts engage in my research? While McAreavey and Das (2013, p. 121) cite altruism as a key motivator of the gatekeeper, it is unlikely that an overall selflessness could be presumed for rural Namibians, or, in fact any research subjects. My last interview question: 'Would you like to ask me anything?' often led toward a discussion of how community members could benefit from contributing to research projects and how they perceived visiting researchers. Based on the maxim of honest disclosure, I acknowledged that direct benefits to participants were unlikely. Still, as one of my hosts articulated, there were associated incentives of partaking in research:

> When we see people are coming to our area, for me, I like it, I *enjoy* it. Because the more these kinds of questions are being asked, at the end of the day, that's how we can grade ourselves as a community, as a conservancy [...] So personally, I feel that it's very important when we see researchers coming into our areas.

Clark's (2010) analysis of how researchers make sense of gatekeepers' engagement differentiates motivators at individual level (for example enjoyment, social comparison, and economic interest) and collective levels such as representation, political empowerment, and informing change. A greater appreciation of the associated incentives to engage in non-compulsory activities may help to reflect on good research practice and, more specifically, the moral obligations toward participants. In my case, I asked myself if I had achieved a fair and just representation of people and place. Also, following Stevens, responsible research carries an obligation to return research findings (2001, p. 72), hence I ensured that my written results reached my hosts. The answer came promptly:

> I received your email, thank you so much for thinking back to Africa and our conservancy and provide us some feedback on your PhD study, very few do that. I will appreciate if you can forward the feedback to the current manager, it's good for the management to see and do some changes in the management system where applicable.

GATEKEEPERS' IMPACT ON DATA COLLECTION AND EMPIRICAL FINDINGS

Apart from enabling physical access to the research setting by helping me to walk 'through the metaphorical gate' (Crowhurst 2013, p. 463), my hosts also legitimized my presence in the village by lending me their authority for continued social access during my stay (De Laine 2000; Mandel 2003). Their 'facilitative style of gatekeeping' (McAreavey and Das 2013, p. 121), as well as their own status, significantly shaped both data collection and analysis. At the time of research, both managers had held their positions for several years and, apart from their seniority within the organization, they were highly regarded individuals in their communities. While many interviews with CBO representatives happened 'naturally' during the conservancy office routine, my hosts also arranged a number of meetings with key people, such as committee members, who were not on-site daily. Although they were never present during any interviews and never enquired about what was said, their intermediary role likely added another layer of complexity to the interview situation.

Stevens points out that researchers need to be aware of the side-effects of collaborating with certain individuals as one 'tends to inherit their enemies as well as their friends and relatives' (2001, p. 71). Similarly, Campbell et al. emphasize that 'co-construction of data will take place in the shadow of the relationship with the gatekeeper' (2006, p. 117), meaning that the route of access determines what experiences are shared and how opinions are voiced. Inferring that subjects at lower levels automatically align to higher-level authorization and opinions, however, may be oversimplified (Mandel 2003). In this context Wanat notes that despite gatekeepers' approval, cooperation from participants still needs to be 'earned' (2008, p. 192). While I am in no position to make judgment calls about my interviewees' unconscious filtering of information, the fact that people turned down interview requests or occasionally voiced strong anti-conservancy attitudes and disillusion with CBNRM, to a certain extent, indicated non-alignment with the manager as a gatekeeper of 'their' conservancy's reputation.

'Distance yourself from your data' was a valuable piece of advice I received after intense fieldwork periods, in order to take a neutral stance towards it. However, taking into consideration how empirical data collection was shaped by my gatekeepers as 'feeders and enablers' (Dutton and Dukerich 2006, p. 26) of the phenomenon under study, I realized that separating methodological approaches in the field, analysis, and actual empirical outcomes was practically impossible—and actually not desirable. Recognizing that my gatekeepers and other CBO members were themselves deeply embedded in the social fabric of the research site, embodying and reproducing power relationships within the conservancy, aided the process of framing and contextualizing the two case studies. One unanticipated research finding related to the significance of the manager position which strongly emerged as one principal driver for overall conservancy progress or stagnation. Undeniably, my hosts'

management style and attitude toward NGO support affected framing and conceptualizing both case studies. The exceptional drive and
resourcefulness of the Kunene conservancy manager reflected the overall development path of the CBO, which somewhat mirrored being an
NGO on its own due their proactiveness in sourcing legal advice and
other NGO support services as needed. Conversely, the manager of the
Zambezi conservancy strongly condemned his own peoples' attitude of
actively using the analogy of having a mother-NGO that had to continue
to provide for them explaining that 'NGOs have fed us *so much* that now,
we feel we cannot do things.'

My aim, in this section, has been to demonstrate the importance of key
individuals in aiding researcher access to 'closed' settings in a rural, developing country context. My experiences show that the gatekeeper assumes
a critical role in legitimizing and facilitating fieldwork by outsiders—
and that this in turn impacts upon the sample composure, respondents'
attitudes and thus ultimately the data collected. But, so far, I have focused
only on the CBO side of my research, what about my other research target, the Namibian NGO community? Due to my own background in
the non-profit sector, I assumed we would be 'more on the same page'
and that the necessity of access through gatekeepers would simply be
redundant. While this is true for gatekeepers in the classic sense, in the
following section I move on to deliberate on another, more collective,
form of gatekeeping that I encountered within the intertwined CBNRM
support NGO network.

ACCESSING THE NAMIBIAN NGO SCENE

Namibian CBNRM support NGOs are at the forefront of promoting
the achievements of the program as 'the greatest African wildlife recovery story ever told' (WWF 2016). Making reference to Brosius et al.
(1998) discussion on the 'proliferation' of CBNRM models in southern
Africa, Sullivan notes that the Namibian program and its protagonists
'have attained something of an iconic status within conservation circles'
(Sullivan 2003, p. 71; see also Sullivan 2002). This is also reflected in
numerous accolades and international conservation awards for various
key individuals and NGOs in the CBNRM network (cf. IRDNC 2016:
'History and Awards').

Based on its international reputation, the Namibian CBNRM program has attracted considerable scholarly interest. The NGO scene was found to be fairly accessible and responsive to interview requests. During my first preliminary trip, snowball sampling based on referrals proved to be very effective in securing interviews with senior Windhoek-based NGO staff, several of them key figures in the Namibian Association of CBNRM Support Organizations (NACSO), as well as NGO field staff who directly interacted with and administered support services to 'their' conservancies.

Differentiating between the first and second fieldwork period helps to elucidate my evolving relationship with the NGO scene. While appearing as an open and accessible network, I encountered an unexpected form of closure during my first visit. A recurring *nota bene* in my field notes and memos was the impression that Namibian NGOs were very protective of 'their' CBNRM program. Repeatedly and vehemently reinforcing the success of the program, at times combined with an alleged defensiveness to more critical enquiries, some NGO representatives were recurrently perceived as being somewhat dismissive despite taking the time to talk to me. Initially, I put this down to a more general sign of research fatigue as a result of being overresearched (Clark 2008). The second fieldtrip one year later shed light upon these felt sentiments toward me as a researcher and the nature of my enquiry.

One aspect of this unexpected closure related to research practice by foreign scholars more generally. Several NGO staff expressed their frustration about researchers visiting for short periods, as one interviewee put it 'some only stay for a day.' The main frustration lay in the fact that these short-time visitors did not re-consult and, more importantly, did not share their research findings with the people and institutions they studied. Stevens (2001, p. 72), stressing the importance of reciprocity and responsibility in field research, refers to this as 'grab-and-run research.' One NGO director explained that she found it difficult to accept research accounts 'from outside,' which articulate shortcomings and criticisms about the CBNRM program, without offering any recommendations for improvement. Not being able to comment or being otherwise consulted in order to respond to critical findings was felt to be unfair. In this way, the establishment of trust, positive rapport and credibility, commonly cited in the literature as essential preconditions for 'good' research relationships, essentially collided with how several research participants perceived research practice.

Revisiting Namibia for another three-month fieldwork period one year later meant that I was a returnee re-consulting with the people that I had already connected with previously. Also, the fact that I had now spent time in the field changed how I was perceived as a researcher. My status as a returnee, I believe, had a significant impact on the manner in which NGO staff chose to share their opinions and also their frustrations, which they seemed to have withheld during our first encounter. Interviewees often mirrored their inherently ambivalent position as development intermediaries. Senior Windhoek-based staff repeatedly stressed how their overall donor dependency and increasingly rigorous reporting requirements affected their work. Field-based staff emphasized the immense pressure with regards to delivering CBNRM support services within certain timelines having to 'keep people in Windhoek happy' as well as meeting the demands of their conservancy clients.

During this second fieldwork period, I came to realize that I had underestimated the politically charged nature of my research topic. My specific enquiry entered an area of concern where the NGO community had a political interest in protecting 'their' program and their specific role in it (Clark 2010; Siwale 2015). Tackling exogenous, NGO-driven development of local community institutions made my enquiry 'inherently political' and collection and analysis of data were 'embedded in such politics' (Campbell et al. 2006, p. 98). Especially with regards to one of my chosen case studies, where one CBO received disproportionally high amounts of financial and in-kind support, I was warned that this particular case was: 'A very prickly issue where everyone pricks up their ears.' My query if this conservancy was promoted as a typical CBNRM success story or somewhat resembled a 'donor darling' apparently was a rather delicate subject matter. One senior consultant cautioned that: 'I wouldn't want to make any conclusions about that because it's quite sensitive ground.'

Against the background of positionality and good research practice, the quest for reality through critical academic enquiry seemed somewhat at odds with representing the 'reality that is congruent to the one held by the group in question' (Clark 2010, p. 494). Sullivan (2003), who has conducted extensive field research in north-western Namibia since the 1990s, wrote about an incident where a local community resisted and protested against NGO involvement in their conservancy formation process. Her below deliberations illustrate the divide between development practitioners and researchers and the effects when the former feel misrepresented, or their work discredited, by the latter:

Academics can appear rather sanctimonious in their writings regarding environment and development: preaching from the margins while avoiding 'getting their hands dirty' with the 'real' work of implementation. In consequence, the possibility of engaging those who 'matter' in the debate–policy-makers, donors, implementers, facilitators and local people–is compromised, especially if those 'on the ground' feel under attack by academic work. In response to my own writings on this region I have experienced resistance and abuse, and threats of libel suits. (Sullivan 2003, p. 83)

GATEKEEPING AS EMPIRICAL OUTCOME

While gatekeeping as methodological consideration, that is gaining and maintaining access to the Namibian NGO network, posed no immediate challenge as its members were accommodating toward my interview requests, NGOs gatekeeping their role as implementers and the program per se constituted a key empirical finding that transpired from my research data. At macro or national level, the NACSO network constituted not only a forum to facilitate CBNRM support but also acted as gatekeeper where new support NGOs wanting to 'come in' had to 'go through' NACSO. Some interviewees described how outside NGOs, which had not followed the 'right' procedures, 'got a cold shoulder.' At meso level, intensely political and competitive conditions stemmed from the fact that certain areas and thus conservancies 'belonged' to different NGOs (Sullivan 2003). NGO support was highly unequal, systematic inclusion and exclusion of individual CBOs was mostly determined by donor requirements regarding the conservancy's economic (tourism) potential based on the occurrence of wildlife. At micro level, the designated support NGO had the power to significantly shape the overall conservancy development path, a senior NGO representative and CBNRM expert reflected:

We quickly become gatekeepers. Gatekeepers of *ideas*. Gatekeepers of *direction*. Gatekeepers of *priorities*. Gatekeepers of *information*. And I think we have to be very *careful* of that. That *our* role is to just *share* knowledge and understanding.

Pressed for the need to demonstrate positive impact, that is to deliver and maintain success stories to secure continued donor-funding, NGOs as principal implementing agents have a vested interest in 'filtering and regulating the flow of information and stabilising representations [that] are necessary for survival' (Mosse 2005, p. 12). Thus, NGOs collectively

gatekeeping the program's, and ultimately *their*, reputation was a conse-
quential outcome. Silverman cautions that when interviewing 'up,' elite
members might object to 'opening up' (2010, p. 196). Yet, the openness
of senior NGO representatives during the second field visit, especially
with regards to their frustration with the 'donor dictate,' almost came as
a surprise:

> Sometimes NGOs have to take donor money for survival—but that
> becomes dangerous because then you become a machine that's just
> feeding the beast.

Field notes, and post-interview additions regarding field-based NGO
staff, recurrently contained descriptions such as 'exhausted' and 'disil-
lusioned' by the actual workings of rural development projects and, in
particular, 'under pressure' to deliver pre-defined training modules for
CBO capacity-building. During all formal interviews with the different
CBNRM stakeholder groups, only members of the NGO community
requested that certain statements were off the record. Each time it was
directly related to dissatisfaction with donor requirements. It seemed I
had become some sort of gatekeeper myself. Campbell et al. define this
transformed position of fieldworkers as that of 'keymaster' (2006, p. 99)
where, as research evolves and more data are assembled, the researcher
gradually assumes the role of the gatekeeper.

CONCLUSIONS

This chapter reflected on the processes and relationships that enabled my
fieldwork and how the methodological aspects of gatekeeping related to
empirical findings. The field and its players provided the furnishings for
my research. They denied access to my original research endeavor but
readily offered another social phenomenon of interest. CBOs as the consumers and NGOs as the implementers of rural development projects
greatly shaped key issues arising and thus the eventual research focus.
They acted as the bridge between my research and the people, institutions and events holding desired knowledge and thus actively influenced
the process of *doing* research and data collection.

So, what are the lessons learnt from all this? Despite the context-specific
nature of this research project, I believe that my fieldwork experiences may
assist future researchers who rely on gatekeepers for access by considering

three key aspects. First, strike a balance between flexibility and persistence in determining access. During the early stages of sussing out the actual focus of a larger research project that heavily relies on the continued cooperation of gatekeepers, one needs to realistically assess the overall feasibility of the project in terms of gaining access. The discouraging experiences of my initial research enquiries into KAZA made it clear that I had misjudged my access options. However, by keeping an open mind and continued engagement, I quite literally found my final research objective in the field. Once I had identified the people who would act as critical door-openers I ensured that contact was maintained in a friendly but persistent manner. The flexibility-tenacity maxim also pertained to the actual research methods used to collect data. For instance, the interview guide was not a static, pre-defined agenda for enquiry, rather it evolved as re-emerging issues, often shaped by gatekeepers, were built in. Once integrated, I was insistent in my enquiry. Being an outsider, especially in a rural community setting, in fact allowed me to make certain enquiries (cf. Bondy 2013). For instance by explaining that an institution like the traditional authority does not exist where I come from, I could ask somewhat naïve but powerful questions about its spheres of influence, whereas a Namibian would have been expected to know or otherwise been deemed ignorant.

Secondly, contemplate how you can achieve 'good practice' in your gatekeeper relationship. While ethical considerations, such as informed consent, were of course covered and approved by my institutional review board, I found that there was limited 'workable' advice for researchers in the field. Review boards seem to treat ethics in a somewhat technical fashion (for example, with questions such as: *Has voluntary participation been achieved, yes or no?*). At the same time, the recommendations from the literature on methodology to nourish trust and rapport seemed difficult to perform as this usually requires much longer fieldwork periods and exposure than most research agendas allow. I therefore propose to ask a number of more applied ethics-related question that pertain to good research conduct with gatekeepers: Did the researcher ensure honest disclosure of her intentions and how the project might, *or might not*, provide benefits to participants? Did the researcher consider the interests of gatekeepers and the 'communities of interest' they provide access to? Were they fairly represented by the researcher? Could someone lose face because of this research account? Was written feedback provided to the people who enabled and continuously facilitated field research? Would they likely take part in the research project again?

Thirdly, acknowledge the influence of gatekeepers beyond simply providing access to the field. The manner in which gatekeepers enable access is likely to have repercussions on the sample population as well as on the key themes and thus research findings that emerge. By recognizing the connection between methodological approaches and empirical findings researchers can enhance the representation and understanding of social phenomena within the research setting. Ultimately, 'it is in the context of the encounter with the researcher that a subject assumes the identity and role of gatekeeper' (Crowhurst 2013, p. 471), likewise the researcher and her positionality vis-à-vis the researched only exists within the relational foundations in the field. Hence, data are not simply collected 'through' gatekeepers, but rather co-constructed within the research encounter. The implication of this is that practical concerns of knowledge production and empirical findings must be considered in relation to the conditions under which the researcher entered and remained in the research setting (cf. Bondy 2013). Not only acknowledging the importance of gatekeepers as methodological consideration when accessing 'closed' membership-based rural settings, but also recognizing gatekeepers/gatekeeping as theoretical consideration, helped me to frame the two case studies and to conceptually relate the empirical findings to the larger topical domain. Finally, and probably most importantly, tackling gatekeepers and *their* interests helped me to make sense of the sometimes confusing personal and political dynamics I encountered in the field.

NOTES

1. More than 90% of registered Namibian tourism businesses are white-owned, and one quarter is foreign-owned (Jänis 2014).
2. In Namibia, community-based organizations are referred to as 'conservancies.' The two terms will be used interchangeably in this chapter.

REFERENCES

Bondy, C. (2013). How Did I Get Here? The Social Process of Accessing Field Sites. *Qualitative Research, 13*(5), 578–590.

Brosius, J. P., Lowenhaupt Tsing, A., & Zerner, C. (1998). Representing Communities: Histories and Politics of Community-Based Natural Resource Management. *Society and Natural Resources, 11*(2), 157–168.

Campbell, L. M., Gray, N. J., Meletis, Z. A., Abbott, J. G., & Silver, J. J. (2006). Gatekeepers and Keymasters: Dynamic Relationships of Access in Geographical Fieldwork. *Geographical Review, 96*(1), 97–121.

Clark, T. (2008). We're Over-Researched Here!' Exploring Accounts of Research Fatigue Within Qualitative Research Engagements. *Sociology, 42*(5), 953–970.

Clark, T. (2010). On 'Being Researched': Why Do People Engage with Qualitative Research? *Qualitative Research, 10*(4), 399–419.

Crowhurst, I. (2013). The Fallacy of the Instrumental Gate? Contextualising the Process of Gaining Access Through Gatekeepers. *International Journal of Social Research Methodology, 16*(6), 463–475.

De Laine, M. (2000). *Fieldwork, Participation and Practice: Ethics and Dilemmas in Qualitative Research.* London: Sage.

Dutton, J. E., & Dukerich, J. M. (2006). The Relational Foundation of Research: An Underappreciated Dimension of Interesting Research. *Academy of Management Journal, 49*(1), 21–26.

Easton, G. (2010). Critical Realism in Case Study Research. *Industrial Marketing Management, 39*(1), 118–128.

Government of the Republic of Namibia. (2015). *Poverty and Deprivation in Namibia 2015,* Windhoek, Namibia: National Planning Commission. http://www.un.org.na/home_htm_files/NPC-Summary%20Report.pdf. Accessed December 10, 2017.

Grant, A. (2017). "I Don't Want You Sitting Next to Me": The Macro, Meso and Micro of Gaining and Maintaining Access to Government Organizations During Ethnographic Fieldwork. *International Journal of Qualitative Methods, 16,* 1–11.

Gummesson, E. (2000). *Qualitative Methods in Management Research.* London: Sage.

IRDNC—Integrated Rural Development and Nature Conservation. (2016). About Us/History and Awards. http://www.irdnc.org.na/history.html. Accessed October 27, 2017.

Jänis, J. (2014). *The Tourism-Development Nexus in Namibia: A Study on National Tourism Policy and Local Tourism Enterprises' Policy Knowledge.* Ph.D. thesis, University of Helsinki, Finland.

Jezewski, M. (1993). Culture Brokering as a Model for Advocacy. *Nursing and Health Care, 14*(2), 78–89.

Jones, B. T. B. (2010). The Evolution of Namibia's Communal Conservancies. In F. Nelson (Ed.), *Community Rights, Conservation and Contested Land: The Politics of Natural Resource Governance in Africa* (pp. 106–120). London: Earthscan.

Kitchin, R., & Tate, N. (2013). *Conducting Research in Human Geography: Theory, Methodology and Practice.* Abingdon: Routledge.

Long, N. (2001). *Development Sociology: Actor Perspectives.* Abingdon: Routledge.

Mandel, J. L. (2003). Negotiating Expectations in the Field: Gatekeepers, Research Fatigue and Cultural Biases. *Singapore Journal of Tropical Geography, 24*(2), 198–210.

McAreavey, R., & Das, C. (2013). A Delicate Balancing Act: Negotiating with Gatekeepers for Ethical Research When Researching Minority Communities. *International Journal of Qualitative Methods, 12*(1), 113–131.

Miles, M. B., & Huberman, A. M. (1984). *Qualitative Data Analysis: A Sourcebook of New Methods*. London: Sage.

Ministry of Environment and Tourism Namibia. (2013). National Policy on Community Based Natural Resource Management. http://www.met.gov.na/files/files/CBNRM_20Policy%20Approved.pdf. Accessed January 10, 2018.

Mosse, D. (2005). *Cultivating Development*. London: Pluto Press.

Mulhall, A. (2003). In the Field: Notes on Observation in Qualitative Research. *Journal of Advanced Nursing, 41*(3), 306–313.

NACSO—Namibian Association for CBNRM Support Organizations. (2017). Conservancies and Conservancies Overview. http://www.nacso.org.na/conservation-and-conservancies. Accessed September 27, 2017.

Peace Parks Foundation. (2017). Kavango Zambezi. http://www.peaceparks.org/tfca.php?pid=27&mid=1008. Accessed October 7, 2017.

Reeves, C. (2010). A Difficult Negotiation: Fieldwork Relations with Gatekeepers. *Qualitative Research, 10*(3), 315–331.

Ribot, J. C. (2002). *Democratic Decentralization of Natural Resources: Institutionalizing Popular Participation*. Washington: World Resources Institute.

Robson, C. (1993). *Real World Research: A Resource for Social Scientists and Practitioners-Researchers*. Oxford: Blackwell.

Scott, S., Miller, F., & Lloyd, K. (2006). Doing Fieldwork in Development Geography: Research Culture and Research Spaces in Vietnam. *Geographical Research, 44*(1), 28–40.

Shaw, I. (2008). Ethics and the Practice of Qualitative Research. *Qualitative Social Work, 7*(4), 400–414.

Silverman, D. (2010). *Doing Qualitative Research* (3rd ed.). London: Sage.

Siwale, J. (2015). Why Did I Not Prepare for This? The Politics of Negotiating Fieldwork Access, Identity, and Methodology in Researching Microfinance Institutions. *SAGE Open, 5*(2), 1–12.

Stevens, S. (2001). Fieldwork as Commitment. *The Geographical Review, 91*(1–2), 66–73.

Sullivan, S. (2002). How Sustainable is the Communalizing Discourse of 'New' Conservation: The Masking of Difference, Inequality and Aspiration in the Fledgling "Conservancies" of Namibia. In D. Chattyand & M. Colchester (Eds.), *Conservation and Mobile Indigenous Peoples* (pp. 158–197). Oxford: Berghahn Press.

Sullivan, S. (2003). Dissent or Libel in Resistance to a Conservancy in North-West Namibia. In E. Berglund & D. Anderson (Eds.), *Ethnographies of Conservation: Environmentalism and the Distribution of Privilege* (pp. 69–86). Oxford: Berghahn Press.

Tushman, M. L., & Katz, R. (1980). External Communication and Project Performance: An Investigation into the Role of Gatekeepers. *Management Science, 26*(11), 1071–1085.

Wanat, C. L. (2008). Getting Past the Gatekeepers: Differences Between Access and Cooperation in Public School Research. *Field Methods, 20*(2), 191–208.

Wolcott, H. F. (2005). *The Art of Fieldwork*. Walnut Creek, CA: AltaMira Press.

WWF—World Wide Fund For Nature. (2016). Namibia: The Greatest Wildlife Recovery Story Ever Told. http://www.worldwildlife.org/pages/namibia-the-greatest-wildlife-recovery-story-evertold. Accessed May 31, 2016.

CHAPTER 9

Failed Fieldwork in Senegal: Give Up or Continue?

Elizaveta Volkova

Nowadays, doctoral research students are given a certain amount of training before they approach the field. This training is intended to equip them with an array of tools to carry out fieldwork with at least some degree of success. These tools might include, among other things, advice and guidance on how to immerse oneself in the culture of one's host country; how to establish the right distance between oneself and one's research participants; and how to negotiate with gatekeepers in order to find helpful, available and responsive local contacts (Aspen 1991; Salamone 1991). With the appropriate research tools at their disposal, researchers head off to conduct fieldwork with a good grounding in how to apply academic know-how to the realities of the field in order to facilitate access to and collection of data. But these realities are often much more complex than those taught in methods training and can often leave a novice researcher confronting feelings of helplessness and failure.

E. Volkova (✉)
Ecole Pratique des Hautes Etudes, Institut des mondes africains,
Paris, France

153

L. Johnstone (ed.), *The Politics of Conducting Research in Africa*,
https://doi.org/10.1007/978-3-319-95531-5_9

It is not uncommon for researchers to feel this way. Doctoral students are often, as novice researchers, balancing coping strategies of being in a new culture with the pressures of getting the research done. During my first foray into the field, I experienced feelings of insecurity as I was confronted with a number of obstacles which made me realize quickly the difference between academic training and the realities of conducting research. In research situations, either in Africa or beyond, there are many obstacles that stand in the way of access to the field site, and to data, these cause researchers to constantly improvise and to readjust fieldwork strategies and research methods (Kovats-Bernat 2002). The success of fieldwork is determined by a number of critical factors of differing levels and of differing kinds. These factors range from planning stage administrative procedures, such as applying for a visa, getting research permits, and finding a host research institution (see, for instance, Pritchard in this volume, or Suzuki (2004) for an example from Iran), to the more practical considerations of establishing contacts in the host country in order to facilitate access to research participants and the collection of data. In addition to these challenges, access to the field its people and their data could be jeopardized when the path to potential fieldwork success is blocked, or heavily controlled. This control might be something that is out of the researcher's hands such as control of the legal kind by government forces (Thomson 2009) or a host institution (Thiongane 2013); alternatively researchers might be faced with control or blockage of a less rigid or tangible but no less complex kind.

The control to which I am referring comes from my own experiences conducting fieldwork in the Enampore village of Senegal with the Joola people. I utilized the assistance of a number of field assistants to provide access to research participants as well as, in some instances, to provide translation. Upon arriving in Enampore, I spent some time familiarizing myself with my surroundings and immersing myself in the local Joola culture. Such familiarization is a natural, and necessary, part of fieldwork, however, I felt that, in the case of my own experience, it had taken up too much time. The time spent on familiarization, such as attending local football games and ceremonies, was time when I felt I could, or should, have been conducting interviews and gathering data. This fear of having wasted valuable time and the anxiety of not having anything in the way of concrete data contributed to my decision to work with research assistants, or gatekeepers as they are commonly referred, but I soon found out that this decision would create obstacles of its own.

Before heading to the field, I had had some training in the importance of field site access and learned some techniques about how to build relationships in order to gain access to research participants. What this training lacked, however, was an understanding of the fact that, no matter how essential the role of field assistants can be to field site access, these key figures commonly approach researchers with their own assumptions and preconceptions about what the research is supposed to be (Wanat 2008; McFadyen and Rankin 2016). This can have a tremendous influence on the progression of one's research, as I found out for myself when, in some instances, my field assistants were selective in their translation of consultants answers. Compounding the anxiety I was already experiencing from wasting too much time, these attempts by my consultants to control the direction of my project left me with the feeling that my research was failing, and I did not know whether to give up or continue.

These feelings were compounded by the fact that, where I might usually have taken solace in other researcher's similar experiences, when it comes to discussing failure, there are few instances in the scholarly literature on fieldwork where researchers remove the filter and discuss their own experiences and anxieties in this area. This failure to tell the 'stories behind the findings' (Thomson et al. 2013, p. 1) means that, more often than not, the only models available to novice researchers heading to the field are of successfully completed fieldwork reported in successfully completed accounts, which tend to emphasize achievements while rationalizing the more problematic obstacles that come along. There are many reasons why researchers might wish to sanitize the realities and anxieties of fieldwork and sift out the more problematic issues that happened on the ground. These might contain, among other things, the more personal issues such as uncomfortable interviews or embarrassing distress to the academically challenging abandonment of the direction of one's originally planned research (Nairn et al. 2005; Jemielniak and Kostera 2010). Whatever the reasons for the tendency to sanitize the research process, I want to push against this here in order to provide a personal narrative of my experiences with feelings of failure in the field in order to offer novice researchers an understanding that the actual experiences of fieldwork nearly always diverge from the idealized versions presented in the literature, and feelings of failure quite often naturally accompany them when they do.

I use the term 'failure' here to refer to the cocktail of experiences that diverted my research from the intended or expected path that I had envisaged and emotions that accompanied these experiences. Over the next three sections, I share my experience and understanding of the emotional and intellectual challenges of fieldwork defeat and discuss how I dealt with these feelings of failure. Through these reflections, I wish to highlight how things take place during the fieldwork process that do not correspond to any of the training that we have received in preparation for the field, or to our previous fieldwork experience. During my time among the Joola in Senegal, I found the first few weeks of fieldwork especially difficult because I could not seem to unlock the secret to accessing the information I had set out to retrieve. Because of this lack of progress accompanied by the frustrations of working with field assistants, who at times acted as gatekeepers to data production, I started to believe that my fieldwork would end up as incomplete. It was only later in the fieldwork, when I decided to face my fears head on, instead of continuing along the same path of slow progress, that I decided to re-evaluate the strategies and methods of data production I was using. By letting go of the frustration and fear, I was able to develop new methods of data collection which as, I will show, took a slightly different, and more interesting, path toward data production.

FIELDWORK: ON THE WAY TO FAILURE?

Since 2011, I have been working on the subject of joking relationships in Casamance, a region in the South of Senegal. The aim of my research is a comparison of the joking relationships among two ethnic groups, the Mandinka and the Joola, from the Casamance region. These groups differ greatly in the ways in which they are socially organized but nevertheless appear to share the similar tradition of joking relations. Joking relationships are relations 'between two persons in which one is by custom permitted, and in some instances required, to tease or make fun of the other, who in turn is required to take no offence' (Radcliffe-Brown 1940, p. 195). The relationships are established between clans (for example, Mandinka Faati and Maanee clans), ethnic groups (Joola and Sereer), villages (Diégoune and Thionk Essyl Joola villages in Casamance), or family members (maternal uncles and uterine nephews among the Joola, cross-cousins among the Mandinka, grandparents and grandchildren among the two groups).

The joking relationship is sometimes connected to the rituals of initiation and can also play a role in mediation and conflict resolution between

families and villages. As people are supposed to obey their joking partners, this position allows intervention to resolve a conflict situation.
People linked by joking relationships are also allowed to adopt some
deviant behaviors. These behaviors are reflected in ritual insults or in
group members making fun of each other. The jokes used to reach these
means are not spontaneous. They are often taken from a narrow inven-
tory of themes and subjects, such as greediness, seniority, wealth, and
development. An important characteristic of joking relations is their sym-
metry (Smith 2006), each of the two members of the joking relationship
makes fun of the other. To tease his or her joking partner, for example,
one can say: 'your village is too poor,' 'I am your grandfather,' 'you are
an uncircumcised boy (speaking to an adult man),' 'I am the king, and
you are here to serve me.' A child might say to their grandmother: 'you
don't have teeth anymore; you are not eating but spoiling your food.'
There is no winner in the joking fight, and one should never be offended
by his or her joking partner.

After beginning my doctoral research project, I carried out several research trips to Casamance, staying mainly in the region's capital Ziguinchor as well as short stays in Mandinka villages. In May
2014, however, I traveled to Enampore village twenty kilometers East
of Ziguinchor, part of Bandial country known locally as *Mof evvi* kingdom, in order to conduct fieldwork that focused for the first time solely
on the Joola part of my project. While there are many works devoted
to the instrumentalization of joking relationships as a political tool for
conflict resolution, and in particular, their application to the conflict
in Casamance,[1] literature that focuses on the more specific joking relations of the Joola people is more difficult to track down. From the small
amount of information I could find, however, as well as my previous
research trips, where I was able to conduct interviews with some members of the Joola community, it seemed clear to me that joking relationships played some role in Joola life.

I arrived in Enampore feeling relatively confident that my knowledge,
albeit brief, of the joking relations among the Joola would be received
with interest by the Joola people themselves. This was because, in my
previous experience of conducting research in the Mandinka areas, I had
had little or no difficulty raising the issue of joking relationships with
the local people as, among the Mande, whether in Mali, Côte-d'Ivoire,
Burkina Faso, or Senegal, joking relations are a common phenomenon
that are easily observed, for example, among family members, neighbors,

at a market, in a neighborhood grocery shop, in a university, or at an administration office.

Joking relations among Mande people are a matter of pride. They are not only considered a widespread tradition but are also a kind of cultural heritage and, it could be argued, are even a symbol of local democracy. This is because these joking relations have an important function—they provide mediation in the way that a joking relation partner or *sananku* is someone to be listened to. When talking about their joking relations in interviews, my Mande participants all gave similar examples: 'If my *sananku* says: "Stop it!," I must stop. I must stop for the honor of the joking relation which links us.' For many of my Mande research participants, joking relations were sacred. As one Mande put this, 'You cannot refuse anything to your *sananku*. For example, if you hit someone because he hurt you, because he wants to kill you, he is wrong...If your *sananku* says: "Leave it.", you must leave it alone.'[2]

During my fieldwork in the Mandinka area, I was able to extract much of my knowledge about the joking relations of the Mande with relative ease through a mixture of participant observation and interview. My proficiency in local languages helped me considerably in observing the joking relations in everyday life both in the rural Mandinka areas and also while listening to the French-speaking townspeople. In general, my interest in learning more about joking relations was greatly encouraged with excitement and enthusiasm by most of my participants. In their opinion, the joking relations tradition continued to play an important role in their society, and this was often described as something very 'useful.' It was this excitement and enthusiasm that I took forward into my preparation for the Joola leg of my fieldwork, and this excitement that led me to expect that I might receive a similar approving attitude from my new research participants in the Joola community. I was all the more confident because, since the time of my fieldwork with the Mande, I had had the chance to develop and improve my interview and observation skills and I felt ready to apply these to the Joola leg of my trip.

Upon my arrival in Enampore, I began to familiarize myself with the field by investigating the history of the village, the area and its population. In accordance with traditions, I conducted my first interviews with what appeared to be the best experts on local tradition—middle-age men and officials who had studied at least to the level of secondary school. I was warmly welcomed by the villagers who talked willingly about different aspects of their culture. I recorded in my notes the foundation story of the village, information about the history of Joola migration to this area, and the settlement of neighboring villages. I learnt a great deal about marriage and dowry, about funeral ceremonies, about childbirth and motherhood, about palm wine and rice production, and about the religious life of the community. Additionally, I was encouraged to join many of the different events and ceremonies celebrating the Joola life-style and culture. Some of these were more private, family events such as ceremonial sacrifices to home shrines. Others were on a larger scale prepared and held by the whole village. These included the first communion ceremony, weddings, funerals, *kacinen* (boys initiation ceremonies), school football games, and an inter village young people dance evening.

While my participation in these Joola ceremonies made me feel like a welcome guest in the village, I began to feel anxious about the progress of my fieldwork. On one hand, I was content with the discovery of my new field. I was beginning to find my bearings in the new environment,[3] learning the language and finding out about historical accounts, traditions, facts, ceremonies, and the everyday life details that my hosts and neighbors wanted to share with me. Yet, on the other hand, the purpose of my stay was to try, in a relatively short period of time, to develop an understanding of the essential information about joking relations among the Joola people. While I had excelled at the former of these two things, my information on the latter was severely lacking.

A few weeks after my arrival in Enampore, I decided that I had now given myself enough time to become familiar with the field and my surroundings, it was time to focus in more closely on the actual subject of my research—joking relations. I began to arrange and conduct interviews with people who were pointed out to me by my local field assistants,[4] but when the interviews were complete and I went over my field notes at the end of each day, they seemed to contain all kinds of information related to Joola life and culture, but nothing at all about their joking relations.

A while after my interviews began, and data production had progressed in a similar manner, I came to the realization that perhaps my research project was in trouble. This fear was enhanced by the fact that many of the people that I had consulted as field assistants and research participants while in Enampore did not consider the joking relationships an integral part of Joola culture. This became clear to me when, during interviews, some of my consultants tried to bring my attention to other aspects and characteristics which, as they saw it, were considered more of a hallmark of the Joola culture than the joking relationships that I was attempting to uncover for my research. These hallmarks included unique cultural characteristics such as shrines and spirit worship, male initiation ceremonies held in the sacred forest, king-priests, and the egalitarian social organization of the Joola community. While these characteristics might have been unique to the Joola, providing interesting background information for my research project, they did not facilitate anything in the way of progress toward my quest to understand in more detail the joking relations culture among the Joola themselves. Everything outside the presumed Joola culture was not worth studying as far as my consultants were concerned.

Precious time in the field had by now passed by and I had not been able to obtain much information at all about joking relationships between the Joola people in the Bandial region of Casamance. Fearing that my fieldwork was turning into a failure, I multiplied my visits to the village 'wise men' expecting to learn something which would help me to expand the perimeters of my research question. Yet, the elders did not seem to approve of my interest in joking relations and encouraged me instead to visit homes, gardens, and rice fields. When I asked questions about joking relations, the reaction was often accompanied by responses such as, 'We don't know it here in Bandial. We don't have such relations. Mandinka do. You'd better go there to study them. Why aren't you interested in circumcision ceremonies?' The more these answers met my questions, the greater I felt the risk of returning home with either too little, incomplete or unanalyzable field data. These very real feelings of failure were enhanced by emotional stress and a feeling of being stuck in a deadlock between what I believed was something interesting in the Joola culture to be explored and what my consultants believed relevant.

When one conducts fieldwork, which is relatively long term, is focused narrowly on a community, and is on a subject closely linked to social relations, everyday contact with the research participants is of crucial importance. At this point in my fieldwork, I felt that I was not only conducting research, but also gaining the valuable experience of relationship building. The feeling of wasting time, however, my research participants' as well as my own, put significant pressure on the fieldwork progress. The sense of responsibility toward my field as a researcher made me feel discouraged and disappointment in my research skills and my fieldwork strategy. As far as I felt at the time, in that situation, my research was failing. But can we really ever say that research fails? For a researcher conducting fieldwork, every experience, even if a negative one, is valuable, but what valuable experience could I take away from my failed fieldwork with the Joola, and what could I possibly do to save this part of my research project? To answer this question, I needed to climb out from under these feelings of defeat and get a better understanding of the issues behind the failure. I reflect on these in the next section.

DETERMINING THE ISSUES

The first step to solving any problem is to determine it. My experience conducting research on the joking relationships of the Joola people led me to the realization that fieldwork is not only a method of collecting information, but it is also a form of communication between a researcher and their research participants before anything else. It is, therefore, crucial to make sure that you and your research participants understand each other well. This understanding does not necessarily refer to speaking the same local language as one's research participants, although it is enormously helpful for integration while, in the field, if one does because, in many areas, European languages are spoken only by locals who have acquired a formal education. For those researchers, such as myself, who are not fluent in the language of the community on which their research is based, it is common to engage gatekeepers or interpreters in order to facilitate and translate the interview process. While this option may be helpful, it can also have its limits, which need to be identified, acknowledged, and taken into consideration.[5]

In my own experience, my basic knowledge of the Joola language consequently led me, on a number of occasions, to ask for help from members of my host family. Yet, even with this assistance, my attempts at interpreting interviews were far from successful. This was largely because, when one relies on the assistance of interpreters to conduct interviews, the conversation and the information relayed are never directly with or from the interviewee, but are passed through the prism of the interpreter's point of view. As a result, both the interviewer and interviewee's control over interview data is at the mercy of the interpreter and, therefore, considerably weak. A pertinent example of this weakness, in my own fieldwork, was when, on one occasion, I was interviewing a non-French speaking elderly man. My interpreter translated my question about joking relations into Joola, and, after a long discussion with the interviewee, the interpreter turned back to me with the response that the

man did not know the answer to my question. Confused by this translation of a conversation which appeared to have lasted around ten minutes in Joola, I asked the interpreter to explain in more detail the elderly
man's response. Once again, the information given to me was the same:
'He said he doesn't know. Maybe his parents did not talk to him about
their culture. Perhaps they did not teach him anything.' Reflecting on
the interpreter's translation later, I came to understand that many of the
reasons why, after weeks of living and working with the Joola community, my knowledge of the joking relations between the Joola had not
progressed, could be traced to my reliance on research assistants and
interpreters during the interview process.

Perhaps, the most important tools in an anthropologist's toolkit are
the ability to react rapidly to answers given by interviewees and adapt
follow-up questions accordingly while at the same time taking into
account research participants' reactions and feelings toward certain questions in order to better analyze what is being said. One's precision with
and handling of these interview tools is rather a difficult task to articulate
when using interpreters in the field because, in cases where interpreters
are used, the person who conducts the interview and the person who
directly asks questions are two entirely different people with different
ways of interpreting situations. Although the use of interpreters for some
researchers might aid the precision of translation, the use of interpreters
in my experience caused only confusion. But while I have noted above
that my lack of progress uncovering information on the joking relationships between members of the Joola community can be traced back to
interpreters, my own relationship with these interpreters is also to blame.

By this I mean that, the way a researcher positions themselves in
the field is an essential factor for the smooth functioning of their field
research. As sincerity and transparency are the best ways to establish relationships of trust, the researcher needs to be very clear, both with themselves and with their research participants, about the aims of the project
under the research lens. In the first few weeks of my fieldwork, I chose to
spend what with hindsight appeared to be an excessive amount of time
collecting general, preliminary information about my surroundings. This
strategy might be reasonable for fieldwork that takes place over a longer
period of time but is not the best use of time when, as with my own situation, a researcher has a shorter, more limited period of time in the field.
Perhaps some of the feelings of failure, discussed in the previous section
of the chapter, could have been avoided if I had gathered introductory

information at the same time as conducting interviews in order to gather the data related directly to my research.

Another aspect of my first few weeks in the field that took a considerable amount of time away from my direct focus on my research subject was courtesy visits. In the early stages of their fieldwork, a researcher inevitably begins to discover the field through courtesy visits to village chiefs, notables, elders, religious leaders, and other important community members. As well as being good manners and following local codes of behavior, these visits present an opportunity for the researcher to introduce themselves, to present their research objectives and discuss the details of their planned fieldwork. Such contacts can also facilitate administrative procedures required to access the field, provide official frameworks for research activities, or aid researchers in finding consultants or assistants. While I understood their usefulness and wanted to follow the local codes of behavior as closely as I could, these courtesy visits took valuable time away from other research activities such as observations, meetings, and interviews with other consultants and turned out to be detrimental to my data collection.

While all of these things—the use of interpreters and poor use of my time—had a considerable effect on the amount of useful data that I was able to collect, there was an additional detail that may have had an effect on the way in which some aspects of the Joola culture were revealed to me, while others remained hidden. Since the 1980s, the Casamance region has been affected by armed conflict waged by a movement seeking independence for the region. This conflict has considerably affected the economy, and as a result, many community development initiatives have been put in place in the Casamance region (Diédhiou 2013). In Enampore, where I conducted my fieldwork with the Joola, priority is given to the development of tourism as a way in which to boost the economy of the region. Initiatives to attract tourism in the area include a traditional *impluvium* hut transformed into a hostel and the organization of a number of cultural festivals every year. These things are driven largely through tourism websites which present the *Mof evvi* kingdom to the world as the land of responsible tourism, cultural activities, unique nature, and welcoming hosts. The outcome of this new cultural dynamic is a new cultural discourse which presents a simplified version of Joola culture focusing on selling a snapshot of Joola local religious beliefs, ritual life, agricultural activities, handicraft, and performance arts to tourists and travelers. Most likely, during my fieldwork, I was regarded by the locals as being one of these tourists or travelers. At the very least, this goes some way to explaining the simplified version of Joola culture that I was offered during my time in the field.

All of the issues that I have determined in this section point to the fact that, while my research was not going in the linear direction I expected it to take—where I drew up my plan, went into the field, and returned home to analyze data—it was not actually failing either. Reflecting on these feelings of failure since leaving the field, I realize that they were actually a catalyst I was able to proactively use to improve my research practice and outcomes and turn my project around.

FAILED RESEARCH: DON'T GIVE UP, CONTINUE

The pressures of conducting fieldwork for novice researchers can often lead to feelings of insecurity and emotional vulnerability, particularly when one feels like on is not mastering the situation (Nilan 2002). These insecurities, as I have shown, add complexity to an already stressful situation and, in turn, can lead researchers to believe that their research is failing. Reflecting on the emotions I experienced during my time in the field, it is clear, with hindsight, that the pressure I had put on myself to produce meaningful data added a layer of complexity to these feelings of failure. And yet, in spite of the complexity of these feelings, my research did not fail, nor was I defeated by the research process. Giving myself time to reflect on and interrogate the issues that were compounding these feelings, I came to realize that the relationships that I had built during my time in the field were not time wasted, as I had originally believed, but, with some adjustments in my research methods, could be developed into strategies for success.

The examples from my fieldwork show that most of the problems that I faced revolved around issues with communication. Once I had realized this, I was able to find solutions to my question of how to unlock the joking relationships of the Joola people. For example, when conducting a more formal interview with my notebook and recorder, I had by now learned to anticipate the official version of the Joola story that my interviewee would no doubt deliver. While the information delivered in this more formal interview setting was useful, I found that the most interesting information that I gathered on the Joola culture was delivered more often than not spontaneously during informal talks. For example,

I recorded some of my best and useful data conversing with my fellow travelers while traveling in a public car from one village to another, and again while helping women to prepare a meal peeling onions, grinding condiments, and so on. These situations, when the conversation flowed naturally, appeared to be the most comfortable option for both the participants and the researcher. Furthermore, engaging in or stimulating such a 'natural' conversation required an absolute focus on the research subject, and moreover a strong motivation and readiness to learn more about the field and especially the people.

From these more comfortable interview experiences, I learnt that in order for my research to be more successful, I needed to broaden the range of participants. Thus, I undertook the task of approaching not only those research participants who were recommended by my field assistants because of their high-ranking social position in the community, but also people from other social groups, additionally expanding the participant net to include women and young people. It is uncommon for a young person or woman to agree to talk in a formal way about traditions or culture, just like in many other West-African communities. This information is traditionally associated with elderly men, who are positioned as experts. Once I had made the decision to approach other groups for interviews, I quickly came to understand that informal talks were a useful way of circumventing this tradition. The contribution that these new groups made to my field research was essential, and the knowledge they agreed to share during our conversations was unconventional compared with the so-called experts in the community.

Despite my initial difficulties of communication in Joola, I forced myself to be attentive to everyday situations, which I thought likely to generate information about joking relations. This ready to observe attitude opened the door to further developments in my understanding by learning more about joking relationships between Joola grandparents and grandchildren. It occurred to me to observe some young children making fun of their elderly grandmother. In one instance, two small Joola girls threw their grandmother's walking cane into the household waste and offered to replace it with a 10-cm-long wooden stick; they then observed that the elderly woman did not deserve to eat dinner since she could no longer walk. Observing such a situation helped me to engage in a conversation about these interactions with other family members as well as my village consultants. My interest was to find out why the children were making fun of the grandmother, whether she was angry at them, if she was also making fun of the children and under what conditions. I noted down all interesting situations linked, or which seemed to be linked, to joking relations and based all further investigations on these examples. From this development, I quickly noticed that questions like: 'What kind of joking relationships do you have here in Bandial?' did not receive anything in the way of informative answers. However, if I referred to the example of the interaction between the grandmother and grandchildren that I had witnessed, more explications about the case followed.

My decision to rethink my research strategies and the subsequent data that this produced is a testament to the fact that no matter how well prepared or well trained we are when heading to the field, field-work is an open-ended process. Once I had accepted that, contrary to the more polished representations of fieldwork in the literature, data production could be a frustrating process that often stands still, I was able to try alternative approaches to what I had been taught. Had I simply continued to grind away at interviews with the elder male members of the Joola community accompanied by my field assistants I would, of course, have produced something in the way of data, but using my failure as a way to re-approach the field, not only was I able to discover new things about the joking relations of the Joola that contributed to our understanding of this culture, but failure became a resource that helped strengthen my research. It follows, then, as many anthropologists will attest through their own experience, once defined, all problems thought to be leading to 'failed' fieldwork can most likely be treated—for example, through flexibility (Agyeman 2005), or by taking a different approach to data collection (Olawale 2005). At the very least, as Davis (2011) aptly points out, though fieldwork never guarantees success, it deserves to be done anyway, because at the very least, there is a personal outcome.

CONCLUSION

Overcoming the obstacles associated with ethnographic research can potentially be overwhelming for researchers who are new to the field, but that does not mean that when things do not go according to plan we should feel that our research is failing, as often such issues are unlikely to compromise an entire doctoral research project. I have shown in this chapter that physical access to the field alone does not guarantee the smooth execution of field research. Fieldwork experience, as I quickly learned, involves a multitude of human contact. This can be something of a traumatizing experience when we first set foot in the field (Pollard 2009), especially because we have not yet built networks, we might not speak the local language well, and we have not yet internalized local codes of behavior. Naturally, our fieldwork strategies have to be planned in advance, but research is an open-ended process. This means that we should approach the field as a learning experience and be ready to encounter something new. Here, I am reminded of Davis' (2011, p. 6) encouraging words that 'Where logic, analysis and self-reflection fail, experience, affection, and time come into play. We do find our feet, become more or less accepted and accepting. Communication happens.' While we may have reservations at first or feel anxious about the outcome, it is often the case that a slight strategy adjustment can remedy the problem. With this in mind, giving up seems to be more of an emotional response then a meaningful solution. In my own experience, I found that flexibility is a prerequisite to field site entry. My advice is to last, and, if not, to come back another time and have another go.

NOTES

1. The Casamance conflict broke out in 1980s and is connected with a separatist movement.
2. Interview with D. C., Ziguinchor, 2010.
3. Furthermore, the 'appearance' of Mandinka villages can be easily distinguished from Joola ones. Joola villages seem to be dispersed in the forest, disorganized, spread out over a large surface area, and do not have any center or periphery, whereas Mandinka villages are well-defined, concentrated and well-structured.
4. The relationship between the researcher and the field assistant and the issues that might arise are analyzed in detail by Molony and Hammett (2007).
5. Temple and Edwards (2002) argue that the positioning of the interpreter in qualitative field research (his gender, social, ethnic identity) may determine his role in the interview. They contend that common/different identities (that of the researcher, interpreter and interviewee) are constantly modified and negotiated during the research process.

REFERENCES

Agyeman, D. (2005). Methodological Lessons: Working with Liberian and Togolese Refugees in Ghana. In E. Porter, G. Robinson, M. Smyth, A. Schnabel, & E. Osaghae (Eds.), *Researching Conflict in Africa: Insights and Experiences* (pp. 56–63). Tokyo: United Nations University.

Aspen, H. (1991). A Novice's Field Experience. In M. Zamora & B. Erring (Eds.), *Fieldwork in Cultural Anthropology* (pp. 97–110). New Delhi: Reliance Publishing.

Davis, S. H. (2011). Introduction: Becoming Human. In S. H. Davis & M. Konner (Eds.), *Being There. Learning to Live Cross-Culturally* (pp. 1–7). Cambridge, MA and London: Harvard University Press.

Diédhiou, P. (2013). La gestion du conflit de Casamance: Abdoulaye Wade et la "tradition" joola. In M.-C. Diop (Dir.), *Le Sénégal sous Abdoulaye Wade: Le Sopi à l'épreuve du pouvoir* (pp. 249–265). Dakar and Paris: Cres-Karthala.

Jemielniak, D., & Kostera, M. (2010). Narratives of Irony and Failure in Ethnographic Work. *Canadian Journal of Administrative Sciences/Revue Canadienne des Sciences de l'Administration, 27*(4), 335–347.

Kovats-Bernat, J. C. (2002). Negotiating Dangerous Fields: Pragmatic Strategies for Fieldwork Amid Violence and Terror. *American Anthropologist, 104*(1), 208–222.

McFadyen, J., & Rankin, J. (2016). The Role of Gatekeepers in Research: Learning from Reflexivity and Reflection. *GSTF Journal of Nursing and Health Care, 4*(1), 82–88.

Molony, T., & Hammett, D. (2007). The Friendly Financier: Talking Money with the Silenced Assistant. *Human Organization, 66*(3), 292–300.

Nairn, K., Munro, J., & Smith, A. B. (2005). A Counter-Narrative of a "Failed" Interview. *Qualitative Research, 5*(2), 221–244.

Nilan, P. (2002). "Dangerous Fieldwork" Re-examined: The Question of Researcher Subject Position. *Qualitative Research, 2*(3), 363–386.

Olawale, I. (2005). Applying Social Work Practice to the Study of Ethnic Militias: The Oduduwa People's Congress in Nigeria. In E. Porter, G. Robinson, M. Smyth, A. Schnabel, & E. Osaghae (Eds.), *Researching Conflict in Africa: Insights and Experiences* (pp. 64–89). Tokyo: United Nations University.

Pollard, A. (2009). Field of Screams: Difficulty and Ethnographic Fieldwork. *Anthropology Matters, 11*(2). https://www.anthropologymatters.com/index. php/anth_matters/article/view/10/10. Accessed January 10, 2018.

Radcliffe-Brown, A. R. (1940). On Joking Relationships. *Africa: Journal of the International African Institute, 13*(3), 195–210.

Salamone, F. A. (1991). Friends in the Field. In M. D. Zamora & B. B. Erring (Eds.), *Fieldwork in Cultural Anthropology* (pp. 67–78). New Delhi: Reliance Publishing.

Smith, E. (2006). La nation "par le côté". Le récit des cousinages au Sénégal. *Cahiers d'études africaines, 184,* 907–965.

Suzuki, Y. (2004). Negotiations, Concessions, and Adaptations During Fieldwork in a Tribal Society. *Iranian Studies, 37*(4), 623–632.

Temple, T., & Edwards, R. (2002). Interpreters/Translators and Cross-Language Research: Reflexivity and Border Crossings. *International Journal of Qualitative Methods, 1*(2), 1–12.

Thiongane, O. (2013). *Anthropologie de la méningite au Niger: Espaces épidémiques, mobilisations scientifiques et conceptions de la maladie,* Unpublished Ph.D. thesis, Ecole des Hautes Etudes en Sciences Sociales, pp. 106–139.

Thomson, S. (2009). "That is Not What We Authorised You to Do… ": Access and Government Interference in Highly Politicised Research Environments. In C. Lekha Sriram, J. C. King, J. A. Mertus, O. Martin-Ortega, & J. Herman (Eds.), *Surviving Field Research: Working in Violent and Difficult Situations* (pp. 108–123). London: Routledge.

Thomson, S., Ansoms, A., & Murison, J. (2013). Introduction: Why Stories behind the Findings? In S. Thomson, A. Ansoms, & J. Murison (Eds.), *Emotional and Ethical Challenges for Field Research in Africa: The Story behind the Findings* (pp. 1–11). London: Palgrave Macmillan.

Wanat, C. L. (2008). Getting Past the Gatekeepers: Differences Between Access and Cooperation in Public School Research. *Field Methods, 20*(2), 191–208.

CHAPTER 10

Negotiating Research Access: The Interplay Between Politics and Academia in Contemporary Zimbabwe

Joshua Pritchard

In September 2015, an American associate professor landed in South Africa en route to neighboring Zimbabwe. Eager to begin an eight-week research project that had been in planning for over a year, his expectation was to spend a couple of days in Cape Town and Pretoria, before continuing up to Harare and the National Archives of Zimbabwe (NAZ) for the bulk of his fieldwork. The South African stage proceeded without a hitch: 'the National Archives in Arcadia (Pretoria) have been unthinkably open to me,' the academic wrote in an email on 26 September 2015. Zimbabwe, however, was already proving to be a more complicated fieldwork location. Over the previous year, the academic had amassed the plethora of necessary documentation that was required by the Zimbabwean government. The single most important item at his disposal was a research permit from the Research Council of Zimbabwe (RCZ), a result of months of emails, phone calls, incalculable form filling, networking, and expensive fees.

J. Pritchard (✉)
University of Cambridge, Cambridge, UK

© The Author(s) 2019
L. Johnstone (ed.), *The Politics of Conducting Research in Africa*,
https://doi.org/10.1007/978-3-319-95531-5_10

A few days before his flight to Harare, the academic was suddenly informed that his institution of affiliation—the University of Zimbabwe (UZ)—had 'declined to host' him. When he urgently enquired why, the response from colleagues in Zimbabwe was an unusual one. As the professor explained in an email on 26 September 2015:

> Unfortunately, your insight about [University of Zimbabwe] closing off affiliations in the last year or two was spot-on correct. There is now a Vice-Chancellor who is rejecting research permits without comment, but whose private statements to angry heads of department indicate that it is because they are from countries "unfriendly to Zimbabwe." [...] My UZ colleagues are mortified by this eleven-month odyssey, but my application is at least still breathing so I remain hopeful.

For many academics who work on Zimbabwe, the frustrations encountered by this professor are depressingly familiar. A research proposal can stumble at any number of hurdles. From securing institutional affiliation and gaining the support of influential Zimbabweans, to negotiating a cumbersome and heavily politicized bureaucratic system, the process of gaining access is costly in terms of finances, effort, and time. It is also a highly individualized experience: while one foreign researcher may find themselves welcomed with open arms in a matter of weeks, another may strive for months or years only to unexpectedly discover their efforts have been in vain. To complicate matters further, applicants are reliant almost entirely on the advice and assistance provided by others to guide them through the process. Thus, there is an overwhelming reliance on the support of the host institution in Zimbabwe to point potential researchers in the right direction and walk them through the required procedures. Yet many of these institutions and their staff are equally as overextended and underfunded as the national research council.

The difficulties that this presents for a foreign researcher, particularly one unfamiliar with the realities of conducting fieldwork in the nation, were summarized most clearly by the African Studies Association (ASA) of the USA in 2012. In a short online piece entitled *Getting Research Permission*, several anonymous academics shared their thoughts and experiences about undertaking fieldwork in Tanzania, Zambia, Rwanda, Zimbabwe, South Africa, and Malawi (see ASA 2012). The most significant point made within the article was the differences between the official processes of obtaining research clearance and the practical, pragmatic considerations that frequently had to be utilized. Most academics noted that the process in their subject nation was simply long and arduous but not especially difficult. One question asked: 'On a scale of 1–10, with 1 being very simple and 10 being very difficult, how easy or difficult was it to get permission to conduct research in the country?' Tanzania received an 8, Rwanda 8.5, Malawi 9, and finally Zimbabwe a 10. Such observations reaffirmed the notion that whatever the specific considerations, gaining research access to these nations was regarded as a genuinely difficult process, and therefore, discussions about these realities are invaluable to all potential researchers.

The foundation of this chapter is to recount the trials and tribulations encountered in pursuit of a research permit in Zimbabwe. These accounts are based primarily on my own experiences and interactions with assorted Zimbabwean institutions during a year-long application process. As a doctoral candidate working on the themes of race and nonracial cooperation during Zimbabwe's liberation struggle, my experiences during application were not atypical, but they were complicated by both my subject matter and personal circumstances. Therefore, to compliment these specific conditions, I have also included assorted interjections from academics with different circumstances but who all faced obstacles in their pursuit of research clearance. Drawing upon these experiences provides a range of examples of the anticipated—and the unforeseen—issues that can arise in securing permission to conduct research in Zimbabwe. By assessing these challenges and discussing how best a researcher can negotiate access despite these restrictions, this chapter also argues the necessity of 'playing the system.' Through a combination of an inoffensive research proposal and an appealing image of the researcher themselves, a large number of these challenges can be easily overcome or simply mitigated. The incalculable benefit that comes from generating a network of local support or contacts is also discussed.

Based upon these foundations, the chapter is subsequently broken down into three parts. First, I briefly discuss the requirements for obtaining a research permit in Zimbabwe as per the official governmental guidelines. In this initial section, I focus on the necessity of institutional affiliation and the accompanying challenges this generates from the formative planning stages for fieldwork through to actually approaching relevant organizations. I also address the important issues of networking and make suggestions as to how best create and utilize the contacts necessary for submitting an application in the first place. Part two considers the official requirements outlined in section one but situates them in the context of a heavily politicized environment, as in Zimbabwe. The interference of politics in academia takes center stage within this section. Indeed, it is the interplay (and conflict) between the ruling ZANU-PF party and the workings of the RCZ and other academic institutions that dictate the nature of negotiating access in the first instance. The third and final part of this chapter discusses how best to tackle factors that are largely outside of a researcher's control. Frequently, it may be the case that even if a researcher meets all the official requirements laid out for research clearance, other elements may still act as an obstruction to them being permitted to actually begin their project. Thus, there is a necessity to consider other research options, as well as other ways of securing a research permit. Whether the use of a research assistant or the support of political sponsors, some suggestions are made as to why alternative or complimentary research methods may be necessary.

Existing literature on field research in Africa has dealt extensively with the challenges faced once in the field but typically pays little attention to the issues that can arise well before the researcher sets foot on the continent. This is evident in the edited volume by Thomson et al. (2013) on the emotional and ethical challenges encountered by researchers in Africa. Throughout the various essays included in the volume, and although the potential problems of access once conducting fieldwork are discussed, the preliminary stages of the research clearance process are almost entirely ignored. Negotiating access is described in terms of something that occurs once in the nation, rather than something that is necessary as a prerequisite (see Ogora 2013). One article by Thomson on research in Rwanda, for instance, discusses how the experience of applying for the necessary research clearance proved beneficial during fieldwork but fails to properly engage with the machinations that were involved in the application procedure itself (Thomson 2013). This absence has been partly redressed by a collection of short working papers edited and published by Engel, Gebauer, and Hüncke in 2015. Covering a range of research applications across the African continent, the brief papers engage with topics from bureaucratic delays to financial considerations present within the procedures. Yet there is still an overwhelming focus on the processes of applying once already in the nation of research, as evidenced in the paper by Schräpel on Rwanda's politicized research environment (see Schräpel 2015). The lack of discussion about the preliminary stages of an application for research clearance weakens the overall picture presented, much to the detriment of otherwise excellent studies which appear to start their accounts already halfway through the story. Consequently, this chapter seeks to redress this absence through a focused look at the entire process of application, from initial planning to on-the-ground efforts. Although the specifics of this chapter discuss Zimbabwe, many of the issues raised are familiar to academics undertaking fieldwork the world over. As Engel has explained, the issue of research access is 'not at all an Africa-typical topic' (Engel 2015, p. 2). Research permits, and the restrictions imposed by research councils vary greatly, even within Africa, and more apt comparisons may be made with nations elsewhere than on the African continent or even in the global south. Thus, the examples within this chapter have common lessons that can be applied to a much broader range of studies and hopefully will be viewed in light of the underlying points rather than the specifics of the Zimbabwean case study.

Following the Rules: Institutional Affiliation

At first glance, the procedure for gaining official permission to conduct research in Zimbabwe seems fairly straightforward. The primary requirement is to obtain a research permit from the RCZ. They define a foreign researcher as 'a non-Zimbabwean national and any person wishing to conduct research in Zimbabwe on behalf of a foreign institution, foreign organization or other foreign person' (RCZ 2017). This broad definition includes not only those seeking to delve into archives but also researchers wishing to conduct any type of interviews or surveys, medical tests, sociological studies, scientific experiments, market research, or any form of investigation that requires access to the Zimbabwe's resources or people.

The criteria which must be met in order to submit an application in the first place are also clearly laid out. An applicant needs to provide evidence of adequate funds, the proposed use of findings, and a detailed explanation of what is being researched. Alongside these, thirteen copies of the application form have to be submitted along with a nonrefundable US$500 fee. None of these requirements are particularly surprising or even unique to Zimbabwe, although a few are somewhat unorthodox. However, the most crucial requirement is also the most frequent stumbling block; a necessity to 'seek an institution of affiliation in the area of the intended research in Zimbabwe' (RCZ 2017).

The reasoning behind such a policy is to reduce the risk of exploitative interactions between researchers and the host nation. In the words of one Zimbabwean academic, the RCZ insists on 'mutual concrete benefit from the research' for Zimbabwe and the researcher.[1] The definition of mutual benefit was expanded further in a meeting with another Zimbabwean academic in December 2014, who explained to me that the relationship is designed to ensure that (a) the researcher will contribute to Zimbabwean academia and the development of students and knowledge within the nation; (b) be under the 'supervision' of a Zimbabwean institution for the duration of their research; and (c) provide a financial contribution to a Zimbabwean institution (as most institutions have a 'fees structure' for research associates). These points are reiterated in the *Directory of Institutions of Affiliation*, first published by the RCZ in 2015 and revised in March 2016.

Until relatively recently, securing institutional affiliation remained only somewhat complicated. The long list of approved institutions included nongovernmental organizations and academic and non-academic trusts, as long as these groups were based in Zimbabwe and authorized by the Zimbabwean state. Affiliation also often meant nothing more than agreeing a status with the host. However, a revision of approved institutions in 2013 narrowed the list considerably. It is now only possible to gain affiliation from a government research station, a government ministry or department, or a Zimbabwean university. Nevertheless, despite this narrowing, these restrictions do not seem too severe. Some forty institutions are listed in the latest RCZ-published directory including most major government ministries and a number of other authorities ranging from the Forestry Commission to the National AIDS Council (RCZ 2017).

The problems begin to arise, however, when the search for an amenable institution takes place. The first port of call for most academics is typically one of Zimbabwe's three largest universities: the University of Zimbabwe (UZ) in the capital city of Harare; the Catholic University of Zimbabwe (CU), also in Harare; or Midlands State University (MSU), located about three hours drive from the capital in Gweru. The most promising option is commonly that of UZ. This is because it is the largest of the three, has the broadest range of faculties that could accommodate a foreign researcher, and is conveniently located near to the National Archives and the other resources of the capital city.

When I began the process of seeking institutional affiliation in late 2014, it was to the UZ that I made my first tentative enquiries. As a historian working on Zimbabwean history, the list of prominent historians who were faculty members within the History and Economic History departments made these faculties an incredibly appealing route to pursue. Already established networks through mutual contacts and encounters at conferences meant that testing the waters was less of a challenge than it would have otherwise been. When Zimbabwean academics visited the UK, I made their acquaintance and spoke to them face to face, thus, ensuring that any prospective or in progress applications could be chased up more efficiently than if we had been limited only to remote channels of communication, like email. This personalization of finding a host institution is an incredibly important factor to consider when assessing which Zimbabwean body would offer the likeliest route to affiliation.

There is, however, something of a Catch-22 at play in utilizing such networks. Potential researchers are advised on the RCZ website that the application for research clearance 'must be made and approved before arrival in Zimbabwe.' In the midst of one British academic's application, she noted with trepidation that despite her desire to visit her potential hosts in person in order to speed up the process, 'they are very clear that if you come to Zimbabwe before clearance is received, it will be denied.'[2] Another American academic lamented that during 'the whole process, from initial feelers to the cusp of approval or denial [...] I have been entirely dependent on my friends at UZ to factor everything.'[3] This presents an issue with the very depersonalization that makes institutional affiliation hard to come by in the first place. A potential host is more likely to dismiss an application—or expand less effort—for a faceless, anonymous foreign researcher than they are from somebody they know personally. As one Zimbabwean lecturer noted in an email to me on 21 December 2015, it is crucial to get your hosts 'interested enough to run around with the papers,' and the best way to do that is to 'talk to these people in person and perhaps collect all the papers that need to be filled yourself and leave them in the paper trail for someone to follow up.'[4] Yet when I discussed the possibility of following this advice with a more experienced American lecturer, the emailed reply was one of caution:

> As far as pushing through a research permit in person, you would be braver than I--it was made very clear to me by a few different people that doing so would disqualify me immediately, the more so because of ZANU ideologues who are eager for a reason to make a political stand and look good at home.[5]

This fear of antagonizing political figures is discussed later in the chapter, but the contradictory advice about how best to proceed with a research permit application is telling of the confusion that surrounds the entire procedure.

While negotiations were ongoing with UZ, I also made approaches to both CU and MSU as a means of providing insurance from an early stage. In December 2014, an academic at CU who had been making enquiries on my behalf indicated that the university was not in a position to provide affiliation for non-Zimbabwean researchers, except as members of the faculty of humanities. As doctoral students were not able to apply for faculty jobs, CU was, thus, rendered impractical despite their interest in a collaborative research project. This restriction was surprising considering the advice received from a colleague who had been hosted by the university only two years earlier. Moreover, it was not immediately apparent, even to the faculty member making the enquiries that such a distinction between doctoral and postdoctoral foreign researchers existed. Nevertheless, it was an early indication that certain opportunities may be open to some foreign researchers but not others and reiterated the advantages of not relying on second-hand information.

While CU policies appeared to close the door on affiliation, MSU appeared to be more amiable, particularly due to the overlap between my research project and the work of a senior lecturer in the history faculty, Gerald Mazirire. Following a chance encounter in June 2015, Mazirire began to petition the university for my becoming a Research Associate for the duration of my fieldwork. As is somewhat typical in these bureaucratic systems, updates were a long time in coming. By September, there had been little progress, allegedly due to the university's lack of a concrete policy on research associate status. As Mazirire recounted in an email on 29 September 2015, 'the MSU is still talking of a buy-into the whole Research Associate concept given the excessive paperwork involved and its previous experiences.'

The legacies of these 'previous experiences' would prove to be something of a major obstacle for researchers attempting to get affiliation with MSU post-2013, and provide another crucial example of how important it is to prepare and plan a fieldwork trip well in advance. During my own application, it emerged that prior to 2014, MSU had accommodated two foreign researchers as research associates with the expectation that they would conduct their fieldwork and simultaneously contribute to the university through teaching, collaborative research, and a simple presence on campus (mainly attendance at seminars, and providing discussions and networking opportunities for Zimbabwean students). Such goals were exactly what institutional affiliation policies were designed to encourage. As a result, MSU's Vice-Chancellor and the Registrar of Human Resources were incredibly keen on the concept and even footed the costs of processing the paperwork and other overheads incurred by the presence of the foreign research associates. Many members of staff similarly hoped that the presence of the foreign researchers and the connections they brought would provide tangible benefits to the relatively young MSU and its students, and were keen to provide their support to the fledgling project.

Unfortunately for all involved, the experience was not a positive one. Both of the research associates simply conducted their Harare-based research projects before departing the country without ever actually carrying out any of the other duties that had been agreed as part of the affiliation agreement. Moreover, as they had failed to fulfill their agreed obligations to MSU, they had left the university out of pocket and frustrated by what the Vice-Chancellor regarded as a breach of the conditions of their affiliation there. As Mazirire noted in an email on 6 November 2015, the actions of these researchers indicated that 'at the present moment MSU does not have an enabling instrument governing terms of reference and obligations of the research associates that would make it worth [the MSU's] while to host any.'

The result of this behavior was an increasing wariness by the MSU of foreign researchers simply using the university as their required host institution and subsequently failing to contribute to the university in any real way. The 300-kilometer distance between MSU and Harare was also raised as a reason why any future research associates would have to prove their research project was to be conducted in the area around MSU, rather than solely in the National Archives in the capital. The vice-chancellor felt particularly affronted by the negative actions of the previous research associates. As the last word on the accommodation of foreign researchers rested with him, getting approval became increasingly difficult. In the aftermath of a meeting held in November 2015, a commission was established to ensure that MSU would 'find value in the presence' of any foreign researchers affiliated with the university. As foreign researcher affiliation required a lot of paperwork, time, and money to organize, the decision was also made to implement a mandatory annual fee for future research associates that would press home the necessity of earning their affiliation with the university. Long term it seemed likely that MSU would begin to take foreign researchers again, but the result, regrettably, was that it would not be able to accommodate any for the immediate future.

With my application at UZ still ongoing, Mazirire and other colleagues recommended that contact be made with two non-university institutions that would still fulfill the requirements set by the RCZ: the Southern African Political Economic Series trust (SAPES) and the Zimbabwe Peace Center—two groups that conduct research within Zimbabwe and are run by Zimbabweans. Both are much smaller than a university, even a relatively young university like MSU, and there are benefits and disadvantages to affiliation with such organizations. One advantage is that affiliation is often provided on the basis of a collaborative research project or assistance with ongoing work rather than on a teaching basis. This gives the researcher more time to conduct fieldwork without having to worry about lesson plans and course materials. An organization inherently focused on a small subject rather than the broad scope of a university or government ministry also provides a potentially better working environment for a researcher. Somebody conducting research into the effects of HIV/AIDs on local communities would be better placed being hosted by the National Aids Council than they would be at UZ. The downside, however, to small organizations is that affiliation is likely more difficult to obtain in the first place. In email correspondence with Dr. Ibbo Mandaza in November and December 2015, he humorously indicated that the biggest issue with SAPES providing affiliation was unfamiliarity with the necessary paperwork they, as the hosting institution, would have to submit to satisfy the RCZ. Approaching a range of different host organizations is, therefore, beneficial as, although some may prove untenable options, a broad approach reduces the risk of encountering the same issues with all.

Nevertheless, as can be seen by the examples above, institutional affiliation is not only the most important part of applying for a research permit for many foreign researchers but also the most time and labor intensive. A researcher may be rejected for any number of reasons, not least a simple lack of ability to host them. The situation worsens when one considers that these decisions are not being made in a vacuum. Even if an academic institution is willing to act as the host for a foreign researcher, there is often a broader, heavily politicized environment to consider. Nowhere is this more apparent than in the University of Zimbabwe.

THE POLITICIZATION OF ACADEMIA

Zimbabwe is a heavily politicized nation. State and party politics—and often the two are one and the same—have a significant influence on almost all aspects of life within the country. Academia has not been spared such interference. Due to what has been termed the 'Third Chimurenga,' meaning the third stage of the liberation struggle, there has been a rewriting of the 'official' Zimbabwean historical narrative in order to favor the ruling ZANU-PF party's political position since the mid-1990s (Ranger 2004; Tendi 2010). Tied in with contemporary issues such as the Fast Track Land Reform Program, the rise and fall of a coherent opposition party (the Movement for Democratic Change), and the collapse of Zimbabwe's economy, the Third Chimurenga saw an attempt to buttress former President Robert Mugabe and ZANU-PF's claims on the nation.

The result is that even supposedly nonpolitical entities like universities or research bodies are well aware of the political environment in which they operate. When approached for guidance, several academics with experience of fieldwork in Zimbabwe all provided the same advice: pursue any opportunities which will give you the best chance of gaining a research permit. Some opportunities are dependent upon the nature of the research proposed. If the project's topic is either benign or unlikely to damage ZANU-PF's dominant narratives, a potential researcher can approach the application entirely in keeping with the guidelines and trust in the system to provide them with a permit. One academic who followed this route elaborated:

> My approach was [...] engaging with the normal machinery and being simply honest about what I do and how I do it--I gather they like my prior work and of course the NGO crowd are supportive--so if and when the permit comes, the doors will swing wide open. Because I will already need to try and bend rules once I am in the Archives, I will need to have all of my papers in order up to that point.[6]

The benefits of following the rules precisely are apparent. It reduces the risks of disqualification, it provides a multitude of chances for local Zimbabweans to charge fees and generate an income in a difficult economic environment, and it ensures that there can be no claims after the fact that any research was carried out illicitly. The downside is that it opens up the applicant to having their application denied for even moderately disagreeable research topics due to the absolute transparency required.

For those whose research is potentially more objectionable, there is a second approach. As an anonymous academic explained in 2012, 'framing is crucial' (ASA 2012). By considering the research proposal in light of contemporary politics in the host nation, it is possible to recontextualize the research in a way that makes it less likely to attract the wrath of ZANU-PF supporters. The most efficient way to do so is to highlight how the quality of the research, regardless of the subject matter, could potentially prove useful for ZANU-PF. One research project on white farmers in Zimbabwe was so well researched and written that the author was able to conduct interviews with senior ZANU-PF figures, despite the contentious nature of the subject (Pilossof 2012).

Why such revisions are necessary is evident in the numerous examples of the political paradigm interfering with the proposed research projects in Zimbabwe. The academic behind a comparative study looking at police brutality under the colonial white settler government and the postindependence African government was told in blunt terms that he would not be granted a permit if he intended to look at police records produced in the years after independence in 1980.[7] Another academic working on farm-workers was 'stripped of their clearance and declared *persona non grata*' because they were interviewing workers who still worked for white commercial farmers (ASA 2012). Even the first draft of my own RCZ research proposal on race in Zimbabwe's liberation struggle, penned back in 2014, was returned by my supervisor with suggestions that I highlight the beneficial nature of work focusing on the history of nonracialism. By doing so, it was hoped that it would reduce any possible opposition from political figures by diminishing its potential usage in contemporary racial discourse or criticisms of ZANU-PF. The revised proposal consequently focused more on the positive elements of the African nationalists' usage of race during the liberation struggle. Furthermore, it omitted all references to surveying documents belonging to the white settler state, as ZANU-PF is somewhat nervous about granting access to those archives. As one academic noted in 2012, 'any work related to politics or to the land reform process is suspect and probably very difficult to pursue' (ASA 2012). Yet that does not necessarily mean such documents cannot be examined: one particularly experienced colleague pointed out in an email in September 2015 that there is always the possibility of 'bending the rules once in the archives' and accessing documents not included in the original proposal.[8] The trick is getting into the archives in the first place.

Political pandering is a necessity in other aspects of the application, even after the proposal itself has appeased the restrictive agendas. Because the application to the RCZ is submitted by the host institution and not by the individual, it is the institution itself that acts in a gate-keeping role. It consequently finds itself under pressure to adhere to politically imposed conditions regarding whom it accepts as affiliated individuals and why. Nowhere has this been more apparent than at the University of Zimbabwe. From the outset of my own attempts to secure affiliation, it was repeatedly emphasized that UZ's close connections to Mugabe (as the university's Chancellor) and ZANU-PF would present problems. This was reflected by the stringent qualifications applied to any foreign researcher approaching the UZ to host them. This included not only the research proposal but also the identity of the researcher themselves. As a lecturer at UZ informed me, 'they want clear evidence of how the university, the department you will be affiliated to and Zimbabwe at large will benefit from you and your research being conducted in our country.'[9] The implication is clear. 'Zimbabwe' in this context refers to the government more than the people itself and any work that could be potentially damaging to the Mugabe regime is therefore painted as anti-Zimbabwean and undesirable. An acquaintance who had spent several years working in Zimbabwe in the late 2000s explained that there is a 'deliberate policy to discourage foreign researchers' if their subject matter has any possible controversy.[10]

The issues generated by these policies are easily seen. Unlike the MSU where willingness to have foreign research associates has been tempered by considerations of practicality, the UZ has gained a reputation for rejecting foreign researchers outright. Since 2013, and against the wishes of numerous faculty members and department heads, the UZ's Vice-Chancellor has allegedly rejected a number of foreign researcher's affiliation applications for undisclosed reasons. A UZ faculty member bitterly noted in an email to me on 3 March 2015 that 'we recently tried two applications with some of the best justifications you can possibly think of but in vain. The higher offices simply rejected the applications and the worst part is that they did not give any reasons for rejection.'

After consulting with other colleagues at the university, convincing evidence of this political interference became clear. One academic whose search for UZ affiliation began in late 2014 reported to me nine months later: 'I'm still waiting on the Vice Chancellor at UZ: every other level, from top to bottom, has indicated support. Here's hoping. They did make me jump through a lot of extra hoops, some of which seemed calculated just to flex their muscles and make demands.'[11] Another noted that she had to be incredibly careful about the language used in describing her work, 'the more so because of ZANU ideologues who are eager for a reason to make a political stand and look good at home.'[12] The American professor mentioned at the beginning of this chapter related in more detail the demanding circumstances that had accompanied their application to the UZ in an email on 22 July 2015:

> The point about UZ being cagey about research affiliation is really spot on. Did I mention that they spent several months trying to decide whether I was a likely CIA agent? If I were, I'd have the very best cover ever, because nobody here would believe it. Even passing that muster, and with apparently the support of each of the two UZ departments I will affiliate with [...] and the national Research Council, the University's Chancellors are demanding all sorts of things. I had to scan my physical degrees, write several letters, get affidavits of financial support from my grant agency and my bank, and whatnot.

This same professor was the one who discovered that against the wishes of the sponsors, his position at the UZ had been rescinded only days before he was due to begin his research. He discovered the Vice-Chancellor had 'declined to host' him due to his nationality and nothing more. The unofficial explanation provided was that he was from a country 'unfriendly to Zimbabwe' with little further elaboration. Such a clear reference to a confrontational nationalism is not surprising, but it is alarming. Applying to the UZ as a British citizen with historical family connections in Zimbabwe and South Africa, my own application was always going to be faced with similar challenges. As one Zimbabwean sponsor within the faculty acknowledged at the receipt of my proposal, 'I fear we are going to be fighting a lost battle.'[13]

Unsurprisingly, the decision was made that UZ could not host me. No official statement was given indicating why. My supporting figures at UZ appealed through nonformal channels and asked for clarification on my behalf, but this was a long and tiresome procedure. As academics around the world know, it is often difficult to communicate with large organizations and especially the decision-makers themselves, so I was willing to let these enquiries be made by others on my behalf. Furthermore, as I wrote to a colleague on 12 December 2015, 'my situation is not important enough for national ZANU people to expend favors dealing with it even though they are privately sympathetic and supportive.' The potential career risks that came with challenging prominent ZANU-PF supporting senior figures within the university were not viewed as worthwhile, particularly given my status as a lowly doctoral student, and a white British one with connections to colonial Zimbabwe at that.

Nevertheless, several weeks later my Zimbabwean sponsors received an answer explaining the UZ's position. The university's higher echelons seemingly did not want to associate with a British researcher whose topic, however, innocuous it may seem within the academic community, was in breach of the UZ's stated goals of 'strengthening Zimbabwe's social and economic fabric' (UZ 2016). My focus on race—regardless of context—would apparently undermine the nonracial society ZANU-PF had built since independence in 1980. All of this of course is purely *realpolitik* and is familiar to many working in nations with a troubled recent history, but it was nevertheless surprising to hear, particularly as it was accompanied by the message that being British was itself a sign of suspect intentions. Zimbabwe's turbulent relationship with its former colonial occupier and her allies has remained divisive within Zimbabwean society for a number of years and had been exacerbated during the land reform program of the early 2000s (Blair 2002). For many ZANU-PF figures, any actions they could take against the former colonial oppressors were seen as significant acts in the Third Chimurenga of Zimbabwe's liberation struggle. Moreover, appeals to the RCZ were futile. As one experienced Australian diplomat in Zimbabwe explained to me during an interview in December 2015, 'the Research Council can't pressure the Vice Chancellor. In fact it is the UZ's council which dictates policy.'

PRAGMATISM AND SOLUTIONS

In light of such obstructions, it is apparent that although an applicant can be thoroughly prepared, well informed, working on a benign subject, and willing to abide by the imposed rulebook, there are still other factors that can entirely derail the pursuit of a foreign researcher's permit. The decision must then be made by the researcher as to how best to proceed. There is no overarching answer, but there is one important, universal pointer: local support.

By the time I realized that the UZ would not be hosting me, I had begun a lengthy and related research project in neighboring South Africa. Acting on the advice of colleagues in Zimbabwe and elsewhere, the decision was made to enter Zimbabwe on a tourist visa and attempt to push through the permit in person, despite the clear warnings not to do so by the RCZ. Yet, as I was not specifically in the nation to conduct research and I was acting with the support of senior Zimbabwean academics, my supervisor agreed it was an acceptable step to take.

The first aim was to secure another host institution. To do so, it was suggested that I utilize contacts, call in favors, and gain support from as many people with potential political sway as possible whilst in the country. Through various family and academic connections, I met with and got the support of several politicians including two MPs, a former cabinet minister, and the Co-Minister of State for National Healing, Reconciliation, and Integration. The former Australian Ambassador to Zimbabwe and a senior figure in Zimbabwe Tobacco provided further support in the form of networking and contacts. Finally, the assistance of a number of private citizens with strong political ties proved invaluable. Judith Todd, daughter of a former Prime Minister, championed my cause on a number of occasions and introduced me to other prominent figures, as did the academics who had supported my initial applications.

Such local assistance was invaluable. Not only were these individuals willing and able to provide signatures and statements of support if needed, but also to introduce me to other contacts who would otherwise have remained closed to me. Being in Zimbabwe also made it easier to leave behind a physical paper trail with documents in people's hands and in their offices, rather than simply in their email inboxes. This approach is undoubtedly effective in an increasingly digital world. I cannot recommend enough the potential that comes with being able to shake someone's hand and allow them to put a face to an otherwise anonymous application. It also permits an opportunity to further a professional relationship through discussions and meetings.

Despite all this, as the days passed and it seemed increasingly unlikely that another institution would be able to make the necessary arrangements and complete the necessary paperwork in time, I decided with my supervisor's and my university faculty's permission to carry out at least some of my research in Zimbabwe. For most municipal and private archives, including trade unions and city libraries, the possession of a British university identity card, combined with letters of support from

Zimbabwean and international academics and an explanation of my situation, was enough to grant me a few hours or days in their collections. It seemed many were unaware of the restrictions that they were supposed to abide by or perhaps were simply more willing to bend the rules for specific cases away from official eyes. It was also possible to carry out informal, casual interviews with a wide range of targeted respondents without attracting attention, largely due to the networking mission I was already engaged with across the country. Obviously, such research is much harder to undertake in certain disciplines than others. The necessity of ethical reviews for medical studies, or the access to large-scale survey date for sociological studies, requires a greater level of cooperation with government bodies and regulations. However, that does not mean that all researchers are unable to conduct small-scale research projects without acquiring a research permit. There is a three-day period of research covered by a standard tourist visa, but this can be extended by classifying the trip as a preliminary visit without genuine research being carried out. Combined with the ability to combine informal interviews with simple networking opportunities, a small-scale research project becomes entirely feasible, albeit not ideal.

The National Archives of Zimbabwe, for instance, remains out of bounds to those without a permit. Even with a tourist visa and the supposed three day window permitted, a number of academics have found themselves denied entry without an official research permit. One explanation given by an American academic who encountered just such a response was that the archivists are being cautious not to attract the dissatisfaction of political figures within the UZ or other institutions by granting archive entry to people they have declared *persona non grata*. Whatever the reason, a valid alternative for those unable to gain access is to use local academics or students as hired temporary research assistants. After the rejection of my affiliation at UZ, a faculty member suggested doing just that, writing:

Your best chance would be to come this side and get a research assistant. You are allowed to get into the National Archives for only three days and these you can use to compile list of references that can help you. We will then get a research assistant to do the data collection.[14]

Another American academic whose application had by the point of their email in 2017 been on-going for over four years had similarly resigned themselves to hiring local research assistants and, thus, by-passing the restrictions on foreign researchers. As they noted to me, a research assistant 'may be my only way in, and colleagues with US as well as Zimbabwean bank accounts may be my only vehicle for paying them.'[15] The economic situation in Zimbabwe has made employment much valued and students, as all over the world, are welcoming of chances to earn hard currency, particularly American dollars. That they can practice research skills and gain valuable networking opportunities at the same time further benefits them beyond simple financial recompense.

CONCLUSION

It is incredibly difficult to produce any work based on Africa without conducting research in the field. Restrictions on access can unnecessarily prohibit some excellent projects from seeing the light of day. However, as this chapter demonstrates, a failure to get research clearance does not mean that project cannot be carried out or that a researcher has permanently been denied access. The politicized nature of some research topics has an impact on the way in which access to a state's resources have to be negotiated, and it is, therefore, necessary to employ various tactics to secure such access. Obstacles outside of an individual's control (such as nationality) can further obstruct efforts to secure access, and the ways in which these can be overcome are discussed, particularly through local support, personal interactions, and persistence. Although the Zimbabwean case study may not be applicable to all, the fundamental issue of negotiating access remains constant in any nation where archives and people reside behind a permit requirement and the lessons learnt share common traits throughout the world. When research focuses on politically sensitive subjects—such as contentious periods or themes in history, or issues like land reform or criticism of the ruling political party—restrictions on academic freedoms can arise far beyond those imposed through 'official' conditions. This closing off of resources or research subjects has an impact not only on the fieldwork actually undertaken, but on the project as a whole as many academic enterprises are designed and planned with specific sources in mind. Consequently, drastic alterations to the entire study are required to compensate for the inaccessibility of the original research materials, the knock-on effects of which can impact travel plans, funding, and numerous other details. Some of these restrictions may be mitigated through careful planning and preparation, but others remain largely unyielding and out of the researcher's control. The considerations a potential researcher must be aware of, the preparations they must undertake, and the networks they must build in order to maximize their chances and produce the best research possible are, therefore, significant and universal factors in relation to the issues of access.

NOTES

1. KU, Email correspondence with the author, November 17, 2014.
2. SA, Email correspondence with the author, March 19, 2016.
3. LB, Email correspondence with the author, July 21, 2015.
4. KU, Email correspondence with the author, November 17, 2014.
5. LB, Email correspondence with the author, September 14, 2015.
6. LB, Email correspondence with the author, September 26, 2015.
7. RP, Personal conversation with the author, September 6, 2017.
8. LB, Email correspondence with the author, September 26, 2015.
9. KU, Email correspondence with the author, November 17, 2014.
10. PF, Personal conversation with the author, November 18, 2015 [Cape Town].
11. JA, Email correspondence with the author, January 1, 2015.
12. SB, Personal conversation with the author, March 18, 2016.
13. KU, Email correspondence with the author, March 3, 2015.
14. KU, Email correspondence with the author, April 7, 2015.
15. LB, Email correspondence with the author, October 13, 2017.

REFERENCES

African Studies Association US. (2012). *African Studies Association News Online 29 May 2012: Getting Research Permission.* http://www.asanewsonline. com/2012/05/29/getting-researchpermission. Accessed October 21, 2017.

Blair, D. (2002). *Degrees in Violence: Robert Mugabe and the Struggle for Power in Zimbabwe.* London: Continuum.

Engel, U. (2015). Introduction. In U. Engel, C. Gebauer, & A. Hüncke (Eds.), *Notes from Within and Without—Research Permits Between Requirements and "Realities"* (Working Papers Series 16). Leipzig and Halle: German Research Foundation.

Ogora, L. O. (2013). The Contested Fruits of Research in War-Torn Countries: My Insider Experience in Northern Uganda. In S. Thomson, A. Ansoms, & J. Murison (Eds.), *Emotional and Ethical Challenges for Field Research in Africa: The Story Behind the Findings* (pp. 27–41). Basingstoke: Palgrave Macmillan.

Pilossof, R. (2012). *The Unbearable Whiteness of Being: Farmers' Voices from Zimbabwe*. Harare: Weaver Press.

Ranger, T. (2004). Nationalist Historiography, Patriotic History, and the History of the Nation: The Struggle over the Past in Zimbabwe. *Journal of Southern African Studies, 30*(2), 215–234.

Research Council of Zimbabwe. (2017). *Research Registration*. http://www.rcz. ac.zw/research-registration. Accessed October 21, 2017.

Schräpel, N. (2015). Getting the Papers Right—Some Reflections on the Politics of Research Permits in Rwanda. In U. Engel, C. Gebauer, & A. Hüncke (Eds.), *Notes from Within and Without—Research Permits Between Requirements and "Realities"* (Working Papers Series 16). Leipzig and Halle: German Research Foundation.

Tendi, B. M. (2010). *Making History in Mugabe's Zimbabwe: Politics, Intellectuals, and the Media*. Oxford: Peter Lang.

Thomson, S. (2013). Academic Integrity and Ethical Responsibilities in Post-Genocide Rwanda: Working with Research Ethics Boards to Prepare for Fieldwork with 'Human Subjects'. In S. Thomson, A. Ansoms, & J. Murison (Eds.), *Emotional and Ethical Challenges for Field Research in Africa: The Story Behind the Findings* (pp. 139–155). Basingstoke: Palgrave Macmillan.

Thomson, S., Ansoms, A., & Murison, J. (Eds.). (2013). *Emotional and Ethical Challenges for Field Research in Africa: The Story Behind the Findings*. Basingstoke: Palgrave Macmillan.

University of Zimbabwe. (2016). *Mission Statement*. http://www.uz.ac.zw//index.php/about-uz/uofz-overview/our-mission. Accessed October 15, 2016.

BIBLIOGRAPHY

Abrahams-Gessel, S., Denman, C. A., Montano, C. M., Gaziano, T. A., Levitt, N., Rivera-Andrade, A., Munguia Carrrasco, D., Zulu, J., Akter Khanam, M., & Puoane, T. (2015). The Training and Field Work Experiences of Community Health Workers Conducting Non-invasive, Population-based Screening for Cardiovascular Disease in Four Communities in Low and Middle-Income Settings. *Global Heart, 10*(1), 45–54. http://doi.org/10.1016/j.gheart.2014.12.008.

Abu-Lughod, J. L. (1988). Fieldwork of a Dutiful Daughter. In C. Altorki & C. F. El-Solh (Eds.), *Arab Women in the Field: Studying Your Own Society* (pp. 139–161). New York: Syracuse University Press.

Acker, S. (2001). In/Out/Side: Positioning the Researcher in Feminist Qualitative Research (1). *Resources for Feminist Research, 28*(1/2), 189–210.

Ackerly, B., Stern, M., & True, J. (Eds.). (2006). *Feminist Methodologies for International Relations.* Cambridge: Cambridge University Press.

African Studies Association US. (2012). *African Studies Association News Online 29 May 2012: Getting Research Permission.* http://www.asanewsonline. com/2012/05/29/getting-researchpermission. Accessed October 21, 2017.

Agar, M. (2006). An Ethnography by Any Other Name. *Forum: Qualitative Social Research Socialforschung, 7*(4). http://www.qualitative-research.net/ index.php/fqs/article/view/177. Accessed December 15, 2017.

Agyeman, D. (2005). Methodological Lessons: Working with Liberian and Togolese Refugees in Ghana. In E. Porter, G. Robinson, M Smyth, A. Schnabel, & E. Osaghae (Eds.), *Researching Conflict in Africa. Insights and Experiences* (pp. 56–63). Tokyo: United Nations University.

L. Johnstone (ed.), *The Politics of Conducting Research in Africa,*
https://doi.org/10.1007/978-3-319-95531-5

Ali, R. (2015). Rethinking Representation: Negotiating Positionality Power and Space in the Field. *Gender, Place and Culture, 22*(6), 783–800.

Alveson, M., & Sköldberg, K. (2009). *Reflexive Methodologies. New Vistas for Qualitative Research* (2nd ed.). London: Sage.

Aradau, C., & Huysmans, J. (2014). Critical Methods in International Relations: The Politics of Techniques, Devices and Acts. *European Journal of International Relations, 20*(3), 596–619.

Arendell, T. (1997). Reflections on the Researcher-Researched Relationship: A Woman Interviewing Men. *Qualitative Sociology, 20*, 341–365.

Aspen, H. (1991). A Novice's Field Experience. In M. Zamora & B. Erring (Eds.), *Fieldwork in Cultural Anthropology* (pp. 97–110). New Delhi: Reliance Publishing.

Attia, M., & Edge, J. (2017). Be(com)ing a Reflexive Researcher: A Developmental Approach to Research Methodology. *Open Review of Educational Research, 4*(1), 33–45.

Autesserre, S. (2014). *Peaceland. Conflict Resolution and the Everyday Politics of International Intervention.* Cambridge: Cambridge University Press.

Autesserre, S. (2017). International Peacebuilding and Local Success: Assumptions and Effectiveness. *International Studies Review, 19*(1), 1–19.

Babbie, E. (2013). *The Practice of Social Research* (14th ed.). Boston, MA: Cengage Learning.

Babcock, B. (1980). Reflexivity: Definitions and Discriminations. *Semiotica, 30*(1/2), 1–14.

Bailey, K. (2008). *Methods of Social Research* (4th ed.). New York: The Free Press.

Banks, J. (1998). The Lives and Values of Researchers: Implications for Educating Citizens in a Multicultural Society. *Educational Researcher, 27*, 4–17.

Barrientos, S., Knorringa, P., Evers, B., Visser, M., & Opondo, M. (2015). Shifting Regional Dynamics of Global Value Chains: Implications for Economic and Social Upgrading in African Horticulture. *Environment and Planning A, 48*(7), 1266–1283.

BBC News. (2002). 'Vampires' Strike Malawi Villages. http://news.bbc. co.uk/1/hi/world/africa/2602461.stm. Accessed December 15, 2017.

BBC News. (2017). *Malawi Cracks Down on 'Vampire' Lynch Mobs.* http:// www.bbc.co.uk/news/world-africa-41692944. Accessed December 10, 2017.

Bell, D. (1995). [Screw]ing Geography (Censor's Version). *Environment and Planning D: Society and Space, 13*, 127–131.

Bell, D. (2007). Fucking Geography, Again. In K. Browne, J. Lim, & G. Brown (Eds.), *Geographies of Sexualities: Theory, Practices and Politics* (pp. 81–88). Farnham: Ashgate.

Benoit, C., Jansson, M., Millar, A., & Phillips, R. (2005). Community-Academic Research on Hard-To-Reach Populations: Benefits and Challenges. *Qualitative Health Research, 15*(2), 263–282.

Beoku-Betts, J. (1994). When Black is Not Enough: Doing Fieldwork Amongst Gullah Women. *The National Women's Studies Association Journal, 6*(3), 413–433.

Bhavnani, K. (1988). Empowerment and Social Research: Some Comments. *Interdisciplinary Journal for the Study of Discourse, 8*(1–2), 41–50.

Billo, E., & Hiemstra, N. (2013). Mediating Messiness: Expanding Ideas of Flexibility, Reflexivity, and Embodiment in Fieldwork. *Gender, Place and Culture, 20*(3), 313–328.

Binnie, J. (1997). Coming Out of Geography: Towards a Queer Epistemology? *Environment and Planning D: Society and Space, 15*, 223–237.

Blair, D. (2002). *Degrees in Violence: Robert Mugabe and the Struggle for Power in Zimbabwe*. London: Continuum.

Bliesemann de Guevara, B., & Kostic, R. (2017). Knowledge Production In/About Conflict and Intervention: Finding "Fact", Telling "Truth". *Journal of Intervention and Statebuilding, 11*(1), 1–20.

Bloch, A. (2007). Methodological Challenges for National and Multi-sited Comparative Survey Research. *Journal of Refugee Studies, 20*(2), 230–247.

Blunt, A. (2005). *Domicile and Diaspora: Anglo-Indian Women and the Spatial Politics of Home*. Oxford: Blackwell.

Bolger, A. (1997, May 9). Unions Call for Code to Protect Flower Workers. *Financial Times*, p. 4.

Bolo, M. O. (2010). '*Learning to Export: Building Farmers' Capabilities Through Partnerships in Kenya's Flower Industry* (Hal Id: hal-00526145). http://hal.archives-ouvertes.fr/docs/00/52/61/45/PDF/Bolo_Learning_to_export.pdf. Accessed January 27, 2018.

Bolo, M. (2012). *Learning and Innovation in Agri-export Industries*. Saarbrucken, Germany: LAP Lambert Academic Publishing.

Bolo, M., Muthoka, N. M., Washisino, R., Mwai, V., & Kisongwo, D. (2006). Research Priorities for Kenya's Cut-Flower Industry: Farmers' Perspectives. *African Technology Policy Studies Network*. Technopolicy Brief 14. https://atpsnet.org/wp-content/uploads/2017/05/technopolicy_brief_series_14.pdf. Accessed January 27, 2018.

Bondi, L. (2009). Teaching Reflexivity: Undoing or Reinscribing Habits of Gender? *Journal of Geography in Higher Education, 33*(3), 327–337.

Bondy, C. (2013). How Did I Get Here? The Social Process of Accessing Field Sites. *Qualitative Research, 13*(5), 578–590.

Bourdieu, P. (1977). *Outline of a Theory of Practice*. Cambridge: Cambridge University Press.

Bourke, B. (2014). Positionality: Reflecting on the Research Process. *The Qualitative Report, 19*, 1–9.

Breen, L. J. (2007). The Researcher 'in the Middle': Negotiating the Insider/Outsider Dichotomy. *The Australian Community Psychologist, 19*(1), 163–174.

Broadhead, R. S., & Rist, R. C. (1976). Gatekeepers and the Social Control of Social Research. *Social Problems, 23*(3), 325–336.

Brosius, J. P., Lowenhaupt Tsing, A., & Zerner, C. (1998). Representing Communities: Histories and Politics of Community-Based Natural Resource Management. *Society and Natural Resources, 11*(2), 157–168.

Brotheridge, C., & Grandey, A. (2002). Emotional Labour and Burnout: Comparing Two Perspectives of "People Work". *Journal of Vocational Behavior, 60*(1), 17–39.

Brown, P. J., & Inhorn, M. (1990). The Anthropology of Infectious Disease. *Annual Review of Anthropology, 19,* 89–117.

Burgess, R. G. (1991). Sponsors, Gatekeepers, Members, and Friends: Access in Educational Settings. In W. B. Shaffir & R. A. Stebbins (Eds.), *Experiencing Fieldwork: An Inside View of Qualitative Research* (pp. 43–52). Newbury Park, CA: Sage.

Butler, J. (1990). *Gender Trouble.* London: Routledge.

Buxton, A. (2012, January). Linking Smallholders To Modern Markets. *IIED.*

Buxton, A., & Vorley, B. (2012, September). The Ethical Agent: Fresh Flowers in Kenya. *IIED.* http://pubs.iied.org/pdfs/16037IIED.pdf. Accessed January 10, 2018.

Campbell, L. M., Gray, N. J., Meletis, Z. A., Abbott, J. G., & Silver, J. J. (2006). Gatekeepers and Keymasters: Dynamic Relationships of Access in Geographical Fieldwork. *Geographical Review, 96*(1), 97–121.

Caplan, P. (1993). Learning Gender: Fieldwork in a Tanzanian Coastal Village, 1965–85. In D. Bell, P. Caplan, & W. J. Karim (Eds.), *Gendered Fields: Women, Men and Ethnography* (pp. 168–181). London: Routledge.

Caretta, M. A., & Jokinen, J. C. (2016). Conflating Privilege and Vulnerability: A Reflexive Analysis of Emotions and Positionality in Postgraduate Fieldwork. *The Professional Geographer, 69*(2), 275–283.

Carroll, K. (2012). Infertile? The Emotional Labor of Sensitive and Feminist Research Methodologies. *Qualitative Research, 13*(5), 546–561.

Cargo, M., & Mercer, S. (2008). The Value and Challenges of Participatory Research: Strengthening Its Practice. *Annual Review of Public Health, 29,* 325–350.

Cerwonka, A., & Malkki, L. H. (2007). *Improvising Theory: Process and Temporality in Ethnographic Fieldwork.* Chicago: Chicago University Press.

Chattopadhyay, S. (2013). Getting Personal While Narrating the "Field": A Researchers Journey to the Villages of the Narmada Valley. *Gender, Place and Culture: A Journal of Feminist Geography, 20*(2), 137–159.

Chereni, A. (2000). Positionality and Collaboration During Fieldwork: Insights from Research with Co-nationals Living Abroad. *Forum: Qualitative Social Research Socialforschung, 15*(3). http://www.qualitative-research.net/index.php/fqs/article/view/2058/3716. Accessed January 27, 2018.

Christian Aid. (2008). *Death and Taxes: The True Toll of Tax Dodging.* http://www.christianaid.org.uk/images/deathandtaxes.pdf. Accessed January 20, 2018.

Clark, T. (2008). We're Over-Researched Here! Exploring Accounts of Research Fatigue Within Qualitative Research Engagements. *Sociology, 42*(5), 953–970.

Clark, T. (2010). On 'Being Researched': Why Do People Engage with Qualitative Research? *Qualitative Research, 10*(4), 399–419.

Clark, I., & Grant, A. (2015). Sexuality and Danger in the Field: Starting an Uncomfortable Conversation. *Journal of the Anthropological Society of Oxford, 7*(1), 1–14.

Clarke, C., & Knights, D. (2015). Negotiating Identities: Fluidity, Diversity and Researcher Emotions. In C. Clarke, M. Broussine, & L. Watts (Eds.), *Researching with Feeling: The Emotional Aspects of Social and Organizational Research* (pp. 35–50). London: Routledge.

Clément, M., & Sangar, E. (2018). Introduction: Methodological Challenges and Opportunities for the Study of Emotions. In M. Clément & E. Sangar (Eds.), *Researching Emotions in International Relations: Methodological Perspectives on the Emotional Turn* (pp. 1–30). Cham: Springer.

Corbin Dwyer, S., & Buckle, J. L. (2009). The Space Between: On Being an Insider-Outsider in Qualitative Research. *International Journal of Qualitative Methods, 8*(1), 54–63.

Cotterill, P. (1992). Interviewing Women. *Women's Studies International Forum, 15*(5/6), 593-606.

Cousin, G. (2010). Positioning Positionality. In M. Savin-Baden & C. Howell Major (Eds.), *New Approaches to Qualitative Research—Wisdom and Uncertainty* (pp. 9–18). London and New York: Routledge.

Crapanzano, V. (2010). "At the Heart of the Discipline": Critical Reflections on Fieldwork. In J. Davies & D. Spencer (Eds.), *Emotions in the Field: The Psychology and Anthropology of Fieldwork Experience* (pp. 55–78). Stanford, CA: Stanford University Press.

Crowhurst, I. (2013). The Fallacy of the Instrumental Gate? Contextualising the Process of Gaining Access Through Gatekeepers. *International Journal of Social Research Methodology, 16*(6), 463–475.

Crush, J. (2008). *South Africa: Policy in the Face of Xenophobia.* Migration Policy Institute. Available at https://www.migrationpolicy.org/article/south-africa-policy-face-xenophobia. Accessed January 15, 2018.

Cupples, J. (2002). The Field as a Landscape of Desire: Sex and Sexuality in Geographical Fieldwork. *Area, 34*(4), 382–390.

Czarniawska, B. (2014). *Social Science Research: From Field to Desk.* London: Sage.

D'Aoust, A. M. (2014). Ties That Bind? Engaging Emotions, Governmentality and Neoliberalism: Introduction to the Special Issue. *Global Society, 28*(3), 267–276.

Davies, S. (2001). Philosophical Perspectives on Music's Expressiveness. In P. A. Juslin & J. A. Slobada (Eds.), *Music and Emotion: Theory and Research* (pp. 23–44). Oxford: Oxford University Press.

Davies, J. (2010). Introduction: Emotions in the Field. In J. Davies & D. Spencer (Eds.), *Emotions in the Field: The Psychology and Anthropology of Fieldwork Experience* (pp. 1–32). Stanford, CA: Stanford University Press.

Davies, T. (2015). Nuclear Borders: Informally Negotiating the Chernobyl Exclusion Zone. In J. Morris & A. Polese (Eds.), *Informal Economies in Post-social Spaces* (pp. 225–245). London: Palgrave Macmillan.

Davies, J., & Spencer, D. (Eds.). (2010). *Emotions in the Field. The Psychology and Anthropology of Fieldwork Experience.* Stanford, CA: Stanford University Press.

Davis, S. H. (2011). Introduction: Becoming Human. In S. H. Davis & M. Konner (Eds.), *Being There. Learning to Live Cross-Culturally* (pp. 1–7). Cambridge, MA and London: Harvard University Press.

De Laine, M. (2000). *Fieldwork, Participation and Practice: Ethics and Dilemmas in Qualitative Research.* London: Sage.

Delamont, S. (2009). The Only Honest Thing: Autoethnography, Reflexivity and Small Crises in Fieldwork. *Ethnography and Education, 4*(1), 51–63.

Denscombe, M. (2010). *Ground Rules for Social Research: Guidelines for Good Practice.* Berkshire: Open University Press.

Denscombe, M. (2014). *The Good Research Guide: For Small-Scale Social Research Projects* (5th ed.). Maindenhead: Open University Press.

Deutsch, N. L. (2004). Positionality and the Pen: Reflections on the Process of Becoming a Feminist Researcher and Writer. *Qualitative Enquiry, 10*(6), 885–902.

Dickson-Swift, V., James, E. L., Kippen, S., & Liamputtong, P. (2008). Risk to Researchers in Qualitative Research on Sensitive Topics: Issues and Strategies. *Qualitative Health Research, 18*(1), 133–144.

Dickson-Swift, V., James, E. L., Kippen, S., & Liamputtong, P. (2009). Researching Sensitive Topics: Qualitative Research and Emotion Work. *Qualitative Research, 9*(11), 61–79.

Diédhiou, P. (2013). La gestion du conflit de Casamance : Abdoulaye Wade et la "tradition" joola. In M.-C. Diop (dir.) Le *Sénégal sous Abdoulaye Wade: Le Sopi à l'épreuve du pouvoir* (pp. 249–265). Dakar and Paris: Cres-Karthala.

Diprose, G., Thomas, A. C., & Rushton, R. (2013). Desiring More: Complicating Understandings of Sexuality in Research Processes. *Area, 45*(3), 292–298.

Dolan, C. S. (2007). Market Affections: Moral Encounters with Kenyan Fairtrade Flowers. *Ethnos, 72*(2), 239–261.

Dolan, C., & Opondo, M. (2005). Seeking Common Ground: Multi-stakeholder Processes in Kenya's Cut Flower Industry. *Journal of Corporate Citizenship, 18*(12), 87–98.

Dolan, C., Opondo, M., & Smith, S. (2004). *Gender, Rights and Participation in the Kenya Cut Flower Industry* (Natural Resources Institute Working Paper No. 2768). London: National Resources Institute.

Duncan, J. S., & Lambert, D. (2004). Landscapes of Home. In J. S. Duncan, N. C. Johnson, & R. H. Schein (Eds.), *A Companion to Cultural Geography* (pp. 382–403). Oxford: Blackwell.

Dutton, J. E., & Dukerich, J. M. (2006). The Relational Foundation of Research: An Underappreciated Dimension of Interesting Research. *Academy of Management Journal, 49*(1), 21–26.

Dwyer, C., & Limb, M. (Eds.). (2001). *Qualitative Methodologies for Geographers: Issues and Debates*. London: Arnold.

Dwyer, S., & Buckle, J. L. (2009). The Space Between: On Being an Insider-Outsider in Qualitative Research. *International Journal of Qualitative Methods, 8*(1), 54–63.

Easton, G. (2010). Critical Realism in Case Study Research. *Industrial Marketing Management, 39*(1), 118–128.

Eichler, M. (1988). *Non-sexist Research Methods: A Practical Guide*. London and New York: Routledge.

Ellis, C., & Flaherty, M. (1992). An Agenda for the Interpretation of Lived Experience. In C. Ellis & M. Flaherty (Eds.), *Investigating Subjectivity: Research on Lived Experience* (pp. 1–16). London: Sage.

Engel, U. (2015). Introduction. In U. Engel, C. Gebauer, & A. Hüncke (Eds.), *Notes from Within and Without—Research Permits Between Requirements and "Realities"* (Working Papers Series 16). Leipzig and Halle: German Research Foundation.

England, K. (1994). Getting Personal: Reflexivity, Positionality, and Feminist Research. *Professional Geographer, 46*(1), 80–89.

Fanow, M. M., & Cook, J. A. (1991). Back to the Future: A Look at the Second Wave of Feminist Epistemology and Methodology. In M. M. Fanow & J. A. Cook (Eds.), *Beyond Methodology: Feminist Scholarship as Lived Research* (pp. 1–15). Bloomington: Indiana University Press.

Faria, C., & Good, R. Z. (2012). The Importance of Everyday Encounters: Young Scholars Reflect on Fieldwork in Africa. *African Geographical Review, 31*(1), 63–66.

Farmer, P., Kim, J. Y., Kleinman, A., & Basilico, M. (2013). *Reimaging Global Health*. Berkeley and Los Angeles: University of California Press.

Feldman, M. S., Bell, J., & Berger, M. T. (2003). *Gaining Access: A Practical and Theoretical Guide for Qualitative Researchers*. Walnut Creek, CA: AltaMira Press.

Finlay, L. (2002). "Outing" the Researcher: The Provenance, Process, and Practice of Reflexivity. *Qualitative Health Research, 12*(4), 531–545.

Finley, S. (2008). Arts-Based Research. In G. Knowles & A. Cole (Eds.), *Handbook of the Arts in Qualitative Research: Perspectives, Methodologies, Examples and Issues* (pp. 71–82). Los Angeles, CA: Sage.

Foley, D. E. (2002). Critical Ethnography: The Reflexive Turn. *International Journal of Qualitative Studies in Education, 15*(4), 469–490.

Freyberg-Inan, A. (2006). Rational Paranoia and Enlightened Machismo: The Strange Psychological Foundations of Realism. *Journal of International Relations and Development, 9*(2), 247–268.

Gallagher, J. (2016). Interviews as Catastrophic Encounters: An Object Relations Methodology for IR Research. *International Studies Perspectives, 17*(4), 445–461.

Ganga, D., & Scott, S. (2006). Cultural "Insiders" and the Issue of Positionality in Qualitative Migration Research: Moving "Across" and Moving "Along" Researcher-Participant Divides. *Forum: Qualitative Social Research, 7*(3), Art 7.

Geissler, P. W., & Pool, R. (2006). Editorial: Popular Concerns About Medical Research Projects in Sub-Saharan Africa—A Critical Voice in Debates About Medical Research Ethics. *Tropical Medicine and International Health, 11*(7), 975–982.

Geleta, E. B. (2013). The Politics of Identity and Methodology in African Development Ethnography. *Qualitative Research, 14*(1), 131–146.

Gibson-Graham, J. K. (1994). "Stuffed If I Know!": Reflections on Post-modern Feminist Social Research. *Gender, Place and Culture, 1*, 205–224.

Gilbert, M. R. (1994). The Politics of Location: Doing Feminist Research "at Home". *Professional Geographer, 46*, 90–96.

Gilchrist, V. J. (1999). Key Informant Interviews. In B. F. Crabtree & W. L. Miller (Eds.), *Doing Qualitative Research* (pp. 70–89). Thousand Oaks, CA: Sage.

Glaser, B. G., & Strauss, A. L. (1967). *The Discovery of Grounded Theory: Strategies for Qualitative Research*. New York: Aldine.

Glucksmann, M. (1994). The Work of Knowledge and the Knowledge of Women's Work. In M. Maynard & J. Purvis (Eds.), *Researching Women's Lives From a Feminist Perspective* (pp. 149–165). London: Taylor & Francis.

Goffman, E. (1990). *The Presentation of Self in Everyday Life*. London: Penguin.

Government of the Republic of Namibia. (2015). Poverty and Deprivation in Namibia 2015. *National Planning Commission*, Windhoek, Namibia. http://www.un.org.na/home_htm_files/NPC-Summary%20Report.pdf. Accessed December 10, 2017.

Grant, A. (2017). "I Don't Want You Sitting Next to Me": The Macro Meso and Micro of Gaining and Maintaining Access to Government Organizations During Ethnographic Fieldwork. *International Journal of Qualitative Methods, 16*, 1–11.

Greene, M. J. (2014). On the Inside Looking in: Methodological Insights and Challenges in Conducting Qualitative Insider Research. *The Qualitative Report, 19*(29), 1–13.

Gregory, D. (2000). Empiricism. In R. J. Johnston, D. Gregory, G. Pratt, & M. Watts (Eds.), *The Dictionary of Human Geography* (pp. 205–206). Malden, MA: Blackwell.

Gregory, I. (2003). *Ethics in Research.* London: Continuum.

Grenz, S. (2005). Intersections of Sex and Power in Research on Prostitution: A Female Researcher Interviewing Male Heterosexual Clients. *Signs, 30*(4), 2091–2113.

Gummesson, E. (2000). *Qualitative Methods in Management Research.* London: Sage.

Halberstam, J. (2011). *The Queer Art of Failure.* Durham, NC: Duke University Press.

Hale, A., & Opondo, M. (2005). Humanising the Cut Flower Chain: Confronting the Realities of Flower Production for Workers in Kenya. *Antipode, 37*(2), 301–323.

Hall, R. (2008). *Applied Social Research: Planning, Designing and Conducting Real-World Research.* South Yarra: Palgrave Macmillan.

Hammersley, M., & Atkinson, P. (2007). *Ethnography: Principles in Practice* (3rd ed.). Abingdon: Routledge Taylor & Francis.

Haraway, D. J. (1988). Situated Knowledges: The Science Question in Feminism and the Privilege of Partial Perspective. *Feminist Studies, 14*(3), 575–599.

Harding, S. (1987). *Whose Science, Whose Knowledge? Thinking from Women's Lives.* Ithaca, NY: Cornell University Press.

Harding, S. (2015). *Objectivity and Diversity: Another Logic of Scientific Research.* Chicago and London: The University of Chicago Press.

Harrowell, E., Davies, T., & Disney, T. (2018). Making Space for Failure in Geographic Research. *The Professional Geographer, 70*(2), 230–238.

Hellawell, D. (2006). Inside-Out: Analysis of the Insider-Outsider Concept as a Heuristic Device to Develop Reflexivity in Students Doing Qualitative Research. *Teaching in Higher Education, 11*(4), 483–494.

Henry, M., Higate, P., & Sanghera, G. (2009). Positionality and Power: The Politics of Peacekepping Research. *International Peacekeeping, 16*(4), 467–482.

Herod, A. (1999). Reflections on Interviewing Foreign Elites: Praxis Positionality, Validity, and the Cult of the Insider. *Geoforum, 30,* 313–327.

Herzfeld, M. (2009). The Cultural Politics of Gesture. *Ethnography, 10*(2), 131–352.

Hill-Collins, P. (1990). *Black Feminist Thought: Knowledge, Consciousness, and the Politics of Empowerment.* Boston: Unwin Hyman.

Hochschild, A. R. (1983). *The Managed Heart: Commercialization of Human Feeling*. Berkeley: University of California Press.

Hockey, J. (1993). Research Methods: Researching Peers and Familiar Settings. *Research Papers in Education, 8*(2), 199–225.

Hughes, A. (2000). Retailers, Knowledges and Changing Commodity Networks: The Case of the Cut Flower Trade. *Geoforum, 31*(2), 175–190.

Hutchison, E., & Bleiker, R. (2008). Emotional Reconciliation: Reconstructing Identity and Community After Trauma. *European Journal of Social Theory, 11*(3), 385–403.

Hutchison, E., & Bleiker, R. (2014). Theorizing Emotions in World Politics. *International Theory, 6*, 491–514.

Hutton, L. (2013). Displacement, Disharmony and Disillusion. Understanding Host-Refugee Tensions in Maban County, South Sudan. *Danish Demining Group*. https://reliefweb.int/report/south-sudan-republic/displacement-disharmony-and-disillusion-understanding-host-refugee. Accessed October 29, 2017.

Ingold, T., & Palsson, G. (2013). *Biosocial Becomings: Integrating Social and Biological Anthropology*. Cambridge: Cambridge University Press.

Integrated Rural Development and Nature Conservation. (2016). *About Us/History and Awards*. http://www.irdnc.org.na/history.html. Accessed October 27, 2017.

Ite, U. (1997). Home, Abroad, Home: The Challenges of Postgraduate Fieldwork "at Home". In E. Robson & K. Willis (Eds.), *Postgraduate Fieldwork in Developing Areas: A Rough Guide* (pp. 75–84). London: RGS-IBS.

ITI. (2015). *The SAFE Strategy*. http://trachoma.org/safe-strategy. Accessed February 21, 2015.

Jackson, M. (2010). From Anxiety to Method in Anthropological Fieldwork: An Appraisal of George Devereux's Enduring Ideas. In J. Davies & D. Spencer (Eds.), *Emotions in the Field: The Psychology and Anthropology of Fieldwork Experience* (pp. 35–45). Redwood City, CA: Stanford University Press.

Jackson, P. T. (2011). *The Conduct of Inquiry in International Relations: Philosophy of Science and Its Implications for the Study of World Politics*. Abingdon: Routledge.

Jacoby, T. (2006). From the Trenches: Dilemmas of Feminist IR Fieldwork. In B. Ackerly, M. Stern, & J. True (Eds.), *Feminist Methodologies for International Relations* (pp. 153–173). Cambridge: Cambridge University Press.

Jacobsen, K., & Landau, L. B. (2003). Dual Imperative in Refugee Research: Some Methodological and Ethical Considerations in Social Science Research on Forced Migration. *Disasters, 27*(3), 185–206.

Jaffee, S., 1992. How Private Enterprise Organized Agricultural Markets in Kenya, *Policy Research Working Paper Series* 823, The World Bank. 347–375.

Jaffee, S. (1995). The Many Faces of Success: The Development of Kenya's Horticultural Exports. In S. Jaffee & J. Morton (Eds.), *Marketing Africa's High Value Foods*. Ames Iowa: Kendall-Hunt Publishers.

Jaffee, S., & Gordon, P. (1993). *Exporting High-Value Food Commodities: Success Stories from Developing Countries* (World Bank—Discussion Paper #198).

James, W. (2015). Perspectives on the Blue Nile. In S. Totten & A. Grzyb (Eds.), *Conflict in the Nuba Mountains: From Genocide by Attrition to the Contemporary Crisis in Sudan.* New York: Routledge.

Jänis, J. (2014). Political Economy of the Namibian Tourism Sector: Addressing Post-apartheid Inequality Through Increasing Indigenous Ownership. *Review of African Political Economy, 41*(140), 185–200.

Jemielniak, D., & Kostera, M. (2010). Narratives of Irony and Failure in Ethnographic Work. *Canadian Journal of Administrative Sciences/Revue Canadienne des Sciences de l'Administration, 27*(4), 335–347.

Jewkes, R., Watts, C., Abrahams, N., Penn-Kekana, L., & Garcia-Moreno, C. (2000). Ethical and Methodological Issues in Conducting Research on Gender-Based Violence in Southern Africa. *Reproductive Health Matters, 8*(15), 93–103.

Jezewski, M. (1993). Culture Brokering as a Model for Advocacy. *Nursing and Health Care, 14*(2), 78–89.

Johnson, N. (2009). The Role of Self and Emotion Within Qualitative Sensitive Research: A Reflective Account. *Enquire, 2*(2), 191–214.

Jones, B. T. B. (2010). The Evolution of Namibia's Communal Conservancies. In F. Nelson (Ed.), *Community Rights, Conservation and Contested Land: The Politics of Natural Resource Governance in Africa* (pp. 106–120). London: Earthscan.

Jones, P. J. & Evans, J. (2011). Creativity and Project Management: A Comic. *ACME: An International E-Journal for Critical Geographies, 10*(3), 585–632.

Kara, H. (2015). *Creative Research Methods in the Social Sciences: A Practical Guide.* Bristol: Policy Press.

Karim, W. J. (1993). Epilogue: The Nativised Self and the Native. In D. Bell, P. Caplan, & W. J. Karim (Eds.), *Gendered Fields: Women, Men and Ethnography* (pp. 248–251). London: Routledge.

Kaspar, H., & Landolt, S. (2016). Flirting in the Field: Shifting Positionalities and Power Relations in Innocuous Sexualisations of Research Encounters. *Gender, Place and Culture, 23*(1), 107–119.

Katz, C. (1994). Playing the Field: Questions of Fieldwork in Geography. *The Professional Geographer, 46*(1), 67–72.

Kay, R., & Oldfield, J. (2011). Emotional Engagements with the Field: A View from Area Studies. *Europe-Asia Studies, 63*(7), 1275–1293.

Kenya Flower Council (Website). Accessed at http://kenyaflowercouncil.org/?page_id=92.

Kenya Human Rights Commission. (2012). *'Wilting in Bloom': The Irony of Women Labour Rights in the Cut-Flower Sector in Kenya.* Nairobi: Kenya Human Rights Commission.

Kilgore, J. (2011). *We Are All Zimbabweans Now: A Novel*. Athens, OH: Ohio University Press.

King, N., & Horrocks, C. (2010). *Interviews in Qualitative Research*. London: Sage.

Kiragu, S., & Warrington, M. (2013). How We Used Moral Imagination to Address Ethical and Methodological Complexities While Conducting Research With Girls in School Against the Odds in Kenya. *Qualitative Research, 13*, 173–189.

Kitchin, R., & Tate, N. (2013). *Conducting Research in Human Geography: Theory, Methodology and Practice*. Abingdon: Routledge.

Kobayashi, A. (2003). GPC Ten Years On: Is Self-Reflexivity Enough? *Gender, Place and Culture, 10*(4), 345–349.

Kovats-Bernat, J. C. (2002). Negotiating Dangerous Fields: Pragmatic Strategies for Fieldwork Amid Violence and Terror. *American Anthropologist, 104*(1), 208–322.

Lal, J. (1996). Situating Locations: The Politics of Self, Identity, and "Other" in Loving and Writing the Text. In D. Wolf (Ed.), *Feminist Dilemmas in Fieldwork* (pp. 185–214). Boulder, CO: Westview Press.

Law, J., Ruppert, E., & Savage, M. (2011, March). *The Double Social Life of Methods*. CRESC *Working Paper Series* (Working Paper 95). The Open University. http://research.gold.ac.uk/7987/1/The%20Double%20Social%20 Life%20of%20Methods%20CRESC%20Working%20Paper%2095.pdf. Accessed January 15, 2016.

Lawless, R., Sutlive, V. H, & Zamora, M. D. (Eds.). (1983). *Fieldwork: The Human Experience*. New York: Gordon and Breach.

Leatherman, T., & Goodman, A. H. (2011). Critical Biocultural Approaches in Medical Anthropology. In M. Singer & P. Erickson (Eds.), *A Companion to Medical Anthropology* (pp. 29–48). Oxford: Blackwell.

Leavy, P. (Ed.). (2014). *The Oxford Handbook of Qualitative Research*. Oxford: Oxford University Press.

Letherby, G., Scott, J., & Williams, M. (2013). *Objectivity and Subjectivity in Social Research*. Thousand Oaks, CA: Sage.

Lewis, D. (1973). Anthropology and Colonialism. *Current Anthropology, 14*(5), 581–602.

Liamputtong, P. (2007). *Researching the Vulnerable: A Guide to Sensitive Research Methods*. London: Sage.

Lipton, M. (1977). *Why Poor People Stay Poor: Urban Bias in World Development*. London: Temple Smith.

Lock, M., & Nguyen, V. K. (2010). *An Anthropology of Biomedicine*. Oxford: Blackwell.

Long, N. (2001). *Development Sociology: Actor Perspectives*. Abingdon: Routledge.

Madge, C. (1993). Boundary Disputes: Comments on Sidaway (1992). *Area, 25*, 294–299.

Mandel, J. L. (2003). Negotiating Expectations in the Field: Gatekeepers, Research Fatigue and Cultural Biases. *Singapore Journal of Tropical Geography, 24*(2), 198–210.

Mandiyanike, D. (2009). The Dilemma of Conducting Research Back in Your Own Country as a Returning Student: Reflections of Research Fieldwork in Zimbabwe. *Area, 41,* 64–71.

Manyika, S., & Szanton, D. (2001). PhD Programmes in African Universities: Current Status and Future Prospects. *A Report to the Rockefeller Foundation.* Berkeley: University of California.

Martin, P. Y. (2003). "Said and Done" Versus "Saying and Doing": Gendering Practices, Practicing Gender at Work. *Gender and Society, 17*(3), 342–366.

Maruyama, G., & Deno, S. (1992). *Research in Educational Settings.* Newbury Park, CA: Sage.

Mattingly, D., & Falconer-Al-Hindi, K. (1995). Should Women Count? A Context for the Debate. *Professional Geographer, 47,* 27–35.

Mauthner, N., & Doucet, A. (2003). Reflexive Accounts and Accounts of Reflexivity in Qualitative Data Analysis. *Sociology, 37*(3), 413–431.

McAreavey, R., & Das, C. (2013). A Delicate Balancing Act: Negotiating with Gatekeepers for Ethical Research When Researching Minority Communities. *International Journal of Qualitative Methods, 12*(1), 113–131.

McCorkel, J. A., & Myers, K. (2003). What Difference Does Difference Make? Position and Privilege in the Field. *Qualitative Sociology, 26*(2), 199–231.

McCracken, J. (2012). *A History of Malawi 1859–1966.* Woodbridge: James Currey.

McDowell, L. (1988). Coming in From the Dark Feminist Research in Geography. In J. Eyles (Ed.), *Research in Human Geography* (pp. 154–173). Oxford: Blackwell.

McDowell, L. (1992). Doing Gender: Feminism, Feminists and Research Methods in Human Geography. *Transactions, Institute of British Geographers, 17,* 399–416.

McFadyen, J., & Rankin, J. (2016). The Role of Gatekeepers in Research: Learning from Reflexivity and Reflection. *GSTF Journal of Nursing and Health Care, 4*(1), 82–88.

Meloni, M. (2014a). How Biology Became Social, and What It Means for Social Theory. *The Sociological Review, 62*(3), 593–614.

Meloni, M. (2014b). Remaking Local Biologies in an Epigenetic Time. *Somatosphere.* http://somatosphere.net/2014/08/remaking-local-biolo-gies-in-an-epigenetic-time.html. Accessed February 25, 2016.

Melrose, M. (2002). Labour Pains. *International Journal Social Research Methodology, 5*(4), 333–351.

Merriam, S. B., Johnson-Bailey, J., Lee, M.-Y., Kee, Y., Ntseane, G., & Muhamad, M. (2001). Power and Positionality: Negotiating Insider/

Outsider Status Within and Across Cultures. *International Journal of Lifelong Education*, 20(5), 405–416.

Merry, S. E. (2016). *The Seductions of Quantification*. London: The University of Chicago Press.

Mertens, D. M. (2009). *Transformative Research and Evaluation*. New York: Guilford Press.

Mertens, D. M., & Ginsberg, P. E. (2009). Frontiers in Social Research Ethics: Fertile Ground for Evolution. In P. E. Ginsberg & D. M. Mertens (Eds.), *The Handbook of Social Research Ethics* (pp. 580–613). Thousand Oaks, CA: Sage.

Merton, R. K. (1972). Insiders and Outsiders: A Chapter in the Sociology of Knowledge. *American Journal of Sociology*, 78(1), 9-47.

Meyer, S. (2007). *From Horror Story to Manageable Risk: Formulating Safety Strategies for Peace Researchers*. Thesis for Master Degree Programme in Peace and Conflict Transformation, Centre for Peace Studies, Faculty of Social Science, University of Tromsø, Norway.

Miller, J., & Glassner, B. (1997). The 'Inside' and the 'Outside': Finding Realities in Interviews. In D. Silverman (Ed.), *Qualitative Research: Theory, Method and Practice* (pp. 99–112). London: Sage.

Mills, M. B., & Huberman, A. M. (1984). *Qualitative Data Analysis: A Sourcebook of New Methods*. London: Sage.

Milner IV, H. R. (2007). Race Culture, and Researcher Positionality: Working Through Dangers Seen, Unseen, and Unforeseen, Educational Researcher. *Educational Researcher*, 36(7), 388–400.

Minh-ha, T. (1989). *Woman, Native, Other: Writing Post-coloniality and Feminism*. Bloomington: Indiana University Press.

Ministry of Environment and Tourism Namibia. (2013). *National Policy on Community Based Natural Resource Management*. http://www.met.gov.na/files/files/CBNRM_20Policy%20Approved.pdf. Accessed January 10, 2018.

Mollinga, P. (2008). Field Research Methodology as Boundary Work: An Introduction. In C. Wall & P. Mollinga (Eds.), *Fieldwork in Difficult Environments. Methodology as Boundary Work in Development Research* (pp. 1–17). Berlin: LIT Verlag.

Molony, T., & Hammett, D. (2007). The Friendly Financier: Talking Money with the Silenced Assistant. *Human Organization*, 66(3), 292–300.

Moreno, E. (1995). Rape in the Field: Reflections From a Survivor. In D. Kulick & M. Wilson (Eds.), *Taboo: Sex, Identity and Erotic Subjectivity in Immersed Anthropological Fieldwork* (pp. 219–250). London and New York: Routledge.

Morton, H. (1995). My Chastity Belt: Avoiding Seduction in Tonga. In D. Kulick & M. Wilson (Eds.), *Taboo: Sex, Identity and Erotic Subjectivity in Anthropological Fieldwork* (pp. 168–185). London: Routledge.

Mosse, D. (2005). *Cultivating Development*. London: Pluto Press.

Mulangu, F. (2016, September). Mapping the Technological Capabilities of Kenyan-Owned Floricultural Firms. *African Center for Economic*

Transformation. Presentation at the ASA—UK Annual Conference, University of Cambridge.

Mulhall, A. (2003). In the Field: Notes on Observation in Qualitative Research. *Journal of Advanced Nursing, 41*(3), 306–313.

Mullings, B. (1999). Insider or Outsider, Both or Neither: Some Dilemmas of Interviewing in a Cross-Cultural Setting. *Geoforum, 30*(4), 337–350.

Muthoka, N. (2008). *A Cross Country Analysis of Cut Flower and Foliage Exports: The Case of Kenya* (Discussion Paper 96). Nairobi: The Kenya Institute for Public Policy Research and Analysis.

Muthoka, N. M., & Muriithi, A. N. (2008). Smallholder Summer Flower Production in Kenya: A Myth or a Prospect? *Acta Horticulturae, 766*, 219–224.

NACSO—Namibian Association for CBNRM Support Organizations. (2017). *Conservancies and Conservancies Overview.*http://www.nacso.org.na/conservation-and-conservancies. *Accessed September 27, 2017.*

Nairn, K., Munro, J., & Smith, A. B. (2005). A Counter-Narrative of a "Failed" Interview. *Qualitative Research, 5*(2), 221–244.

Nast, H. J. (1994). Opening Remarks on "Women in the Field". *Professional Geographer, 46*, 54–66.

Newton, E. (1993). My Best Informant's Dress: The Erotic Equation in Fieldwork. *Cultural Anthropology, 8*, 3–23.

Nilan, P. (2002). "Dangerous Fieldwork" Re-examined: The Question of Researcher Subject Position. *Qualitative Research, 2*(3), 363–386.

Nordstrom, C., & Robben, A. (Eds.). (1995). *Fieldwork Under Fire: Contemporary Studies of Violence and Survival.* London: University of California Press.

Oakley, A. (1981). Interviewing Women: A Contradiction in Terms. In H. Roberts (Ed.), *Doing Feminist Research.* London: Routledge.

O'Connell-Davidson, J. (2008). If No Means No, Does Yes Mean Yes? Consenting to Research Intimacies. *History of Human Sciences, 21*(4), 49–67.

Ogora, L. O. (2013). The Contested Fruits of Research in War-Torn Countries: My Insider Experience in Northern Uganda. In S. Thomson, A. Ansoms, & J. Murison (Eds.), *Emotional and Ethical Challenges for Field Research in Africa: The Story Behind the Findings* (pp. 27–41). Basingstoke: Palgrave Macmillan.

Okely, J. (1992). Anthropology and Autobiography. Participatory Experience and Embodied Knowledge. In J. Oakely & H. Callaway (Eds.), *Anthropology and Autobiography: ASA Monographs 29* (pp. 1–28). London and New York: Routledge.

Olawale, A. I. (2005). Applying Social Work Practice to the Study of Ethnic Militias: The Oduduwa People's Congress in Nigeria. In E. Porter, G. Robinson, M. Smyth, A. Schnabel, & E. Osaghae (Eds.), *Researching Conflict in Africa. Insights and Experiences* (pp. 64–89). Tokyo: United Nations University.

Opondo, M. (2006). *Emerging Corporate Social Responsibility in Kenya's Cut Flower Industry*. http://www.unisa.ac.za/contents/colleges/col_econ_man_science/ccc/docs/Opondo.pdf. Accessed December 20, 2017.

Oxfam. (2004). *Trading Away Our Rights: Women Working in Global Supply Chains*. https://policy-practice.oxfam.org.uk/publications/trading-away-our-rights-women-working-in-global-supply-chains-112405. Accessed January 10, 2018.

Oxfam. (2013). *Upper Nile Refugee Crisis: Avoiding Past Mistakes in the Coming Year*. http://www.oxfamblogs.org/eastafrica/wp-content/uploads/2010/09/bp171-upper-nile-sudan-refugee-crisis-050413-en.pdf. Accessed October 29, 2017.

Paechter, C. (2012). Researching Sensitive Issues Online: Implications of a Hybrid Insider/Outsider Position in a Retrospective Ethnographic Study. *Qualitative Research, 13*(1), 71–86.

Parker, M., & Harper, I. (2006). The Anthropology of Public Health. *Journal of Biosocial Science, 38*, 1–5.

Parr, H. (1996). *Mental Health, Ethnography and the Body: Implications for Geographical Research*. Paper Presented at a Conference on Feminist Methodologies, Nottingham.

Parrado, E., Flippen, C. A., & Metzger McQuiston, C. (2005). Migration and Relationship Power Among Mexican Women. *Demography, 42*, 347–372.

Pasura, D. (2014). *African Transnational Diasporas: Fractured Communities and Plural Identities of Zimbabweans in Britain*. London: Palgrave Macmillan.

Patai, D. (1991). US Academic and Third World Women: Is Ethical Research Possible? In S. Gluck Berger & D. Patai (Eds.), *Women's Words: The Feminist Practice of Oral History* (pp. 137–153). London: Routledge.

Patai, D. (1994). Response: When Method Becomes Power. In A. Gitlen (Ed.), *Power and Method* (pp. 61–73). New York: Routledge.

Peace Parks Foundation. (2017). *Kavango Zambezi*. http://www.peaceparks.org/tfca.php?pid=27&mid=1008. Accessed October 7, 2017.

Pfeiffer, J., & Nichter, M. (2008). What Can Critical Medical Anthropology Contribute to Global Health? A Health Systems Perspective. *Medical Anthropology Quarterly, 22*(4), 410–415.

Pike, K. (1967). *Language in Relation to a Unified Theory of the Structures of Human Behavior* (2nd ed.). The Hague: Mouton.

Pillow, W. S. (2003). Confession, Catharsis, or Cure? Rethinking the Uses of Reflexivity as Methodological Power in Qualitative Research. *International Journal of Qualitative Studies in Education, 16*, 175–196.

Pilossof, R. (2012). *The Unbearable Whiteness of Being: Farmers' Voices from Zimbabwe*. Harare: Weaver Press.

Pollard, A. (2009). Field of Screams: Difficulty and Ethnographic Fieldwork. *Anthropology Matters, 11*(2). https://www.anthropologymatters.com/index.php/anth_matters/article/view/10/10. Accessed January 10, 2018.

Polzer, T. (2012). Together Apart: Migration, Integration and Spatialized Identities in South African Border Villages. *Geoforum, 43*(3), 561–572.

Porter, E., Robinson, G., Smyth, M., Schnabel, A., & Osaghae, E. (Eds.). (2005). *Researching Conflict in Africa: Insights and Experiences.* Tokyo: United Nations University Press.

Punch, S. (2012). Hidden Struggles of Fieldwork: Exploring the Role and Use of Field Diaries. *Emotion, Space and Society, 5*(2), 86–93.

Rabinowitz, V., & Weseen, S. (2001). Power, Politics, and the Qualitative/ Quantitative Debates in Psychology. In D. L. Tolman & M. Brydon-Miller (Eds.), *Qualitative Studies in Psychology: From Subjects to Subjectivities: A Handbook of Interpretive and Participatory Methods* (pp. 12–28). New York: New York University Press.

Radcliffe-Brown, A. R. (1940). On Joking Relationships. *Africa: Journal of the International African Institute, 13*(3), 195–210.

Raftopolous, B., & Savage, T. (Eds.). (2004). *Zimbabwe: Injustice and Political Reconciliation.* Cape Town: Institute for Justice and Reconciliation.

Rager, K. (2005). Compassion, Stress and the Qualitative Researcher. *Qualitative Health Research, 15*(3), 423–430.

Ranger, T. (2004). Nationalist Historiography, Patriotic History, and the History of the Nation: the Struggle over the Past in Zimbabwe. *Journal of Southern African Studies, 30*(2), 215–234.

Rancatore, J. (2010). It Is Strange. *Millennium: Journal of International Studies, 39*(1), 65–77.

Reeves, C. (2010). A Difficult Negotiation: Fieldwork Relations with Gatekeepers. *Qualitative Research, 10*(3), 315–331.

Reger, J. (2001). Emotions, Objectivity and Voice: An Analysis of a "Failed" Participant Observation. *Women's Studies International Forum, 24*(5), 605–616.

Reinharz, S. (1997). Who Am I? The Need for a Variety of Selves in the Field. In R. Hertz (Ed.), *Reflexivity and Voice* (pp. 3–20). Thousand Oaks, CA: Sage.

Research Council of Zimbabwe. (2017). *Research Registration.* http://www.rcz.ac.zw/research-registration. Accessed October 21, 2017.

Ribot, J. C. (2002). *Democratic Decentralization of Natural Resources: Institutionalizing Popular Participation.* Washington: World Resources Institute.

Riisgaard, L. (2009). Global Value Chains, Labour Organization and Private Social Standards: Lessons from East African Cut Flower Industries. *World Development, 37*(2), 326–340.

Riisgaard, L. (2011). Towards More Stringent Sustainability Standards? Trends in the Cut Flower Industry. *Review of African Political Economy, 38*(129), 435–453.

Robson, C. (1993). *Real World Research: A Resource for Social Scientists and Practitioners-Researchers*. Oxford: Blackwell.

Romero, M., & Stewart, A. (Eds.). (1999). *Women's Untold Stories: Breaking Silence, Talking Back, Voicing Complexity*. New York: Routledge.

Rose, G. (1997). Situating Knowledges: Positionality, Reflexivities and Other Tactics. *Progress in Human Geography, 21*(3), 305–320.

Rossman, G. B., & Rallis, S. (1998). *Learning in the Field: An Introduction to Qualitative Research*. London: Sage.

Ryan, L. (2015). "Inside" and "Outside" of What or Where? Researching Migration Through Multi-positionalities. *Forum: Qualitative Social Research Socialforschung, 16*(2). http://www.qualitative-research.net/index.php/fqs/article/view/2333/3785. Accessed January 20, 2018.

Saether, E. (2006). Fieldwork as Coping and Learning. In M. Heimer & S. Thogersen (Eds.), *Doing Research in China* (pp. 42–57). Honolulu: University of Hawai'i Press.

Salamone, F. A. (1991). Friends in the Field. In M. D. Zamora & B. B. Erring (Eds.), *Fieldwork in Cultural Anthropology* (pp. 67–78). New Delhi: Reliance Publishing.

Sampson, H., Bloor, M., & Fincham, B. (2008). A Price Worth Paying? Considering the "Cost" of Reflexive Research Methods and the Influence of Feminist Ways of "Doing". *Sociology, 42*(5), 919–933.

Sandgren, D. (2012). *Mau Mau's Children: The Making of a Postcolonial Elite*. Madison: University of Wisconsin Press.

Savin-Baden, M., & Howell Major, C. (2010). *New Approaches to Qualitative Research—Wisdom and Uncertainty*. London and New York: Routledge.

Schaffer, F. C. (2015). Ordinary Language Interviewing. In D. Yanow & P. Schwartz-Shea (Eds.), *Interpretation and Method: Empirical Research Methods and the Interpretive Turn*. Abingdon: Routledge.

Schaffer, F. C. (2016). *Elucidating Social Sciences Concepts: An Interpretivist Guide*. London: Routledge.

Schräpel, N. (2015). Getting the Papers Right—Some Reflections On the Politics of Research Permits in Rwanda. In U. Engel, C. Gebauer, & A. Hüncke (Eds.), *Notes from Within and Without—Research Permits Between Requirements and "Realities"* (Working Papers Series 16). Leipzig and Halle: German Research Foundation.

Scott, S., Miller, F., & Lloyd, K. (2006). Doing Fieldwork in Development Geography: Research Culture and Research Spaces in Vietnam. *Geographical Research, 44*(1), 28–40.

Seear, K., & McLean, K. (2008, December). Breaking the Silence: The Role of Emotional Labor in Qualitative Research. In *The Australian Sociological Association (TASA) Annual Conference Proceedings*. Melbourne: University of Melbourne.

Serrant-Green, L. (2002). Black on Black: Methodological Issues for Black Researchers Working in Minority Ethnic Communities. *Nurse Researcher, 9*(4), 30–44.

Shaw, I. (2008). Ethics and the Practice of Qualitative Research. *Qualitative Social Work, 7*(4), 400–414.

Shepherd, G., Parsonage, M., & Scharf, T. (2010). Social Inclusion: Research and Evidence-Based Practice. In J. Boardman, A. Currie, H. Killaspy, & G. Mezey (Eds.), *Social Inclusion and Mental Health* (pp. 279–294). London: Royal College of Psychiatrists.

Sherif, B. (2001). The Ambiguity of Boundaries in the Fieldwork Experience: Establishing Rapport and Negotiating Insider/Outsider Status. *Qualitative Inquiry, 7*(4), 436–447.

Shore, C. (2010). Beyond the Multiversity: Neoliberalism and the Rise of the Schizophrenic University. *Social Anthropology, 18*(1), 15–29.

Sidaway, J. (1992). In Other Worlds: On the Politics of Research by "First World" Geographers in the "Third World". *Area, 24*(4), 403–408.

Silverman, D. (2010). *Doing Qualitative Research* (3rd ed.). London: Sage.

Silverman, D. (2013). *Doing Qualitative Research* (4th ed.). London: Sage.

Singer, M. (2011). The Development of Critical Medical Anthropology: Implications for Biological Anthropology. In A. H. Goodman & T. Leatherman (Eds.), *Building a New Biocultural Synthesis: Political-Economic Perspectives on Human Biology* (pp. 93–126). Ann Arbor: The University of Michigan Press.

Singh, S., & Wassenaar, D. R. (2016). Contextualizing the Role of the Gatekeeper in Social Science Research. *South African Journal of Bioethics and Law, 9*(1), 42–46.

Siriam, C. L., King, J., Martin-Ortega, O., & Herman, J. (Eds.). (2009). *Surviving Field Research: Working in Violent and Difficult Situations*. London: Routledge.

Siwale, J. (2015). Why Did I Not Prepare for This? The Politics of Negotiating Fieldwork Access, Identity, and Methodology in Researching Microfinance Institutions. *SAGE Open, 5*(2), 1–12.

Smith, L. T. (1999). *Decolonising Methodologies: Research and Indigenous Peoples*. London: Zed.

Smith, E. (2006). La nation "par le côté". Le récit des cousinages au Sénégal. *Cahiers d'études africaines, 184*, 907–965.

Smith, D. (2015). Johannesburg's Foreign Shop Owners Close up Early Amid Threats of Violence. *The Guardian*. Available at https://www.theguardian.com/world/2015/apr/15/johannesburg-threats-violence-foreign-shop-owners-close-early. Accessed January 10, 2018.

Srivastava, P. (2006). Reconciling Multiple Researcher Positionalities and Languages in International Research. *Research in Comparative and International Education*, 1(3), 210–222.

SSR. (2013). Humanitarian and Human Rights Situation of the IDPs and War-Affected Civilians in the SPLM/A-North Controlled Area of South Kordofan and Blue Nile States. *Sudan Relief and Rehabilitation Association*.http://www.kpsrl.org/browse/browse-item/t/humanitarian-and-human-rights-situation-of-the-idps-and-war-affected-civilians-in-the-splm-a-north-controlled-area-of-south-kordofan-and-blue-nile-states-second-issue-six-monthly-report-january-june-2013. *Accessed October 29, 2017.*

Stevens, S. (2001). Fieldwork as Commitment. *The Geographical Review*, 91(1–2), 66–73.

Sullivan, S. (2002). How Sustainable Is the Communalizing Discourse of 'New' Conservation: The Masking of Difference, Inequality and Aspiration in the Fledgling "Conservancies" of Namibia. In D. Chatty & M. Colchester (Eds.), *Conservation and Mobile Indigenous Peoples* (pp. 158–197). Oxford: Berghahn Press.

Sullivan, S. (2003). Dissent or Libel in Resistance to a Conservancy in North-West Namibia. In E. Berglund & D. Anderson (Eds.), *Ethnographies of Conservation: Environmentalism and the Distribution of Privilege* (pp. 69–86). Oxford: Berghahn Press.

Sultana, F. (2007). Reflexivity Positionality and Participatory Ethics: Negotiating Fieldwork Dilemmas in International Research. *ACME: An International E-Journal for Critical Geographies*, 6(3), 374–385.

Sundberg, J. (2003). Masculinist Epistemologies and the Politics of Fieldwork in Latin Americanist Geography. *The Professional Geographer*, 55(2), 180–190.

Suzuki, Y. (2004). Negotiations, Concessions, and Adaptations During Fieldwork in a Tribal Society. *Iranian Studies*, 37(4), 623–632.

Taggart, J. M., & Sandstrom, A. R. (2011). Introduction to "Long-Term Fieldwork". *Anthropology and Humanism*, 36(1), 1–6.

Temple, T., & Edwards, R. (2002). Interpreters/Translators and Cross-Language Research: Reflexivity and Border Crossings. *International Journal of Qualitative Methods*, 1(2), 1–12.

Tendi, B. M. (2010). *Making History in Mugabe's Zimbabwe: Politics, Intellectuals, and the Media*. Oxford: Peter Lang.

Tevera, D. (1999). Do They Need Ivy in Africa? Ruminations of an African Geographer Trained Abroad. In D. Simon & A. Narman (Eds.), *Development as Theory and Practice* (pp. 134–145). Harlow: Addison Wesley and Longman.

Thiongane, O. (2013). *Anthropologie de la méningite au Niger: Espaces épidémiques, mobilisations scientifiques et conceptions de la maladie*. Unpublished Ph.D. thesis, Ecole des Hautes Etudes en Sciences Sociales, pp. 106–139.

Thoen, R., Jaffee, S., Dolan, S., & Ba, F. (2000). *Equatorial Rose: The Kenyan— European Cut flower Supply Chain.* Washington, DC: World Bank.

Thomson, S. (2009). "That is Not What We Authorised You to Do... ": Access and Government Interference in Highly Politicised Research Environments. In C. Lekha Sriram, J. C. King, J. A. Mertus, O. Martin-Ortega, & J. Herman (Eds.), *Surviving Field Research: Working in Violent and Difficult Situations* (pp. 108–123). London: Routledge.

Thomson, S. (2013). Academic Integrity and Ethical Responsibilities in Post-Genocide Rwanda: Working with Research Ethics Boards to Prepare for Fieldwork with 'Human Subjects'. In S. Thomson, A. Ansoms, & J. Murison (Eds.), *Emotional and Ethical Challenges for Field Research in Africa: The Story behind the Findings* (pp. 139–155). Basingstoke: Palgrave Macmillan.

Thomson, S., Ansoms, A., & Murison, J. (Eds.). (2013). *Emotional and Ethical Challenges for Field Research in Africa: The Story Behind the Findings.* Basingstoke: Palgrave Macmillan.

Thomson, S., Ansoms, A., & Murison, J. (2013). Introduction: Why Stories behind the Findings? In S. Thomson, A. Ansoms, & J. Murison (Eds.), *Emotional and Ethical Challenges for Field Research in Africa: The Story behind the Findings* (pp. 1–11). Basingstoke: Palgrave Macmillan.

Tiller, S., & Healy, S. (2013). Have We Lost the Ability to Respond to Refugee Crises? The Maban Response. *Humanitarian Exchange, 57.* Humanitarian Practice Network at ODI. http://odihpn.org/magazine/have-we-lost-the-ability-to-respond-to-refugee-crises-the-maban-response/. Accessed May 21, 2016.

Tindana, P. O., Kass, N., & Akweongo, P. (2006). The Informed Consent Process in a Rural African Setting: A Case Study of the Kassena-Nankana District of Northern Ghana. *Ethics and Human Research, 28*(3), 1–6.

Tushman, M. L., & Katz, R. (1980). External Communication and Project Performance: An Investigation into the Role of Gatekeepers. *Management Science, 26*(11), 1071–1085.

University of Zimbabwe. (2016). *Mission Statement.* http://www.uz.ac.zw/index.php/about-uz/uofz-overview/our-mission. Accessed October 15, 2016.

Unluer, S. (2012). Being an Insider Researcher While Conducting Case Study Research. *The Qualitative Report, 17*(58), 1–14.

Valentine, G. (2002). People Like Us: Negotiating Sameness and Difference in the Research Process. In P. Moss (Ed.), *Feminist Geography in Practice: Research and Methods* (pp. 116–126). Oxford: Blackwell.

Visser, G. (2000). In Other Worlds: On the Politics of Research in a Transforming South Africa. *Area, 32,* 231–235.

Wanat, C. L. (2008). Getting Past the Gatekeepers: Differences Between Access and Cooperation in Public School Research. *Field Methods, 20*(2), 191–208.

WHO. (2013). *Country Profile Malawi*. http://www.who.int/countries/mwi/en/. Accessed February 21, 2016.

Wilkinson, C. (2008). Positioning "Security" and Securing One's Position: The Researcher's Role in Investigating "Security" in Kyrgyzstan. In C. Wall & P. Mollinga (Eds.), *Fieldwork in Difficult Environments: Methodology as Boundary Work in Development Research* (pp. 43–67). New Brunswick, NJ: Transaction Publishers.

Wilkinson, R., & Marmot, M. (2003). *Social Determinants of Health the Solid Facts* (2nd ed.). Copenhagen: World Health Organization Europe.

Wiles, R. (2013). *What Are Qualitative Research Ethics?* London: Bloomsbury Academic.

Williams, B. (1996). Skinfolk, Not Kinfolk: Comparative Reflections of the Identity of Participant Observation in Two Field Situations. In D. Wolf (Ed.), *Feminist Dilemmas in Fieldwork*. Boulder, CO: Westview Press.

Wolcott, H. F. (2005). *The Art of Fieldwork*. Walnut Creek, CA: AltaMira Press.

Wolf, J. (1997, May 10). Report on Flower Industry Unearths Dangers to Workers. *The Guardian*, p. 16.

Wolfe, D. (1996). Situating Feminist Dilemmas in Fieldwork. In D. Wolfe (Ed.), *Feminist Dilemmas in Fieldwork* (pp. 1–55). Boulder, CO: Westview Press.

WWF—World Wide Fund for Nature. (2016). *Namibia: The Greatest Wildlife Recovery Story Ever Told*. http://www.worldwildlife.org/pages/namibia-the-greatest-wildlife-recovery-story-evertold. Accessed May 31, 2016.

Zakri, A. H. (2006). Research Universities in the 21st Century: Global Challenges and Local Implications. *Global Keynote Scenario at the UNESCO Forum on Higher Education, Research and Knowledge: Colloquium on Research and Higher Education, 60*, 17–39.

Zuckerman, A. (1991). *Doing Political Science: An Introduction to Political Analysis*. Boulder, CO: Westview Press.

INDEX

A

Academic squeamishness, 78, 91
Access, 116–119, 125, 126
  blocked, 2
  blocked by gatekeepers, 154
  challenges of, 9, 116
  challenges of negotiating, 136
  link to positionality, 7
  to research participants, 138, 154,
      155
  to the field, 148, 154, 167
African researchers, 4
  positionality challenges of, 3
African researchers researching 'back
      home', 129
African Studies Association (ASA),
      172, 182
African women's voices, 14, 17
  as researchers, 14, 17
  as research participants, 14, 18, 25,
      27, 28
  lack of in the literature, 15, 17, 19,
      20
Agency, 80, 82, 83, 87, 92
Anthropology *of*, 58

B

Bias, 117, 121, 123, 127, 128
  affect on interviews with research
      participants, 123
  challenges of in research 'back
      home', 127
Biomedical construction of disease, 55
Blocked access, 2
Butler, Judith, 88

C

Casamance region, 156, 163
Community-based natural resource
      management (CBNRM),
      134–136, 141–146
Critical biosocial perspective
  affect on positionality, 53
  definition of, 54
  in medical anthropology, 53, 55
  Leatherman and Goodman's synthe-
      sis, 55, 56
  social turn in life sciences, 55
Critical Medical Anthropology
      (CMA), 55, 56

213

D
Diaspora citizenship, 115–129
    research on, 116, 126, 128, 129

E
Emotions
    affect on data production, 3
    affect on future method choices,
        97
    affect on method selection, 8
    emotional labor, 100, 107, 108
    experienced by the researcher,
        101
    Hochschild, A.R., 100
    missing from International Relations
        research, 97
    repressed, 99
Ethics
    issues with, 120
    verbal permission, 120
    with vulnerable research partici-
        pants, 120
Ethnographic turn, 97

F
Failure, 1, 2, 8, 9
    emotional aspects of, 156
    feelings of during fieldwork, 2
    feelings of in the field, 155
    lack of acknowledgement in the
        literature, 155
    sanitized research process, 155
Flirtation
    affect on data collection, 80, 82,
        83, 92
    during interviews, 83
    explicit, 80, 83, 90, 92
    mild, 78, 86, 89, 91
    reciprocated, 83, 89, 91

G
Gatekeepers, 3, 7, 8, 153, 154, 156,
        161. *See also* Senegal
    affect on data collection, 136, 138,
        140, 156
    affect on data production, 3
    challenges of working with, 8
    evolving relationships with, 137
    negotiation with, 137, 138
    own ideas of research, 153
    power of, 137
    problems of working with, 156
    reconceptualizing relationships with,
        137
    unidirectional portrayals of, 137

H
Haraway, Donna, 76, 80, 87
    positioning, 87
Hidden agendas
    affect of on data collection, 163
Hidden migrants, 116. *See also*
        Zimbabwe
    emotional trauma of, 121
    giving a voice to, 116, 118
    in South Africa, 116–118, 122
Home
    African researchers returning to, 13,
        14, 20, 23
    alienation experienced when
        researching back, 14, 28
    problematizing the idea of, 14
    returning to as a Cambridge
        University research student, 20
    rootedness in, 13
Hybrid insider/outsider
    advantages of being, 39, 40
    affect of being on data production, 5
    challenges of being, 35, 38, 41, 49, 51
    definition of, 40

I

Imagined community of biomedics, 63, 64

Insider
advantages and disadvantages of being, 39, 40
affect of being on data collected, 50
closeness to the researched group, 38
complete, 39–41, 43, 46–48, 50
difficulties with bias, 5
difficulty of boundaries, 38
narrow view of research relationships, 39, 42
partial, 36, 39, 43, 46–48, 50

Insider status, 126

Institutional affiliation, 172, 173, 176, 177, 179, 180
requirement for research permit, 173

Interpreters, 161–163
challenges of working with, 162
problems with communication, 161

J

Joola culture
in Senegal, 156
joking relations between community members, 162

K

Kavango-Zambezi Transfrontier Conservation Area (KAZA), 133, 134, 147

Kenya
conducting research in, 14
cut flower industry in, 15, 20

Kristeva, Julia, 77

L

Local biologies
Lock's conception of, 56

Local support and contacts, 173
advantages of for application for research permit, 173

M

Malawi
challenges of conducting research in, 6
conducting medical anthropological research in, 53
researching Trachoma in, 54, 57, 60, 63–65, 69, 71
working with Yao communities, 54

Methodologies, 3, 9
adaption of, 3, 9

Methodology
positionality affect on choices of, 100

N

Namibia
conservancies in, 135, 136
reciprocity, 137
working with CBOs and NGOs as gatekeepers, 137

National Archives of Zimbabwe, 171, 187
three-day window of access, 187

NGO support for CBO development implications of, 135

O

Objectivity
of researchers, 99, 108

Outsider

advantages and disadvantages of
being, 39, 40
challenges of unfamiliarity, 38, 45
complete, 39–41, 45–48, 50, 51
language barriers, 38
narrow view of research relationships, 38, 42
partial, 39, 40, 46–48, 50

P
People Against Suffering Oppression
and Poverty (PASSOP), 117, 118,
120, 123, 124, 126
Performance
as a key feature in data production,
86
Politicization of academia, 181–185
Positionality, 115, 116, 126–128
affect on access, 15, 16, 25, 26, 36,
63, 79, 81
affect on data production, 3
affect on knowledge production,
148
alienating, 14
anxiety around, 57
challenges of, 43, 46, 51, 115, 116
changing over time, 53, 60, 62, 71
class, 15, 16, 25, 42
ethnicity, 15–17, 28, 54, 59
evolving, 42, 49, 51
gender, 2, 3, 6, 15–17, 25, 27, 59,
75, 79–81, 87, 88, 91, 92
gendered misperceptions with male
research participants, 23
hybrid insider-outsider, 5
identity, 2, 4
impeding data production, 116
in public health spheres, 58
insider/outsider dichotomies, 5
insider/outsider dichotomy, 35, 39,
42

intersecting identities, 13
knowledge exchange, 13–16, 25, 28
language, 62
multi-positionalities, 6, 70, 71
navigating privilege, 59
otherness, 15, 20
performance, 15, 28
race, 2, 7
sexualized identity, 75, 79, 82, 88,
92
slipping between, 15, 16, 21, 22, 28
spectrum of insider and outsider, 35
temporal aspect of, 42, 43
transient boundaries, 54
Positivism
in medical training, 57
reductionist ideology, 57
sense of obligation, 57
underpinning biomedical paradigms,
57
Post-Positivism
feminist research methods, 6
'god trick', 76
messiness of research, 76
Power relations, 75, 79, 81, 87, 123
between interviewer and interviewee, 78, 80, 123
gendered, 123

Q
Quantitative methods, 109

R
Reciprocity, 13, 15, 16, 22, 25, 28
institutionalizing knowledge, 25
Reflexivity, 15–18, 25, 36
consideration of own position on
research outcomes, 36
Reinharz, Shulamit, 13, 15–18, 22
Research, 13–29

African researchers conducting research
    'back home', 13, 15, 17, 25
conducting 'back home', 5
messiness of, 9
polished and sanitized style, 9
Research diary, 102
Researcher, 35–42, 44, 48–51
    third category of, 36
Researcher wellbeing, 98, 108
Research permit application process
    difficulties with, 172
    pragmatic considerations, 172
    requirements for, 173, 175
    research associate position, 178
Research settings
    'closed or private', 136
    'open or public', 136
Rwanda, 76, 77, 81, 83, 90
    conducting interviews in, 76, 77

S
Senegal
    conducting research in, 157
Sexualized behavior, 81, 82
Social interaction
    between NGOs as implementers and
        CBOs as consumers, 135
    in rural development projects in
        Namibia, 135
South Africa
    challenges of conducting research
        in, 116
    conducting research as a
        Zimbabwean in, 122
    conducting research in townships
        in, 122
    xenophobia towards Zimbabweans,
        116, 126
South Sudan, 98, 102, 103, 106, 109.
    See also Emotions

conducting research in, 100
emotional responses to interviewees,
    108
Jamam and Gendressa refugee
    camps, 98
refugee camps in, 102, 103, 108
Subjectivity, 122, 127, 128. *See also*
    Bias

T
Tourist lodges, 139

U
Uganda, 35, 40, 42–46, 48, 49
    conducting research in, 42
    researcher as former public servant
        in, 40, 42–44, 49

V
Violence, 116, 119, 122
    fear of for researcher, 119

Z
Zanu-PF, 174, 181–183, 185
    interference of politics in academia,
        174
Zimbabwe, 76, 77, 81, 83–87, 90,
    116, 119, 127
    application for research permit for,
        171–173, 175, 178
    conducting elite interviews in, 81
    conducting research in, 76, 180
    relationship between Britain and,
        76
    vulnerable migrants from, 116
Zimbabwean research assistants
    working with local, 181

Printed by Printforce, the Netherlands